BIBLE Counseling:

Equipping Christians for an Evangelistic Counseling Ministry

Doug Mallett
and
Debra A. Read

xulon PRESS

Copyright © 2003 by Doug Mallett and Debra A. Read

BIBLE Counseling
by Doug Mallett and Debra A. Read

Printed in the United States of America

ISBN 1-594670-81-1

All rights reserved. No part of this publication may be reproduced or transmitted in any form or by any means without written permission of the author.

Unless otherwise indicated, Bible quotations are taken from the Holy Bible, New International Version®. NIV® Copyright © 1973, 1978, 1984 by International Bible Society. Used by permission of Zondervan.

Portions of this book are also published on the Open Arms Ministry Website, http://www.oaim.org.

Xulon Press
www.XulonPress.com

Xulon Press books are available in bookstores everywhere, and on the Web at www.XulonPress.com.

We would both like to dedicate this work to Charlotte:
A very special thank you for all the meals, the patience and the support to help us finish this book. We know it's been a long time in the making, but we thank you for helping us to maintain our focus and to continue in the work.
A big thanks also to the Open Arms Internet Ministry staff who stepped up to the plate and took on more than their share of counseling, e-mails, and posts so we could finish this.
And a special thanks to Wvstarwolf for her enthusiasm and dedication to OAIM, and to Daizychain1981 for helping us edit the manuscript.

Table of Contents

❖❖❖

Introduction ix

Part 1: The Basics of BIBLE Counseling
    Chapter 1: What Is BIBLE Counseling?..............................13
    Chapter 2: The Many Faces of Pharisaism.........................35
    Chapter 3: Biblical Self-Esteem...47
    Chapter 4: Depression 59
    Chapter 5: Suicidal Thoughts..75
    Chapter 6: Helping the Sexually Abused 79
    Chapter 7: Are Disorders Real? 87
    Chapter 8: The Fraud of Deliverance Ministries................93
    Chapter 9: The Great Addiction..113
    Chapter 10: Till Death Do We Fight 137
    Chapter 11: Integrating BIBLE Counseling Into the
          Local Church..155

Part 2: The Gospel and Its Defense
    Chapter 12: The Basics of Christianity 161
    Chapter 13: Going on the Defensive 175
    Chapter 14: The Root of All Cults 187
    Chapter 15: Paganism, the Fad Religion 193
    Chapter 16: How Paganism Has Infiltrated the Church.....201
    Chapter 17: Pseudo-Christian Forms of Paganism 219
    Chapter 18: Jehovah's Witnesses and the Impossible
          Dream..225
    Chapter 19: Mormonism: On the Road to Godhood?.....237
    Chapter 20: Penance, Purgatory and Paganism................245

Chapter 21: The Faith of Our Fathers?...............................259
Chapter 22: The God of Abraham, Isaac and Jacob...........277
Chapter 23: The Unknown God 287
Chapter 24: The Evolution Delusion..................................295

Part 3: Introduction to Internet Ministry
    Chapter 25: The Cutting Edge of Mission Fields...............307
    Chapter 26: How Our Ministry Is Structured.....................319

Appendices: Practical Aids to Ministry
    Appendix A: A Word About Disrupters.............................327
    Appendix B: Most Frequently Asked Questions (FAQs)...333
    Appendix C: Burnout and Internet Ministry 339
    Appendix D: Homefires 343
    Appendix E: A Wife's Letter to Her Husband on
                    Pornography..347
    Appendix F: Helpful Links 355
    Appendix G: Recommended Reading List 359
    Appendix H: Record Keeping..365
    Appendix I: Confidentiality, 911 and Other Legalities 369
    Appendix J: How to Lead Someone to Christ....................375

Index 397

Introduction

◆◆◆

This book is a breath of the fresh air of grace when it comes to biblical counseling. Through over five years of counseling online and working with over 2000 people individually, we, as the team of Parepidemos (Doug) and Chalkbrd (Deb), have developed a new style of biblical counseling, called BIBLE Counseling: Biblical Insights for Basic Living Everyday. We have discovered that many of the counseling texts on the market today fall either into the category of being based on secular psychological premises or on a legalistic type of counseling that focuses primarily on behavior instead of first and foremost on our relationship with God. We believe there is another biblical alternative.

Beginning with the concept of the Bible as the ultimate authority in the lives of Christians, as clearly stated by Dr. Jay Adams in his works, BIBLE Counseling moves the reader from a more legalistic standpoint to one of grace. This is brought about by turning from a focus on changing the behavior of a person first and expecting the beliefs to follow to working with a person's beliefs and, by doing so, helping them to line up those beliefs with what the Bible says about God. Behaviors change when our hearts are in tune with God's intention for our lives. Through the material in this work, it is our desire to reveal to the reader the "secret of being content in any and every situation," which is spoken of by the Apostle Paul in Philippians 4:12.

We invite you to follow along with us as we expose the thread of Paganism, woven through both secular situations as well as in today's Bible-believing churches. As this type of false belief turns hearts from fully trusting in the God of the Bible, as He reveals Himself therein, we intend to show how these false teachings become ingrained and absorbed into mainstream Christianity, leading to all sorts of spiritual, emotional and mental problems.

Gone is the day of accepting at face value the validity of anyone who claims to be a Christian. Because of the proliferation of information on the Internet, false teachings that might have once had only a couple of lines in history have gained tremendous followings. Anonymous chat IDs allow people to dabble in witchcraft, Satanism and other cultic groups that they might never have approached in person in the past.

This landmark work pulls together Biblical counseling and working with cultic beliefs and marries them into one and the same ministry. At the root of depression, anxiety, and other problems that are considered "mental illnesses" is really the spiritual issue of false beliefs about God. If one is to be healed of these emotional issues, we must first rebuild our idea of God to fit what the Bible says: God is all-knowing; God is all-powerful; God is all-loving. Forming a powerful combination, these three aspects of God's unchangeable character allow the Christian to be confident that God knows what their situation is in perfect detail and what is best for them at that time to bring about the characteristics that He wants to build in them. Once we know this, and truly believe that God is both powerful enough to change the situation if it were not for our best and loving enough to *always* do what is for our ultimate best (Romans 8:28), then the problems we face are no longer overwhelming because it is a loving God who has allowed them. This is the "secret" that Paul, in Philippians 4:12, claimed to have learned. God *can* be trusted to do what is for our ultimate best.

Throughout this work, the reader will see how this basic, biblical truth can be used to help those caught up in specific cults as well as those with emotional and mental difficulties. This is an absolutely essential reference manual for any Christian involved in counseling, and it will personally change the life of anyone who reads it as it challenges them to examine their own foundational beliefs about God.

Part 1:

The Basics of BIBLE Counseling

Chapter 1:

What Is BIBLE Counseling?

◆◆◆

The typing on the screen paused. We could tell she was struggling to put her feelings into words. We knew the tears were clouding her eyes, keeping her from seeing the screen and the words we typed in to tell her how much we cared for her, how we longed for her to be safe, to be away from the man who was hurting her so badly. We were crying too, our hearts breaking because it was so frustrating to see her hurt again and again and have no way to shield her from this man, nor to get her away from the situation.

The story was not new. She had no money. She had children about whom she worried. She had no job, no way of supporting herself and her children. We felt so helpless. Women's shelters in her area were full and had no room for a woman with children. What could we do but sit there with her and type away on a cold, lifeless keyboard, giving her advice that became merely words without form? Who else could she turn to when he watched her every move, monitoring her phone calls and keeping track of every mile put on the battered car sitting in the driveway? Did God really have answers that could help her out of this terrible situation?

We are BIBLE counselors who do a unique brand of counseling: working with those who might not find their way into a traditional biblical counselor's office. Ours is an Internet counseling ministry, which is completely based in the world of Cyberspace. In this world, we find intellectuals who want sound, logical answers for their questions, but also we find wounded spirits, begging to be bandaged and longing to find a reason for living and loving.

The Internet, however, is merely a reflection of the local church of today. An epidemic of mental and emotional problems eats out the heart of many churches, leaving only a shell of their members, as they struggle to put on an appearance of the abundant Christian life. Is the abundant life spoken of in John 10:10 merely an unattainable pipe dream?

Paul tells us in Philippians 4:12 that there is a secret to being content and that he has learned it. In this book, we will explore that secret, how it is available to every Christian, and how it can become a vitalizing factor to the local church.

Although this book may cover some subjects on which many other authors have already written, there is a basic thread that seems to have been missed. We will follow this thread of a focus on sound doctrine as we show the invasion of Paganism into even the local church, and its serious effects on the lives of our brothers and sisters — and possibly even our own selves. In this first section we will give the foundational tenets of BIBLE counseling, what it is and how to put it into practice in both your own life and the lives of those around you. A clear understanding of these basics will be important for understanding the rest of the book.

The Three Marks Of a Cult

With the dawn of time, a plot was unleashed. Satan, one of the creatures, consumed by his pride, dared to deny the sovereignty of the Almighty. Unfortunately, although we know that Satan is alive and well in the Earth today, we often forget that he has one specific, persistent theme in all he does: to usurp the glory of God. It should come as no surprise that he is constantly presenting humans with his own set of teachings, designed expressly for tearing their eyes off of their Creator and seducing them away from worshipping Him. These teachings often come as "new" or as "enlightened" doctrines that will help bring you to a higher state of being. They appeal to our fallen nature and always seem a delight to our hearts, completely in keeping with Paul's warning in 2 Corinthians 11:14-15: "Satan himself masquerades as an angel of light. It is not surprising, then, if his servants masquerade as servants of righteousness."

With this satanic plot in mind, we will be doing a brief study of some false teachings of which a BIBLE counselor needs to be aware. Throughout this study, you will find one basic thread, composed of three strands, in which all of these teachings always either deny or alter biblical truth. This thread, intricately woven through time and territory, links all false teachings together. As you work with those who have mental, emotional or spiritual problems, you will see that these are the three issues that are at the root of these problems.

1. The Trinity
   a. The denial of the triune nature of God by denial of the person of the Eternal Son and the person of the Eternal Holy Spirit as God.
   b. The Son and/or the Holy Spirit is altered to distort the nature of God.
   c. The Trinity's nature of God.

2. Challenge the Authority of the Scriptures
   a. Extra-biblical writings (e.g., the Book of Mormon) will be added as equal to or above the Bible's authority.
   b. Placing a church or a person above the Scriptures and making them the new source of authority.
   c. Adding and taking away Scriptures through changing the meaning of words and/or ignoring certain passages and emphasizing certain other passages.
   d. Altering words in the Bible through actual changing of words (e.g., New World Translation, the translation created by the Jehovah's Witnesses), or through adding footnotes that reflect a person's particular beliefs instead of the meaning of the passage.

3. Denial of salvation by grace alone through faith in Christ alone.

    a. Changing the definition of the word "grace" by calling it limited grace, irresistible grace, saving grace, etc., or any other qualifying term that indicates other than pure and lasting grace.
    b. Mingling works and grace by viewing grace as a kick start (after which you are no longer under grace).
    c. Denial of grace in its totality. In other words, adding absolutely any works to the finished work of Christ on the cross.

These elements will always be present in false teachings and when one can see this link clearly, it becomes easy to spot false teachings, some of which might be found in the most unlikely places. As we continue on in this book, you will begin to see how the diabolical plan unfolds before you, weaving these same threads over and over in a variety of facets, to snare those who choose to blind themselves to the truth.

Another thing that is important to notice is that since these three things are always at the root of false teachings, your answers should emphasize these to the one who is caught up in that false teaching. As you will see later, attacks on these three basic principles are in reality attacks on the very nature of God Himself.

The Authority of the Bible

The 19th century ushered in many dramatic changes to the life of the everyday person. Machines began to make their mark, providing the means for mankind to reach possibilities that before could only have been imagined. Communication became swifter with the telegraph and the telephone. The number of publications rose significantly.

As other reading materials became more available, the Bible slowly took a backseat to the new literature that was flooding the market. By the 20th century, the Bible was completely phased out of the educational process and out of many people's lives as well. Allusions to Bible stories in literature waned as the knowledge of those stories faded in the minds of the general populace.

The philosophies of Darwin, Freud, Jung and others undermined the authority of the Bible on every matter, even matters of faith. We were soon left with a religious tradition that stood on the "tenuous" legs of a book that the "real intellectuals" considered a collection of myths and stories on the same level of validity as the *Iliad* and the *Odyssey*.

Yet for those who are willing to look at the evidence, the Bible towers over any other literature in its accuracy, its historicity, its moral values and the testimonies to its life-changing power.[1] The Christian of today must grapple with this foundational issue: Is the Bible truly sufficient for living the Christian life or do we need more in order to live the life God requires of us?

In 2 Timothy 3:16-17 we read, "All Scripture is God-breathed and is useful for teaching, rebuking, correcting and training in righteousness, so that the man of God may be thoroughly equipped for every good work." Here Paul begins to unfold the place of Scripture in the life of the believer by assuring us that the Bible *is* useful for equipping us to do all the good works we should be doing.

Peter also helps to show us God's provision for living the Christian life. "His divine power has given us everything we need for life and godliness through our knowledge of him who called us by his own glory and goodness." (2 Peter 1:3) We do indeed have access to all we need in order to live the life God has set before us by our knowledge of Him. And where do we go to increase our knowledge of God? To the Bible, of course.

Throughout the New Testament, we see believers encouraging, exhorting, rebuking, reproving, and admonishing each other with their knowledge of God, guiding each other into a deeper relationship with Him. But does the Bible really have the answers for the problems and challenges we face everyday? The above passages indicate a strong positive to that question.

As the lack of knowledge of the Bible has decreased during the 19th and 20th centuries, there has been a dramatic increase in mental and emotional problems, as well as in false teachings and involvement in cults. Christians cannot, and should not, ignore the connection between these two.

BIBLE Counseling is a counseling that is grounded in the Bible and deals with the misconceptions about God that people have, whether from their lack of knowledge of the Bible, past experiences, or false teachings to which they've been exposed. It differs from the counseling of the biblical counseling movement because it focuses on exposing and correcting the beliefs of an individual instead of working to alter the behaviors. In traditional biblical (nouthetic) counseling, it is believed that you need to change the behavior (stop the sin) and the beliefs will soon follow, emphasizing holiness as the goal of the Christian life. BIBLE Counseling, however, believes that when you help the person change their basic beliefs about God, they will naturally, through the power of the Holy Spirit, change their behavior to line up with their beliefs about God, showing that the goal of the Christian life is relationship with the God who created us.

BIBLE Counseling is an acronym that stands for **B**iblical **I**nsights for **B**asic **L**iving **E**veryday. As this chapter unfolds, we believe it will become obvious why we stress that these truths are basic, intended for any Christian, and how they are available to anyone through the study of the Bible. The type of counseling we present here is not a "new" concept, but is precisely what has been practiced by biblical teachers throughout the centuries.

How Credible Are Official Credentials?

We believe that counseling from the Bible is a basic skill to which all Christians should have access. Too many times we reserve this type of help for the "professionals" and those who have the proper "credentials." God's view of qualifications, however, does not seem to be rooted in university classes and degrees. In the Old Testament, we see God delivering the Israelites from the Midianites. What was God's choice in leadership for them? It was none other than Gideon, who cowardly hid in a winepress (Judges 6:11). God chose Saul to be king of Israel, even though he hid himself on his coronation day (1 Samuel 10:21). God also chose Amos and David (the shepherds), Jonah the bitter-hearted rebel, and even Balaam's donkey was chosen by God to further His will in the earth. And, of course, Jesus chose plain, ordinary fishermen to be responsible for carrying the Gospel to all nations.

In Philippians 3, Paul, the New Testament writer with the highest credentials, guides us in how to put our accomplishments into a godly perspective.

> If anyone else thinks he has reasons to put confidence in the flesh, I have more: circumcised on the eighth day, of the people of Israel, of the tribe of Benjamin, a Hebrew of Hebrews; in regard to the law, a Pharisee; as for zeal, persecuting the church; as for legalistic righteousness, faultless.
> But whatever was to my profit I now consider loss for the sake of Christ. What is more, I consider everything a loss compared to the surpassing greatness of knowing Christ Jesus my Lord, for whose sake I have lost all things. I consider them rubbish, that I may gain Christ and be found in him, not having a righteousness of my own that comes from the law, but that which is through faith in Christ—the righteousness that comes from God and is by faith. I want to know Christ and the power of his resurrection and the fellowship of sharing in his sufferings, becoming like him in his death, and so, somehow, to attain to the resurrection from the dead. (Philippians 3:4b-11)

Even though Paul was the ultimate "professional" of his day, he considered his degrees as rubbish, trash, and garbage, compared to knowing the Lord Jesus Christ. It is not how many degrees we have that make us able to help others, but the commitment of our heart to Christ. Make no mistake, God's perfect will will indeed be accomplished in this world, even if God has to use a donkey to do it. It is always a matter of willingness of the heart.

Are we then competent to help others with their emotional and mental problems? If we are grounded in a strong knowledge of our Lord and Savior through God's written word, most assuredly. Paul tells the Romans in Romans 15:14, "I myself am convinced, my brothers, that you yourselves are full of goodness, complete in knowledge and competent to instruct one another." Through the work of the Holy Spirit inside of us, all Christians with a good understanding of the written word of God are competent to help others through the difficulties of life.

What About Trained Psychologists?

Instead of asking ourselves whether or not the Bible is a reliable source for mental and emotional help, perhaps a better question we as Christians must ask ourselves is, how reliable is secular psychology? Psychology is fond of touting its authority and authenticity yet even its own people are having difficulties believing in the evidence. R. Christopher Barden who is a psychologist and also president of the National Association for Consumer Protection in Mental Health Practices in a press release voiced his fears regarding the reliability of psychology: "It is indeed shocking that many, if not most forms of psychotherapy currently offered to consumers are not supported by credible scientific evidence." [2]

It appears that the author of the article "What Is Vulgar?" from *The American Scholar* has summarized the reliability of psychology very well when he said, "Psychology acts as if it is holding all the theoretical keys, but then in practice reveals that it doesn't even know where the doors are." [3]

There have been a few studies done on the efficacy of psychology, but they are not widely publicized. In their book, *PsychoHeresy* by Martin and Deidre Bobgan, the Bobgans cite a study done in 1952 by Hans J. Eysenck, a prominent English scholar, who "found that a greater percentage of patients who did not have psychotherapy improved over those who did undergo therapy." [4]

In fact, Eysenck examined over 8000 cases and here is the conclusion he drew:

> "...roughly two-thirds of a group of neurotic patients will recover or improve to a marked extent within about two years of the onset of their illness, whether they are treated by means of psychotherapy or not." [5]

It is interesting to note that the same percentage of mentally ill people get well as was the case over a hundred years ago in asylums where treatments were more violent than mere talk. In the studies that have been done, the deciding factor in a patient's recovery does not seem to be methodology, training, credentials or expertise, but only the friendly personality of the therapist and his interpersonal relating skills.

The Bobgans also cite a study done by Dr. Joseph Durlak who compared the effects of counseling done by paraprofessionals (with less than 15 hours of training) and professionals, such as psychiatrists, psychologists and social workers. The outcome of this study was that the paraprofessionals were more effective, by a significant degree, than the professionals.[6]

We encourage you to research the validity of psychology's claims for yourself. In Appendix G, we have included a list of books that will give you some solid, documented resources with which to begin. Your own personal study of this subject will prepare you for answering others who have questions about this subject. Do you need to know about psychology to do BIBLE Counseling? No, but, just like in dealing with any false belief, you will want to study it so you can be prepared to give answers when the questions do arise. Unfortunately, the most difficult thing about practicing BIBLE Counseling is having to continually defend the sufficiency of the Bible against those Christians who want to cling to the fallacies of psychology.

The Root of Psychology

Psychology has become a very important factor in the lives of all of us, even in ways of which we are not aware. Teachers are required to take psychology classes for their teaching degree. Ministers take psychology courses in order to help their congregations. At work, we are given personality tests to determine what kind of employee we will be.

But should modern psychology and the Bible co-exist in the lives of today's Christians? Throughout all of Christian History, the popular theology of the day has moved like a pendulum, swinging away from what the Bible teaches and then back with equal passion, burying itself in the pages of the written word of God. Where on the pendulum does psychology lie? Is it *for* God? *Against* God? Or is it found somewhere in the middle of the two extremes?

In order to compare the compatibility of psychology with biblical teachings, we must first determine our method of measuring this. Since we are fundamentalists, we choose to measure any teachings according to the infallible written word of God, the Bible. Men can change, and society may waver from side to side, but God's word remains true and steady, an unchangeable ruler by which to accurately measure truth and error in today's world.

Psychology permeates much of our culture in such a way that it has become as common to place our minds in the hands of a "professional" psychologist, as it is to place our bodies in the hands of a "professional" medical doctor. Yet in our spirit we should hear 1 Thessalonians 5:21 constantly ringing, "Test everything. Hold on to the good." Let's take a look at what the basics of psychology are and compare them to the unchanging standard of what God has to say and see if it can measure up.

The word psychology comes from two Greek words, *psuche*, which means "soul," and the word *logos*, which means "word" or "teaching." Putting these two together, we have the Greek meaning of psychology as, "teaching about the soul." The first thing to ask ourselves is, "To whom does the area of teaching about the soul belong?" If psychology teaches us about our souls, we need to make certain that the "professional" we go to is skilled in the care of, and is knowledgeable about, the soul. When we have a broken ankle, we do not go to the dentist. When we need a good haircut, we do not go to an electrician. And for the care of the soul, we should certainly make sure we have the right professional for the job.

Basically, the soul is the seat of our mind, will and emotions. What type of professional does it seem best to go to for help with your soul? What type of qualifications should you look for when you want to have help dealing with your soul?

Until the 17th century, the only professional who was considered qualified to help people deal with their mind, will and emotions was the local clergy. In fact, this was an integral part of the Church's responsibility. However, the 17th century led a tremendous change in the way people thought about the role of religion in their lives.

René Descartes, famous for his quote, "I think therefore I am," was one of the first to begin the separation of mind, will, and emotions from the territory of the Church. He advocated the nativist view, which tells us that our intellect, what our will chooses and does not choose, and even what we feel, are merely products of nature, heredity or genetics.

This view, however, opposes the Bible in two key factors. First, it snatches our creation out of the hands of God and places it in the hands of a nebulous being called, "nature." It places nature on the throne, crowning it king of kings, empowering it to move our lives around like life-sized chess pieces, robots who can only do what we have been "pre-programmed" to do. This view exalts the creation yet denigrates the Creator. It is born out of the heart of paganism, as we shall see more clearly as this book progresses. But the Bible tells us that we are creations of Almighty God (Genesis 1-3) and have been created in His likeness. We have been given the incredible gift of free will by our Creator so we can choose whether or not we will love Him.

This leads us into the second way this nativist view contradicts what the Bible has to say. If we believe that our heredity and genetics direct our mind, will and emotions, then we become incapable of making independent choices, and changing our "pre-programmed" behavior turns into a complete impossibility.

However, God tells us that there most certainly *is* a way of altering our mind, will and emotions. Hebrews 4:12-13 is very plain: "For the word of God is living and active. Sharper than any double-edged sword, it penetrates even to the dividing soul and spirit, joints and marrow; it judges the thoughts and attitudes of the heart. Nothing in all creation is hidden from God's sight. Everything is uncovered and laid bare before the eyes of him to whom we must give account." Why would we have to give an account to God if our soul was determined by heredity, a factor we cannot change? Surely the Creator of the human soul would see no reason to judge our thoughts and attitudes if those thoughts and attitudes were merely part of our genetic makeup, formed on the day we were conceived.

Moreover, if our behavior cannot be changed, how can 2 Corinthians 5:17 be true? "Therefore, if anyone is in Christ, he is a new creation; the old has gone, the new has come!" God is in the business of making new creations of people; this is His very nature. God is a change-maker.

Also during the 17th century, John Locke promulgated his view of *tabula rasa*. These Latin words for "blank slate" tell us that Locke believed that men were born amoral (morally neither bad nor good), and it is society and experiences that shape the morality of any given individual. This view is much like the basis of Buddhism and eastern thought, which we will deal with later on in this book.

It's a pleasant thought to say that we can't be blamed if we don't know what is right and what is wrong in life because we've never been taught or our experiences have shown us differently than someone else. This type of belief eases our consciences and assuages our guilt. How can we be held responsible for knowing something we've never been taught? How can we know God unless He shows Himself to us?

Romans 1:18-20, however, makes it obvious that none of us has an excuse in this area. Being created in the image of God, He has stamped the knowledge of His very essence into all of humankind, and since we know Him, we know what moral good really is. "The wrath of God is being revealed from heaven against all the godlessness and wickedness of men who suppress the truth by their wickedness, since what may be known about God is plain to them, because God has made it plain to them. For since the creation of the world God's invisible qualities — his eternal power and divine nature — have been clearly seen, being understood from what has been made, so that men are without excuse."

The idea of our morality being shaped by society and our experiences is called an empiricist view. The observable nature of this, watching as moralities are shaped, led to the word empiricism taking on a more in-depth meaning, which has become the heart of modern science. Empirical science must have observable facts, experiences and information to back up their claims.

Can the Soul Be Observed?

But can the soul be observed? Can one soul be compared to another equally? What does a soul look like? What being can see into another person's soul?

The Bible gives us the answer to these questions. "The heart is deceitful above all things and beyond cure. Who can understand it? I the LORD search the heart and examine the mind, to reward a man according to his conduct, according to what his deeds deserve." (Jeremiah 17:9-10) We can easily see that it is only God who created us who can look into our souls.

Since the soul is not something we can see, touch, or experience in any way with our senses, the study of the soul has nothing to do with empirical science. In Psalm 62:1 we read: "My soul finds rest in God alone; my salvation comes from him." The Bible is very clear that the realm of the soul belongs to God alone, and the logical conclusion then is that only someone who is trained in what God says in His written word can give you adequate insight into your soul.

Because of this, we believe that a secular person, one who does not believe in God or who has not committed his or her life to God and has not studied God's written word has very little to offer the souls of people. However, one who understands God's plan for mankind, who is familiar with God's character and nature, who has an intimate knowledge of God's written word, will have the qualifications we need to direct us to the real, life-changing Source of help to heal our souls.

The Founders of Modern Psychology

If we asked you to give one famous name in psychology, the most likely response would be Sigmund Freud. Yet if we inquired further about his life, his morals, his values, or his teachings, we doubt if you could give us any details. While knowing psychology's theories is not necessary to do BIBLE Counseling, it *is* necessary to know what you are up against. When it comes to Freud, we definitely believe there are some details about him that a Christian should know.

From early in his life, Freud had problems with the very idea of religion, and especially with Christianity. In his work, *The Future of an Illusion*, Freud calls religion "the obsessional neurosis of humanity."[7] His idea was that religions are illusions and myths that people invent in order to cope with life. In his opinion, religions do much damage to people and should be eliminated from people's lives if they were to become well-adjusted human beings.

"One of Freud's most powerful motives in life was the desire to inflict vengeance on Christianity for its traditional anti-Semitism,"[8] says Dr. Thomas Szasz, professor of psychiatry. Doesn't it follow that if Freud was so anti-Christian his views would also be anti the Christian God? Freud believed his view of the world had the answers to end the miseries of mankind. But with all of Freud's theories and philosophies, his secular wisdom was not enough, however, to stop him from committing suicide.

Freud's protégé, Carl Jung, was also anti-Christian in his beliefs. Jung, though, took a different perspective on religion. Growing up in a Christian family, Jung became disillusioned with Christianity at an early age and soon repudiated it completely. Jung did not share Freud's opinion of religion. He believed that religion was not evil, but was a collection of myths that helped people deal with reality and, as such, should be encouraged — that is, all religions except biblical Christianity.

"In cases of difficult diagnosis, I usually get a horoscope."[9] Jung was particularly into mysticism and the occult. In fact, he had his own personal spirit guide named Philemon, through which he received special revelations and even some of his counseling theories. True to life in the occult, Jung was enticed deeper and deeper into occult practices including necromancy, which is calling up spirits from the dead. As Christians we need to remember God's condemnation of King Saul in the Old Testament for just such a sin.[10]

The tie between psychology and the occult doesn't end there. Carl Rogers is a more recent founder of psychological thought, whose teachings permeate counseling offices today. He also openly repudiated Christianity and was involved in the occult, specifically necromancy.

Each of the founders of the most popular psychological thought that is taught in both secular and Christian colleges today had one major thing in common. They were all very anti-Christian and wanted to find a way of helping people to deal with their problems without having to acknowledge the God of the Bible. As Christians, those who are indwelt by God the Holy Spirit, we must ask ourselves what these men have to offer us in regards to our soul.

When the fall occurred, sin entered the world. Because of sin and the sin nature we all have within us, our thinking processes are distorted. What we consider human wisdom must always be evaluated with the understanding that our perspective is heavily influenced and distorted by sin. This causes our own thinking to always need to be readjusted so we line up with the truth of God's word.

In dealing with our problems, let us go first to the wisdom of God that should rule our behavior instead of relying on the words of mere men who opposed God with every fiber of their being.

What Is the Biblical Solution?

Biblical counseling is a bold twist on what today's society thinks of as counseling because it dares to work on the premise that the Bible contains all the information we need to deal with the problems we face. Are we really in need of Freud's psychoanalysis to be healed of our "mental" diseases or does God give us the answers we need contained within Scripture? We believe the Bible does indeed have the answers to the mental and emotional problems we deal with in our everyday lives, totally apart from the secular "wisdom" of psychology. Does this mean that we believe a biblical counselor can replace a "trained" psychologist? We definitely believe this is true and should be the therapy of choice for Christians.

Many people say that mental and emotional problems should only be dealt with by a trained psychologist and that a pastor is not qualified to help anyone in these areas. We disagree strongly. Who better to deal with the soul of human beings than someone who has at his or her disposal the very wisdom of the God of the universe?

There are some serious flaws in the root beliefs of secular psychology that need to be examined before one puts confidence in its methodology. The major premise of psychology is that man is basically good and that the answers to our problems lie within our own selves. This concept is not reconcilable with Romans 3:10, "There is no one righteous, not even one," and Romans 3:23, "For all have sinned and fall short of the glory of God," which tell us that it is our nature itself that is flawed and that we are not basically good, but instead basically sinful.

Biblical counseling, on the other hand, is based on the foundation of God's truth that all men are sinners and that the troubles we are faced with in our daily lives are the result of our own sin and the sins of those around us. With this foundation, we go to the One who knows us, who created us, for the remedy to the consequences of sinful behavior.

Counseling was originally the church's responsibility because it was generally known that the evils in our lives are sin-based. Today, however, many pastors are buying into the secular mindset. They consider themselves incompetent to give counsel in other than specifically spiritual matters and will immediately refer the members of their congregations to a "professional" who can help them in a way they can't. Since problems are sin-based, both emotional and mental problems that people are struggling with have spiritual roots, and if the spiritual problems are dealt with, the emotional and mental problems will be solved as well.

The biblical counseling perspective that we will be using for this section is often difficult for many people to accept at first. Our society, both Christians and non-Christians, have bought into the many falsehoods perpetuated by psychology, which often blatantly contradict what God has said in His written word. Again, the purpose of this book is not to give a complete theological basis for biblical counseling, but to provide a tool for those who feel led to a BIBLE counseling ministry. The reason we present this stance is because of the study we have done on this subject. We encourage anyone who is skeptical about our position to do the research themselves. In Appendix G you will find some excellent resources for a study in this area.

Psychology is rooted in a false pretense that Man can find the solutions to his problems within himself. Many who are connected with psychology (both Christians and non-Christians) are taught to have the counselee determine answers for themselves, to remain aloof from the counselee and turn all questions that are asked them back into questions for the one being counseled. Man can solve his own problems if given the right tools, according to psychological thought.

Those who are rooted in knowledge of the Bible, however, know that this is a fallacy. Mankind can never solve our own problems because we are at heart sinful people. Where secular counseling spends months delving into "why" did this happen, the biblical counselor doesn't need to ask why. We already know why. Man is sinful. The Bible tells us this (Romans 3:10, 23; Jeremiah 17:9). Because of this premise that is grounded in the truth of God's word, we can take a different route to help the people we work with as they heal.

All pain in this world is caused by sin.[11] If there were no sin, there would be no problems, no hurts. But sin does indeed exist, whether in our own lives or in the lives of those around us, and it is the effect of sin that must be dealt with in order for healing to occur. *No other solution* will work because this is the *only* reason for mental and emotional pain according to the Bible.

What a biblical counselor does is what God has commanded Christians to do since His Son came into this world: look to God's word for the answers. We are told in 2 Timothy 3:16, "All Scripture is God-breathed and is useful for teaching, rebuking, correcting and training in righteousness, so that the man of God may be thoroughly equipped for every good work." These ideas of teaching, rebuking, correcting and training in righteousness are what a biblical counselor does and are, in fact, the truest sense of the meaning of the word, "counselor" (one who gives advice in order to help direct the judgment of another).

Since all pain is connected to sin, God is the one with the answers, not popular psychology. How can someone who is lost and doesn't believe in the God of the Bible have any answers about healing the effects of sin in our lives? Why should we go to them for any answers? Isn't that exactly what a pastor is for? Shouldn't the answers be found within the church instead of with someone outside of the church who might not even believe in God?

Those who use secular psychological precepts as the root of their counseling instead of biblical principles (whether they be Christians or non-Christians) will spend months and years accomplishing much less than a biblical counselor can do in days and months. This is because the problem is not that people need to "work through" their problems or "role play" situations or "relive" their abuse. The problem is that we are sinful. We do sinful things that hurt others. We react to things that happen to us in sinful ways. When we deal with the effects of sin, the problems are taken care of. This gives the people we work with the hope of saying, "I have learned the secret of being content in any and every situation" (Philippians 4:12) along with the Apostle Paul.

The success of biblical counseling as opposed to secular means is incredible. What it takes secular counseling years to accomplish somewhat, the Holy Spirit can accomplish in months and He always guarantees His work. He promises to complete the work He has begun in us (Philippians 1:6), if we allow Him.

Does the Bible Speak of Mental Illness?

We need to take a moment here to discuss our beliefs concerning mental illness. Again, this is not a popular belief nowadays, but we believe it is very biblical. It is very interesting to note that the Bible speaks to physical illness and to demonic possession, but there is never a mention of a situation where Jesus encountered anyone who was "mentally ill" (other than demon possessed, which is not an illness, but a spiritual condition). This is a fact we cannot overlook.

Because we cannot find a precedent for this type of "illness" in the Bible, we are led to three possibilities. The first one is that Jesus didn't care about "mentally ill" people. We know this to be a false conclusion because Jesus, being God, was the embodiment of love. A man who even touched the forbidden lepers would certainly never have ignored someone who was "mentally ill."

The second conclusion is that Jesus never encountered any "mentally ill" people. In the June 2000 issue of *Psychology Today*, it is estimated that 44 million Americans should be classified as "mentally ill."[12] This would mean that approximately one in six people in the United States are under this classification. An article in the Chicago Sun-Times quoted the Surgeon General as saying that the percentage was higher, at one in five Americans.[13] It seems highly unlikely then that with the thousands of people Jesus met (at least 4000 one time and 5000 another time not to mention the many others who crossed His path) and with the many He healed that He would never have encountered even one person who was "mentally ill." Odds would say that out of 9000 people, He should have had over 1400 "mentally ill" people in the crowd if the rate was the same as it is in the United States today. It doesn't appear logical that He would not have met even one during His three-year ministry here on earth.

The third possible conclusion would be that God chose not to include any instance of healing a mental illness in the Bible. If this is so, then one must wonder why this is. The Bible has been carefully crafted by God's own hand to give us all we need to know here on earth for godly living. In 2 Timothy 3:16-17 we read: "All Scripture is God-breathed and is useful for teaching, rebuking, correcting and training in righteousness, so that the man of God may be thoroughly equipped for every good work." This doesn't say partially equipped, but it says *thoroughly* equipped. This means that it contains all that we need in order to do the good works that He asks of us. The Bible shows Jesus healing the blind and the lame and raising people from the dead but there is not even one instance of Jesus even encountering someone who was "mentally ill."

If "mental illness" is as rampant as described in the above two sources, then why would God leave this out? Why is there no record of Jesus acknowledging "mental illness" as a valid condition, as He did physical illnesses and demon possession? Did God forget to include it? Did He figure it just didn't matter? Did He not foresee that we would need examples like that in the present? No, God doesn't forget things, and He can see the past, present and future, so He would have known if it was something we would need to see examples of now. The reason is because God sees the "mental illness" problems as the result of sin so there was no need to include more about it than He'd already said. Jesus did indeed work with "mentally ill" people all the time. Every person He touched needed Him to heal his or her "mental illness" because "mental illness" is really a spiritual matter.

To take it a step further even, we have found that those who are classified as "mentally ill" in reality have a distorted view of who God is, whether through incidences in their past, or through present doctrinal errors to which they are clinging. If they are non-Christians, they need to face the reality of their sinful nature and the payment Jesus made for those sins on the cross. If they are Christians, they need to face the reality of their own responses to the situations God has allowed to happen in their lives, which determine whether they will trust that God is all He says He is or whether they will be working from a false idea of God. For instance, many women who have been physically abused by their parents will view God as someone who they must fear and try to placate in order not to be punished for their attempts to live godly lives. When they fail in something they do, there is a fearfulness that often keeps them from accepting the loving grace of God who has covered us with His blood.

It is for this reason that our book is composed of two parts, yet they essentially are one. In dealing with people online who have come to us for counseling, we have found that many of them are mixed up in cultic beliefs that effect the very way they live their lives, their health and their mental state. For example, a person caught up in the word faith movement can often be devastated emotionally and sink into a deep depression when something he was claiming by faith fails to materialize. When the trials and testings come, God winnows out the false beliefs by their obvious failures and the person needs firm yet gentle guidance back to the true path again.

There are some who will read this book and feel more drawn to work with those who are depressed or who have been sexually abused or who have marital problems than with those caught up in cults, but these two are not exclusive. Sound doctrine *is* biblical counseling. When you are talking with a person and he tells you that he is a Christian, you will need to examine what exactly he means by the term "Christian." Many who come for biblical counseling will believe they are Christians, but as you dig deeper, you will find that perhaps the Jesus they are following is not the Jesus of the Bible. Remember, there are many cults that claim to be Christians and who use Christian terminology but who are very far from the true gospel as set forth in the Bible. And this is usually the root of the problems they are having.

What About a Degree?

Do you have to have a degree in counseling in order to do biblical counseling? That doesn't seem to be in keeping with Colossians 3:16 where we are all told: "Let the word of Christ dwell in you richly as you teach and admonish one another with all wisdom, and as you sing psalms, hymns and spiritual songs with gratitude in your hearts to God" (see also Romans 15:14, Ephesians 4:2, Ephesians 4:32, 1 Thessalonians 5:11, Hebrews 3:13, Hebrews 10:24, 25). We are exhorted to help one another in living the Christian life by admonishing, rebuking, encouraging, teaching and loving each other. These are all the very heart of biblical counseling, spurring "each other on to love and to good deeds." (Hebrews 10:24)

What is important in helping people through their problems is a good, solid foundation in biblical truth and a sensitivity to the leading of the Holy Spirit. When we help people biblically, we offer God's word to them and then rest in the power of the Holy Spirit to work His work in their lives and draw them closer to Him as He continues to mold them into His image. This is especially true when we are helping people online. We cannot see their facial expressions and we cannot hear the tone of their voices. We need to rely heavily on the Holy Spirit and His leading to determine truth from lie, sincerity from pretense. We must constantly remember that we are merely sowing the seed and it is *always* God who gives the harvest.

Cult Check

Let us hold psychology up to our three marks of a cult and see how it measures up. Do these teachings hold the true nature of God in high esteem? No. In much of psychology, such as the "Anonymous" support groups that are flourishing, God becomes a nebulous "higher power," Jungianly encouraged as a mythological crutch to help us cope with life.

Do psychological teachings challenge the authority of the Scriptures? Most decidedly yes! The writings of mere humans take precedence over the wisdom of God, or at minimum, are expected to be considered on a level of equality with the divinely inspired Bible.

The final mark of cultic teaching is whether or not it adds human works to what Christ has already done for us. Once again, we can say a resounding "yes" to this question as well. Psychology is built on the foundation that man, in and of himself, has the answers to life's problems. The emphasis is on man's works to the exclusion of the finished work of Christ on the cross.

Does psychology see itself as a means of salvation? Here is a quote from one of Jung's students as he summarized the root of this type of therapy. "Jungian psychotherapy is...a *Heilsweg*, in the twofold sense of the German word: a way of healing and a way of salvation. It has the power to cure....in addition it knows the way and has the means to lead the individual to his 'salvation.'"[14]

A BIBLE counselor needs to be constantly on the look-out for false teachings, whatever the source of them might be. We cannot merely accept a teaching, whether it be termed "religious" or not, without testing it against the infallible written word of God. Let us remember the words of the Apostle Paul in 1 Timothy 6:3-4 when he told Timothy, "If anyone teaches false doctrines and does not agree to the sound instruction of our Lord Jesus Christ and to godly teaching, he is conceited and understands nothing." Secular psychology offers the starving person a piece of old shoe leather, dressed up to look like a Thanksgiving turkey. As Christians, we should not be fooled by this poor imitation, but let us look to God for the wisdom we need. "To God belong wisdom and power; counsel and understanding are his." (Job 12:13)

Chapter 2:

The Many Faces of Pharisaism

◆◆◆

In BIBLE Counseling, we are trying to help people move closer to God by challenging them to line up their beliefs about God to what He reveals to us about Himself in His written word. As we said before, this is the major difference between BIBLE Counseling and most other biblical counseling thought. When we change our beliefs about God, our behavior will naturally fall into place. Those who focus on having people change their behavior first lead the person they are helping into a form of legalism.

Because this same type of thinking permeates churches today, legalism is often at the root of many Christians' problems today. Living under the Law causes a hopelessness and despair for which God's grace is the only remedy. Why are so many Christians struggling with the same issues and on the same level as non-Christians? We believe that legalism, the spirit of Pharisaism, is a foundational misconception about God with which a BIBLE counselor should be prepared to deal.

When you hear the word Pharisee, what kind of picture comes to your mind? We don't know what your experience has been, but for most of us, if we ever suggest that someone is a Pharisee, we should be prepared to have some not-so-kind words thrown back at us. Why would someone be offended at being identified as a Pharisee? Isn't it because of this picture we have of a Pharisee as to why it would be offensive?

When we think of a Pharisee, the first word that comes to our minds is pride. Our image of a Pharisee is one who has a prideful, arrogant, self-righteous attitude as he looks down his nose at those who are less spiritual than himself. From the Bible we see that a Pharisee is one who views himself as the standard by which everyone else should measure their religiosity.

Jesus said in Luke 12:1, "Be on your guard against the yeast of the Pharisees, which is hypocrisy." Yeast, also called leaven, is used in baking bread. A good cook knows that it only takes a little bit of leaven to permeate the entire loaf. Jesus used the illustration of leaven both positively and negatively. In one instance, He used leaven in a positive way to equate it to the faith like a grain of mustard seed as it grows into a mighty tree (Luke 13:19-21). However, on the negative side, Jesus said to beware of the doctrine (teachings) of the Pharisees and Sadducees (Matthew 16:5-12). It is this negative aspect we wish to examine so we can be prepared to obey Jesus by avoiding this type of teaching.

What is the doctrine or teaching of the Pharisees? The entire doctrine of the Pharisees can be summed up in this one word: "self-sufficiency." What this means is that we rely on our own works of righteousness in obtaining our own salvation through doing the works of the law. When one believes we can earn our salvation through self-effort, there is no need or acknowledgment of the righteousness of God. It is essentially saying, "I don't need a Savior. I *am* my own savior, and I will trust in my own works of righteousness that will please God and make me acceptable."

This is called legalism: the belief that through strict adherence to the laws one can earn his own salvation. Legalism breeds pride and arrogance and is exactly the mindset of Pharisaism of which Jesus was speaking. What always follows is the ability to see the sins in others but a blindness to one's own sins. This is why Jesus said that He did not come to call the righteous (meaning self-righteous) but to bring sinners into repentance (Mark 2:17).

Those who believe they are justified through the works of the law seldom, if ever, see themselves as sinners in need of repentance. This is why Jesus said to the Pharisees, "I tell you the truth, the tax collectors and the prostitutes are entering the kingdom of God ahead of you." (Matthew 21:31) Only those who see themselves as sinners in need of salvation will be able to (or will desire to) receive salvation. The Pharisees and Sadducees were always there to oppose Christ's associating with "sinners." They believed that if Jesus really was God, He surely would associate with the "religious" instead of with "sinners." However, this thought can really only come to a person if he actually believes he is without sin himself. Paul tells us that this is because of ignorance: "Since they did not know the righteousness that comes from God and sought to establish their own, they did not submit to God's righteousness." (Romans 10:3)

If we would ever get just a small glimpse of God's perfect righteousness and holiness, we could do nothing but lament as Isaiah, "Woe to me!...I am ruined! For I am a man of unclean lips, and I live among a people of unclean lips, and my eyes have seen the King, the LORD Almighty." (Isaiah 6:5) Isaiah saw the Lord of hosts in all His glory and saw His righteousness compared to his own righteousness and declared in Isaiah 64:6, "All of us have become like one who is unclean, and all our righteous acts are like filthy rags; we all shrivel up like a leaf, and like the wind our sins sweep us away."

The Pharisees focused on the outward appearance of man and judged according to the letter of the law. They supposed if the behavior was changed, the person would become righteous and, by one's own works, be in right standing with God. Jesus, however, did not agree with this attitude. "Woe to you, teachers of the law and Pharisees, you hypocrites! You clean the outside of the cup and dish, but inside they are full of greed and self-indulgence. Blind Pharisee! First clean the inside of the cup and dish, and then the outside also will be clean. Woe to you, teachers of the law and Pharisees, you hypocrites! You are like whitewashed tombs, which look beautiful on the outside but on the inside are full of dead men's bones and everything unclean. In the same way, on the outside you appear to people as righteous but on the inside you are full of hypocrisy and wickedness." (Matthew 23:25-28)

Jesus emphasized it again in Luke 11:39, 46: "Now then, you Pharisees clean the outside of the cup and dish, but inside you are full of greed and wickedness.... And you experts in the law, woe to you, because you load people down with burdens they can hardly carry, and you yourselves will not lift one finger to help them."

The root of legalism is attempting to cleanse the inside from the outside in, focusing on the behavior instead of the root of the behavior. The only solution is a heart change from within. The reason the Pharisees were angered at the words of Jesus was because they knew they had no intention of changing their hearts. Their focus was on the outward appearance because by focusing on this, they did not have to acknowledge their own sinful behavior and could hide behind the laws to give the appearance of righteousness.

Christianized Pharisaism

Now that we understand what Pharisaism is, let us move on towards *Christianized Pharisaism*. There are many various ways this can happen, but essentially it is a form of Christianity that mingles works and grace. One way this is done is to replace the laws of the Bible with a church's own set of laws that one must adhere to in order to remain in a right standing with God. These can be anything that states rules of dress and acceptable conduct according to what is stated by the church. It can also include the manner of worship and any or all of the following: frequency of attendance, prayer life, tithing, involvement in the church, which translations of the Bible are to be used and such other things of this manner.

Some replace the laws with the "Sermon on the Mount" (Matthew chapter 5) as the acceptable and expected Christian code of ethics for Christians to follow in order to remain in good standing. No matter how it may be labeled, it is works in believing that if the behavior is changed, then the person will change from the outside in. If the focus remains on Jesus, He is the one who brings the change from the inside out. Churches don't have to form their own set of commandments, nor should they.

We all need to be careful that we do not have a little Pharisaism in ourselves. If we are really honest with ourselves, we all have this tendency to look down on others whom we may feel are not quite as righteous as we may believe we are.

That old sin nature of pride is a tough one because it is always right there lurking beneath the surface and can be ugly when it manifests itself. We can never forget who we are and where each one of us came from. The moment we ever begin to entertain thoughts that we were saved because of something in us that God saw great value in is to deceive ourselves. Salvation is made possible only because of the grace of God, and we can never lose our focus on that fact. We need to be constantly reminded of it. This is the only thing that will keep us humble before God and towards others.

Seventh-Day Adventism

One group that fits into mingling the works of the law with grace is Seventh-day Adventism. Although Seventh-day Adventists claim salvation by grace, in actual practice it is denied. When works are added to grace, it is no longer grace as the Apostle Paul states in Romans 11:6, "And if by grace, then it is no longer by works; if it were, grace would no longer be grace."

Adventists claim only the ceremonial laws were abolished by Christ and that the Ten Commandments are still in effect. The truth is, however, that the Bible gives absolutely no such distinction between the ceremonial laws and the Ten Commandments. Those who desire to live under the Law are obligated to keep the whole Law. There are a total of 613 laws in the Mosaic laws that must be kept with perfection if one is to trust in their own works of righteousness to obtain or to maintain their salvation. God knew we would not be able to keep all of those laws, though. The laws were intended to bring Man to the point of realizing our total hopelessness in trying to earn our salvation. Yet legalism teaches that one must always add one's own works of righteousness to the finished works of Christ upon the cross to be complete.

When we add our own works to what Christ has already done, it diminishes what He did and reduces His sacrifice on our behalf to only a partial payment for our sins. The unspoken implication of this thought is saying that His sacrifice was not complete and I must add my own works of righteousness to complete what Christ was unable to do. The confusion comes when believers believe the practice of obedience to the law is the same as earning or keeping our salvation. Satan knows the futility of becoming righteous by our own works and desires to keep man in bondage by having us prove ourselves holy through the works of the Law. He also knows that God gave us the laws to prove we are sinners and need a Savior.

In the entire book of Galatians, Paul is addressing those who mingle works with grace. "Again I declare to every man who lets himself be circumcised that he is obligated to obey the whole law. You who are trying to be justified by law have been alienated from Christ; you have fallen away from grace." (Galatians 5:3-4) Somehow, legalistic churches pervert this passage, transforming it into a warning for those who do not keep the laws. They tell their people that if they do not keep the laws they set down for them, they are the ones who will fall from grace. But the passage makes it very clear that it is those who supposed they could in the flesh finish what had begun in the spirit are the ones who fall from grace. Christ had become of no effect because they had resorted back to trusting in themselves to earn their salvation and no longer had any need of grace.

With all extremely legalistic teachings, we have two basic groups within the church that mingle works and grace. Some will continue on in the false belief that they are more righteous than others and, if they have not already obtained sinlessness, they are very close to it. This attitude gives them a feeling that they are earning their salvation, and this strongly appeals to our fallen nature of pride. It becomes something to boast about with the end result of this attitude being a critical, judgmental nature, void of love, mercy and grace. Those who are works-oriented feel they are in a position to judge others, yet are blind to their own unrighteousness.

Those in the other group are the ones who silently suffer and are trapped with fear, guilt and intimidation. This group knows they cannot obtain the requirements set forth by the church and the laws and before long, a sense of hopelessness and despair sets in. Some call this clinical depression, and the secular "solution" is to receive medication for the depression. More often than not, the false doctrine is not even questioned or thought about as being at the root of the depression.

Although not involved in Seventh-Day Adventism specifically, this type of legalistic catch-22 was at the root of the Andrea Yates' tragedy. Through her own testimony and what has been written about her, one sees the portrait of a woman who had been taught that her salvation was based on how good a mother she was. Inside her heart, she knew that she had failed her children in many ways, as does every mother at one time or another, but yet her only hope of avoiding hell was to be a perfect mother. How could she ever reconcile these two pieces of knowledge? Without grace, it is impossible, and unfortunately, the preacher who acted as her family's spiritual mentor does not understand the grace of God. His teachings are based on exactly the legalism we are speaking against in this chapter.

We have seen many set free from the bondage of the laws by challenging them to rethink this trap of legalism that has hold of them. When they grow to have a proper understanding of who Jesus is and the message of the gospel of salvation by grace and not of works, their supposed clinical depression is replaced with the joy of the Lord in their new found freedom in the Lord Jesus.

Does this sound too simple? It shouldn't. The Bible says, "For God hath not given us the spirit of fear; but of power, and of love, and of a sound mind." (2 Timothy 1:7 KJV) The Bible also says, "There is no fear in love; but perfect love casteth out fear: because fear hath torment. He that feareth is not made perfect in love. We love him, because he first loved us." (1 John 4:18-19 KJV)

We believe this with all our hearts that God is the answer, but one has to have the proper view of who God is and what the gospel is all about. We believe the gospel of Christ is summed up in Ephesians 2:8-9, "For it is by grace you have been saved, through faith—and this not from yourselves, it is the gift of God— not by works, so that no one can boast."

There can be no mingling of works and grace. This is the doctrine of the Pharisees, salvation by our own works and not by God's grace. Any portion of works is like a little leaven that permeates the entire loaf because any time one trusts in the works of the law for our justification is to trust in "self." Falling back into the works of the Law brings bondage and keeps us from the freedom in Christ that Jesus paid for by His own blood.

Oneness Pentecostalism

Oneness Pentecostalism[15] not only falls under the category of a works based salvation, but they also teach another Jesus, another gospel and another spirit (2 Corinthians 11:4).

Oneness Pentecostals teach a strict adherence to the laws for our justification. It is also taught that speaking in tongues is required for evidence of salvation, and if one does not speak in tongues, they are not saved. Water baptism, in the name of Jesus only, is also a requirement for salvation. The UPC church has very strict dress codes and rules of conduct that must be met to remain in right standing with the church and with God. To leave the UPC church is to abandon the faith and results in a loss of salvation.

With Oneness Pentecostals, the divinity of the Father, the Son and the Holy Spirit is not denied, but they do deny the doctrine of the Trinity. The Oneness belief is that the Father, the Son and the Holy Spirit are not three persons who are the One true God but that God manifested Himself first as the Father, then as the Son and then as the Holy Spirit. Although He can be in any one of these forms at any time He chooses, the three are not co-existent.

They deny the eternal existence of the Father, the Son and the Holy Spirit as three persons but describe the Eternal God as the Father, the Son and the Holy Spirit. To the Oneness Pentecostal, God would best describe Himself as me, myself and I and not the Father, the Son and the Holy Spirit. The confusion of the Oneness belief is that when the Bible speaks of the "One" true God, they think of the numerical "one" rather than "one" in purpose, power and glory.

It would stand to reason that if they do not understand the triune nature of God, they cannot know God as He is and have received another Jesus and another spirit. With this being so, then by whose spirit would they be speaking in tongues?

The answer for the Oneness Pentecostal is to have a solid understanding of the Trinity and let the Oneness Pentecostal know that you also believe there is only One true God. Oneness Pentecostals believe Trinitarians worship three gods and it needs to be made clear that there is only One true God, God the Father, God the Son and God the Holy Spirit who are the One true God.[16]

Oneness view the Trinity in this manner, 1+1+1=3 gods, while as the triune nature of God is 1x1x1=1 God. This mathematical illustration may help aid a Oneness Pentecostal in understanding the Trinity. Once they come into that understanding, then introduce them to Jesus and the gospel of Christ, salvation by grace and *not* of works.

Cult Check

Pharisaism (legalism) is found in so very many forms throughout the world today. In its more intense forms such as Seventh-Day Adventism and Oneness Pentecostalism, we see it does fall under the three marks of a cult that we have previously listed, although they primarily focus on the salvation by works issue. As such, legalism becomes a form of Paganism where we replace the authority of the God of the Bible with our own authority, measuring the standards of everyone else by our own impossible standards that even we are unable to keep. It undermines the sufficiency of the cross as we see Paul warning in Galatians 2:21, "I do not set aside the grace of God, for if righteousness could be gained through the law, Christ died for nothing!"

With this in mind, we can begin to see the difference between the judging Paul referred to in 1 Corinthians 5:12, where he tells us that we have a responsibility to judge those within the Church, and the judging condemned by Jesus in Matthew 7:1. The judging which Jesus spoke against was where we judge according to our own standards, the standards that we believe have to be met in order for someone to be acceptable. We are never to measure people according to our own standards, whether they are wearing the right clothes, or they give enough money to the church, or they go to church enough.

The type of judging Paul commanded is a type of judging that we *must* do within the church and is done in the form of rebuking, correcting and admonishing our brothers and sisters. This is where we hold each other accountable, not to our own standards or the standards our church has set up, but only according to the perfect standards of God. Judging of this sort does not effect our salvation, but spurs us all on to "love and to good deeds" as Hebrews 10:25 encourages us to do.

Nevertheless, it is very important to note the differences between these two perspectives. The first is done with a goal of elevating oneself by exposing the inadequacies of another. The goal of the second is to encourage each other in our relationship with God. In comparing these two types of judging, we can more clearly see the difference between legalism (works based) and grace. In Pharisaism there is an attitude of arrogance. In grace, there is an attitude of humility. With legalism, we squash our brother under our own heavy burden of laws. Under grace, we move alongside him and hold out our hand to help pick him up when he has fallen.

Although by far not all those who are caught up in Pharisaism are involved in a cult, when we allow ourselves to fall into legalistic thinking, we are putting a wedge between ourselves and God. We become like a cranky child who desperately needs rest from the day's activities, but who fights the parent's attempts to lay him down. Look at what effect the writer of Hebrews attributes to missing this grace in Hebrews 12:15, "See to it that no one misses the grace of God and that no bitter root grows up to cause trouble and defile many." Missing grace and thereby falling into legalism can often cause souls to be disillusioned in the goodness of God and to exude a bitterness that will saturate those around them.

Jesus has already given us the rest from our work and there is nothing more we can add to what He as done. This is why the Sabbath is no longer one day out of the week, but every day, every moment of our lives. The Sabbath, the day of rest, was the day Man was to cease from his own labor and rest in God. Since the cross, how can this possibly be confined to merely one day? There is no more labor for us. There is only the work Christ already did. Hebrews 4:9-10 tells us, "There remains, then, a Sabbath-rest for the people of God; for anyone who enters God's rest also rests from his own work, just as God did from his." Let us enter into God's rest and beware of any attempts of our own or of those with whom we counsel to rely in any way on our own works.

Legalism breeds fear of acceptance and a pride in our own works, but grace produces love and gratefulness through a humble heart. For this reason we obey, not out of fear of loss of salvation, but out of gratefulness for receiving the wonderful gift of God that we in no way deserved. Leaving legalism behind us, let us rejoice when people are freed from legalism "so that the grace that is reaching more and more people may cause thanksgiving to overflow to the glory of God." (2 Corinthians 4:15)

Chapter 3:

Biblical Self-Esteem

◆◆◆

Self-esteem is a term that is very familiar to everyone today. Our schools teach it to our children. Parents are told to encourage their children's self-esteem. Psychologists get paid for building the self-esteem of their clients. The friend who came to you with her problems yesterday obviously needed a better self-esteem. But, as Christians, we have to ask ourselves just how biblical is the concept of self-esteem.

The phrase "self-esteem," as it is used in the common English language, means, "to regard oneself highly." This concept, however, does not appear in the pages of the Bible, or at least does not appear in a positive light in the pages of God's word. It was invented fairly recently by the secular psychological community in order to alter man's focus from God as the one to be esteemed (regarded highly) to ourselves who are the ones to be esteemed. This type of refocusing our esteem is an important distinction that we cannot overlook.

Secular "professionals" have told many people that they have low self-esteem and that if they raise their self-esteem, their life will be so much better. At first glance, this might appear to make sense to us. However, this is Man's view of how to make our lives happier and more fulfilled. As Christians, though, we must look beyond Man's view because we know that mankind is sinful and as such, there is an inherent distortion in how mankind sees the problems we have. The opinions of Man mean nothing if they do not match up to the wisdom of God. Let us look to the Bible as the source for our conclusions about self-esteem.

Our Penchant For Pride

From the beginning of Genesis through the end of Revelation, there is one sin that is obvious to all: the sin of pride. This is the sin of Satan, the sin of Eve, the sin of Adam, the sin of Cain, the sin of Sodom and Gomorrah. Satan wanted to usurp God's place in creation. The pride of Eve, Adam, Cain, and all humans who have come after them made us believe that we know better than the Creator. We think we deserve more than someone else. Pride. We think we deserve to have our own needs met even if it hurts others. Pride. We think we are better than others. Pride. We think we are worse than others are (and so we have a legitimate excuse for our selfish behavior). Pride. We think about committing suicide. Pride (because we've set ourselves up as wiser than God Himself in regards to how our life should be run).

What we think of as a low self-esteem is in reality a type of pride. When we have a "low self-esteem" we focus on ourselves and become quite self-centered, looking to our own needs before we look to the needs of others. We become caught up in ourselves. We fill with a type of pride that allows us to be excused from our present selfish behavior because we are so down on ourselves. We "allow" ourselves not to pick up the phone and wish someone a happy birthday. We "permit" ourselves to ignore that friend who needed someone to talk to. It becomes "okay" that we don't get all our work done around the house because we have low self-esteem. We begin to think that we are special and deserve a special consideration because of our low self-esteem. Pride.

The Bible gives us insight to the idea of self-esteem in many places, but the biblical concept is quite different from what secular psychology would have us believe. In Philippians 2:3-4 we are told: "Do nothing out of selfish ambition or vain conceit, but in humility consider others better than yourselves. Each of you should look not only to your own interests, but also to the interests of others." This passage indicates that Paul knew the Philippians were dealing with pride issues by putting their own motives ahead of anyone else's interests. Had they not been struggling with pride, Paul would not have needed to include these verses.

In Romans 12:3 we are told, "For by the grace given me I say to every one of you: Do not think of yourself more highly than you ought, but rather think of yourself with sober judgment, in accordance with the measure of faith God has given you." In both of these passages, Paul's assumption is that the churches would be dealing with those who were driven by pride and not by the humble spirit required to be able to understand and truly experience grace.

This vein of thought continues throughout the Bible in passages such as Luke 16:15, Deuteronomy 17:14-20, 1 Kings 19:3-18, Proverbs 16:19, Proverbs 25:6,7 and Luke 14:7-11 to name a few. A point to note is that on the contrary side, there is no example in the Bible of an admonition to someone to think *higher* of himself than he already does.

When we go back to the root of the self-esteem movement, we find that it follows the same basic premise of psychology: man is basically good. As we have stated before, this goes against God's position of the depravity of man and keeps us from understanding what grace really is. A proud spirit cannot understand grace because pride keeps us from humbling ourselves to the point of recognizing our sin and our inability to change ourselves to match up to God's standard.

How do we help someone who appears to think very little of themselves? As with all the emotional problems we will be discussing, we believe it goes down to the heart of Man, to the deep beliefs we have about God. We must draw them back to what the Bible tells us about mankind. After the flood, God told us of the state of our hearts when He said, "Never again will I curse the ground because of man, even though every inclination of his heart is evil from childhood." (Genesis 8:21) In Jeremiah 17:9 we see the bottom line of it all: "The heart is deceitful above all things and beyond cure. Who can understand it?" This decisively tells us that Man is basically evil and apart from God has no intrinsic value of his own.

And this is the key. By ourselves, on our own, we stand without value, without worth, except for a few cents worth of chemicals that make up our bodies. However, in God's eyes we have great worth, great enough that He gave His very life to redeem us even before we cared anything for Him. Our worth is not dependent on anything inside of us, but merely because of what is inside of God. God is love and His love shed on us grants us a value that we could never have on our own and is, in fact, the only true value we have.

Everyone knows that Picasso's paintings are worth quite a lot in the open market today. In fact, most of them sell for millions of dollars. But, if you know anything about oil painting, you know that you can purchase the canvas, paints and brushes for less than $30. So, why would anyone pay $1 million for something that really only costs $30? Obviously the reason is not that the paints and canvas themselves are so special. It is purely because of the touch of the master's hand. It is only because God has chosen to love us that we are valuable. Within ourselves, we have no value.

Once we really understand this, it humbles our souls and forces us to see both the worthlessness of man and the awesome grace of our loving God. These two concepts must run in tandem for them to be completely understood. Unless we know that we are worthless except for God's love and grace, we cannot appreciate how incredible it is that a holy and perfect God who created all that exists reached down to us, His rebellious creation, and became as one of us to pay the price for our rebellion by His own death on the cross. If we believe ourselves to be worth much, then we see little need for a Savior and cannot treasure His grace, which comes to rescue us from ourselves and the sins in which we wallow. "He who has been forgiven little loves little." (Luke 7:47)

Neil Anderson's[17] popular deliverance ministry is known for urging Christians to earn victory over sins by "knowing who you are in Christ." We think he has this backwards. It doesn't really matter who *we* are in Christ, but only who *Christ* is in *us*. Self-esteem is the root of most, if not all, of the problems that people face emotionally. The answer does not lie in us thinking more of ourselves, however, but of us thinking more soberly of who Christ is in us and putting our confidence in the worth Christ has given us and not the worth we or others place on us.

A correct esteem of ourselves is based on the unshakable foundation that God loves us as we are, flaws and all, and that He loved us long before we were even a glint in our father's eye. When our esteem is rooted in the God who is love, we look to Him for our meaning and significance in life and are never disappointed. This adds a securely stable confidence in us that is neither boastful nor selfish. We see our gifts and talents as being given to us of God and humbly turn all praise to Him when people compliment us.

Many proponents of biblical counseling work from the standpoint of having the counselee work on changing their behavior and to some degree this might help, but the real changes begin when the person's understanding of God lines up with who He really is. The Bible tells us that "Above all else, guard your heart, for it is the wellspring of life" (Proverbs 4:23). What we do in life, how we behave and what we say comes out of the spring of our heart. The word heart here does not mean the blood-pumping organ in your chest, but is used in the sense of our inner being, all that makes us who we are.

Therefore, it only follows that when we line up our inner being to match what God expects of us, our behavior will change as well. Jesus confirms this in Matthew 12:34, 35: "You brood of vipers, how can you who are evil say anything good? For out of the overflow of the heart the mouth speaks. The good man brings good things out of the good stored up in him, and the evil man brings evil things out of the evil stored up in him." The inner changes must come before the exterior changes will occur.

How do the inner changes happen? These happen by the power of the Holy Spirit living inside of the person. We can help to guide them in replacing faulty thinking about God with the truth of the Bible, but the Holy Spirit will be the one to effect the changes in His timing. When presented with the idea that they might have an incorrect view of who God is, some people grasp this right away and the changes you will see will be immediate. Others will reject the concept totally. Still others will gradually come to realize the truth of what you are saying to them. The thing to do, though, is be patient and faithful to do what God asks of you and let His Holy Spirit do the work inside of the counselee.

The Misconception About God

When dealing with someone who appears to have "low self-esteem," the major flaw in their beliefs about God is that they cannot believe that God loves them as they are now, without any change they could make, and that He will always do what is for their ultimate best. If someone can grasp these two truths, it transforms their image of themselves into a more biblically higher esteem because of who God is (taking the focus off of who they are to themselves and rooting it in the fact that God is love).

The reason the topic of this chapter stands by itself is because it is so intricately woven throughout the other issues we will deal with that a basic understanding of this is essential to helping others through the various problems mentioned. When someone says he is a bad person, he usually wants us to bolster him with some nice comments about how good he is. But when we do offer them the words they want to hear, they are not satisfied. Many who are caught in this "low self-esteem" trap are rather like bottomless pits where all the nice comments in the world will never satiate their hunger for more. The reason behind this is because they are searching for an infallible, 100% reliable source for their own self-worth. This is the perfect time to point them to the reality of our sinfulness and God's wonderfully faithful grace that loves us in spite of our being sinful.

Those who question God's love for them need to be brought back to the Bible. Show the person Jeremiah 31:3, "I have loved you with an everlasting love; I have drawn you with loving-kindness." (Among other verses to use are: Exodus 34:6; 1 Chronicles 16:34; 2 Chronicles 5:13; Psalm 6:4; Psalm 13:5; John 3:16; 1 John 3:1; 1 John 4:11 and a myriad of others.) Once they see this verse, ask them if God is a liar. If they are Christians, they will most likely say, "Of course not!" (If they say God *is* a liar, then you need to deal with that flawed thinking.) Point out to them that if God said this in the Bible and God is not a liar then this is a true statement no matter how we might feel about it. From here you need to guide them to make a choice between whether they will trust God or trust what their feelings are telling them.

This change of thinking might take several instances of this procedure, but if you are consistent, they will see that when it comes down to it, the choice is whether we will believe what we *feel* or believe what we *know* to be true about God. "Low self-esteem" always comes back to whether the person will believe what God through the Bible tells us or put their trust in themselves.

Chasing the Elusive Dream

Cars, jobs, children, spouses, money, clothes, fame, sports, health, love — where we spend our time and energies speaks volumes about the depths of our hearts. What is it we are pursuing in life? For what inaccessible goal are our empty hands grasping?

More than ever before in history, hedonism has saturated every aspect of our daily lives. From the commercials we watch to the books we read to the clothes we wear, we are chasing after the elusive dream of our own happiness. Yet our quest always seems to fall short of the goal after a temporary happiness ends and leaves our hearts feeling void, still searching for the pot of gold at the end of the rainbow. The closer we think we are getting, the farther away we find ourselves.

Many who come for counseling will unabashedly give their own unhappiness as the reason they are looking for someone who can help them. "I just want to be happy," is their heart cry. "Doesn't God want me to be happy?"

Because God created us for His pleasure and a relationship with Him, we must examine what His goal is for our lives. Is God's major goal for our lives our own happiness? Or does He have something else in mind for us?

Does God want us to be happy? Yes. However, we must understand that He has not called us to be happy, but to be in relationship with Him. This relationship comes about by holy living (1 Peter 1:16).[18] Our goal should not be happiness, but the goal we strive for should be the imitation of our holy God who calls us to be like Him so we can be in closer relationship with Him.

Take a moment and look at the beatitudes. The word blessed means "happy." In giving the beatitudes, did Jesus give the goal of being happy? Or the goal of relationship with God? What is the key He gives to being happy?

"Blessed are the poor in spirit, for theirs is the kingdom of heaven." (Matthew 5:3) What is it Jesus tells us will bring us happiness? A humble heart. The happiness Jesus speaks of comes from striving for this relationship with God through holiness. "Blessed are those who hunger and thirst after righteousness, for they will be filled." (Matthew 5:6) When we are filled with righteousness, we move closer in our relationship with God, and thereby gain the happiness for which we long.

Too often, though, today we are tempted to gain our happiness through the situations around us. Do I have a loving spouse? Do I have a good-paying job? Do I have talented children? Are things going well for me now or are there troubles in my life?

Happiness that stakes its presence on what is going on around us will change from moment to moment as the "weather" around us changes. We receive a promotion at work and we are happy. The driver in front of us cuts us off and we are not happy. Our son's team wins the basketball game and we are happy. We sprain our ankle and we are not happy. We live on a roller coaster of happiness ups and downs. But is this really the type of happiness Jesus meant when He told us that He came to give us "life to the full?" (John 10:10)

Whenever we focus on happiness as the goal we are to attain, we will find it eludes us, much like trying to pick up mercury with our bare hands. It always seems to be just out of our reach, sliding this way and that, almost within our grasp yet at the last moment disappearing.

This is because God never intended us to have happiness as our goal. God's goal has never been to make us into people who live our lives happy at the expense of living our lives holy because God knows that the only true happiness comes as a result of our relationship with Him and is a by-product of holy living.

In fact, this is the "secret" of contentment that Paul was talking about in Philippians 4:12, "I know what it is to be in need, and I know what it is to have plenty. I have learned the secret of being content in any and every situation, whether well fed or hungry, whether living in plenty or in want. I can do everything through him who gives me strength." It is when our focus is on pleasing Christ that we learn to be content in the things around us. The more we focus on pleasing God and strive to be like Him in His holiness, the more we will find the happiness we seek.

When people come to us for help to be happy in their lives, we need to help them see the reality God wants them to see: we are created to please God, with a by-product being our happiness. Once they understand this basic tenet, we can help them to rebuild their faith centered on this foundation instead of the foundation of their own happiness. Focusing on their own happiness is again merely a form of the self-esteem pride, choosing their own happiness over God's goal for their lives, our holiness through our relationship with Him.

There is a fear, however, in many helping people, to confront others about their striving for happiness. We forget that our own goal in working with them should not be to ensure our relationship with them, but to move them into a closer relationship with God. Too often we are more interested in maintaining our friendship with the person than in challenging them to view their actions from a godly perspective.

A great confusion about what love is exists in our society. We think it is love to help people to be happy at the expense of their relationship with God. Any truly loving action, though, will be motivated by a desire to see the loved one grow in their relationship with the Almighty God who created them. This is where we see true love in action. Sometimes this might require us to deny people the help they *think* they need in order to give them what they really *do* need to draw them to God.

Treating people in this way is not at all being unloving. Imagine a parent with a three-year-old child, who wants to play in the street. A truly loving parent will set up rules that do not allow the child to play in the street, not because the parent wants to deny the child happiness, but because the parent knows that it would not be loving to place the child in danger like this.

If we have a friend who is a drug addict, loaning them money would most likely not be the best thing we could do for them. Even if they tell us the money was going to go for their rent or food or other necessities, the reality we must face would be that our money would be helping them to support their life-style, not challenging them to turn from what was harming them and turn instead into one of life.

We find this misunderstanding of loving behavior especially in women who are being abused. They allow their abuser to continue his abusive acts because they do not feel it is their place to keep him from doing what he wants. The most loving action, however, is not to stand by and allow him to continue in his sin. The most loving thing that can be done for such a man is to help him come face to face with his sinful behavior and how it violates God's desires for marriage. We will talk more about this in the chapter about marriage, but the basic principles are in play. The wife makes her goal the happiness of her husband instead of the godliness of the man and his relationship with God.

As we make ourselves aware of this false goal in both ourselves and others, we can begin to see why we have been disappointed in our relationship with God. When we chase our own happiness, we quickly become disillusioned when things happen to us that do not seem (in our opinions) to be for our happiness. Our car breaks down. We lose our job. We contract a debilitating illness. Our view of God becomes distorted because we momentarily cannot see His hand in these unfortunate situations. Disappointment with God overwhelms us as we begin to question His goodness at times like these. This is when we must bring ourselves back to what we *know* to be true and to trust that, rather than to trust what we are presently *feeling* to be true. When we remember the truth of the Bible, we become confident that God will indeed carry on His work in us until it is complete (Philippians 1:6) — and sometimes that involves a different route than what we would choose for our own happiness.

We see this very principle at work in Paul's second letter to the Corinthians. "Even if I caused you sorrow by my letter, I do not regret it. Though I did regret it—I see that my letter hurt you, but only for a little while— yet now I am happy, not because you were made sorry, but because your sorrow led you to repentance. For you became sorrowful as God intended and so were not harmed in any way by us. Godly sorrow brings repentance that leads to salvation and leaves no regret, but worldly sorrow brings death."

(2 Corinthians 7:8-10) Confrontation can sometimes be the most sincere form of love for another, as long as it is fueled by our desire to see that person move closer to the presence of God.

This is the goal we must strive for in the lives of all those we touch as well as in our own lives. Our desire should always be to move ourselves and our beloved into a closer relationship with our loving Father in holiness and godliness, even if it means we will be rebuffed for our stance. The relationship with God must always be top priority if we are to truly love those around us and move them towards happiness as a result of holiness.

Chapter 4:

Depression

◆◆◆

Without doubt, we have encountered more people suffering from some degree of depression than any other problem online. There have been some recent studies that say they believe that the Internet is causing this depression in people, but we believe that the contrary is true: depressed people are drawn to the Internet. The Internet is seen as a way of temporarily escaping the problems that they have or of finding someone, somewhere, who has answers to what they are going through, or even merely finding someone who will listen to them.. It is a way of connecting with people in a more distant way than in a face-to-face relationship. It allows them to interact with others yet still maintain a safe cushion around their heart so they will not get hurt.

There are various levels of depression that people experience. Some experience a light depression that manifests itself in a lack of luster for life and a general sadness. Others experience a depression that effects many parts of their lives but which still allows them to function in daily routine ways such as their job, taking care of children, etc. More and more we are seeing those who have a deep sense of depression where life as usual becomes more than they can handle. These are the ones who often have suicidal thoughts (which we will deal with in the next chapter).

Depression can last for a couple of days to years, depending on the type of help the person is getting for it. As biblical counselors, we are in a perfect position to help depressed people because we have the very source of hope at our disposal. We know that God has the answers for the depressed soul.

Look For Physical Reasons First

When we first meet a depressed person, the first thing we do is try to question them about their physical state. Depression can sometimes be physical in nature. An unbalanced thyroid function, out of control diabetes, lack of sleep, poor nutrition, and other malfunctions of the body can cause a person to be depressed. Although it is difficult to do with people online, if it is possible, it is good to ask them to see a doctor to rule out any physical problems that might be causing the feelings they are having.[19]

Another important factor to rule out if you are talking with a woman is whether the depression seems to be connected to PMS. Ask the woman if this depression seems to come and go and if it might possibly be something connected with her menstrual cycle. This is a delicate area to discuss because some women do not like to admit the control their hormones have over their bodies, yet this can be a significant reason for a woman's depression. If you are working with her over a couple of months, you might ask her to keep track of how she is feeling and what day of her cycle that might be and see if there is a correspondence to the second half of her cycle (when PMS happens). Sometimes just the understanding that this is a symptom of PMS can help a woman to deal with it by being prepared for these feelings. Hormonal treatments may also be a help.

If you are a man working with a depressed woman, there are two things to remember. Do not avoid this issue because you are not comfortable in talking about it, but also do not believe that all of a woman's problems are caused by her menstrual cycle and PMS. There is a balance in the middle and each woman is different on this. Some women are free from PMS while others suffer a great deal because of it, and the symptoms can vary widely from woman to woman.

Hormones may indeed be a factor if a woman has just miscarried or has just had a baby. We talked with a woman who had miscarried at 12 weeks and was so deep in depression she was suicidal. This was a direct result of the loss of her baby, both emotionally and especially physically because of the hormones in her body. Helping her was just a matter of getting her through a few weeks and allowing her hormones to balance themselves out again. The same can sometimes be true with those who have recently delivered a baby. Most people have heard of Post-Partum Depression, which they believe is caused by a change in the woman's hormones.

The reason we are spending time on this area is because the majority of the people who are depressed and seek counseling will be women, and this is a factor you must take into consideration. This is a physical matter, and she is often powerless to control it, just as a diabetic cannot control his body without insulin. A trip to a gynecologist might be the first thing to suggest to a woman who is depressed and indicates there might be a hormonal connection. If it is a medical issue, this does not mean you cannot help the woman with her beliefs about God. Depression is often not a clear-cut condition based on only one factor. As you work with her understanding of who God is, this will most likely help her a great deal even if the depression is hormonally-based.

One other physical reason for depression can be a medication that the person is taking for some other physical reason. Again, if this might be the case, you can have the person call their doctor or pharmacist and ask if this is a possible side-effect and if so, ask for a possible substitution for the medication.

If you can rule out physical reasons for the depression, then we can move into a realm where the biblical counselor can help. Every other reason for depression, other than the actual physical reasons, will be a spiritual reason.[20] We know that sounds like a rather audacious statement, but we have found it to be true.

Depression and Drugs

This is one of the most hotly contested areas of debate with which BIBLE counselors need to deal. What role should antidepressants play in biblical counseling? Should we laud them or renounce them?

The following is a true experience Deb had recently that gives a good illustration of the ease of obtaining an anti-depressant and how it is often prescribed without a proper diagnosis.

Delusions of Grandeur

I looked over the doctor's shoulder as he wrote the diagnosis: Fibromyalgia. He grabbed a prescription form and began to write a script for a common anti-depressant.

"But it's just a reaction I'm having to another medication, I'm sure," I told him yet again. Three days earlier, I had started a prescription for an anti-spasmodic for some abdominal pain I'd been having and soon after beginning it, every place on my skin began to hurt when touched as if it were bruised. My appointment with the internist had been set up a couple of weeks before that, and it just happened to coincide with this other medication given to me by my regular doctor.

I walked out of the office in frustrated tears, looking at the two slips of paper I was holding: one a prescription for an anti-depressant I had no intention of having filled and the other a bill for the five minute appointment. Why wouldn't he listen to what I was telling him? It seemed like his mind was closed to what I was saying. Within a day after stopping the antispasmodic, my "Fibromyalgia" was miraculously cured.

During the past year of my life, I had struggled with a physical problem of extreme fatigue,[21] for which none of the local doctors could find a cause. I was amazed at how few tests they were willing to give me and how little they cared about what I had to say. They made a quick diagnosis in their minds and anything I had to add after that was useless chatter on my part. They heard the word "fatigue" and the immediate diagnosis was "depression."

What qualifications did these medical doctors have to diagnose me with depression? What objective information were they relying on to prove that I was indeed depressed? Had they asked me anything about my present life situation? Did they offer names of good counselors I could go to for help? Were there any biological tests that were done that proved such a diagnosis?

These doctors were not trained in psychology. They had no

objective proof from any tests that depression was my problem. They had not asked even one question about what life was like for me. I was given two blood tests, looking for thyroid malfunction, with the results showing normal thyroid functioning. And no offers of counseling were forthcoming. At one point I was told that I might have depression and not even know it. If I were depressed, wouldn't I be the first person to become aware of it?

Unfortunately, my situation is not at all unusual. Antidepressants are being dispensed by regular medical doctors in alarming amounts, before adequate information is collected. They have become the panacea for anyone who complains of fatigue or other vaguely ill feelings. A 94-year-old woman in normally good health began to feel ill. When she visited her doctor, he diagnosed her with depression, and she was sent home with a prescription for an anti-depressant. She was a lady who was still living on her own, capable of taking care of herself, and who rarely complained of physical ailments. A couple of days later in talking with a friend, she told how she was feeling, nothing specific, but she said she just did not "feel right" and was very tired. This time the friend went with her and insisted that the doctor do tests to find out what the problem was. The lady was diagnosed with cancer on Friday and she died the following Monday.

Is Depression a Physical Disease?

The psychological community would have you believe that depression, along with other mental illnesses, are actual biological diseases that need to be treated by medications. If you think about it, you can see how this is to their advantage and to the advantage of the drug companies as well. However, in actual truth, there is no test a person can be given to diagnose him as mentally ill. Dr. Gary Almy, a psychiatrist for several years, clearly supports this:

> The way I think about mental illness...this means someone is having trouble with their thinking, or their feeling or their behaving. And the only thing a psychiatrist like myself has to go by in terms of assigning somebody a diagnosis or putting a label on them is what they're thinking and what

they say and what they do. That's all we've got. We don't have any blood tests; we don't have any skin tests; we don't have anything that is objective other than listening to what people say and watching what they do and hearing about it from their relatives and friends...You shouldn't be deluded into thinking that psychiatrists are like infectious disease doctors where they can actually treat a real disease and watch it go away. Psychiatrists very rarely have that privilege to treat a real disease and watch it go away.[22]

Dr. Peter R. Breggin, in his book, *The Anti-Depressant Fact Book*, concurs with Dr. Almy. "Depression is never defined by an objective physical finding, such as a blood test or brain scan. It is defined by the individual's personal suffering and especially by the depressed thoughts and feelings that the person expresses....Based on that alone, it makes little sense to view depressed feelings , or the emotional state of depression, as a disease or disorder."[23]

So, if this is true, why are we led to believe that depression and other mental illnesses are caused by "chemical imbalances?" What is the *real* story about chemical imbalances, especially low serotonin levels? Why is it we are being led to believe that doctors can tell someone is depressed by seeing whether or not they have a low serotonin level?

The first thing we must understand is that serotonin is a chemical our body produces that carries signals across tiny spaces in our brains called synapses. Because of the complexity and intricacy of this set up, science itself is still much in the dark about what exactly is the process of serotonin in our brains. The drug companies, however, as well as modern psychiatry, have used the media to convince people of theories that they are hoping will be found out to be true. Dr. Breggin states, "Overall, the functioning of the serotonin system is complex beyond our imagination. Science has hardly stuck its big toe into this ocean, and yet biopsychiatry avidly continues to recruit millions of patients into what is essentially an out-of-control societal experiement [sic]."[24]

When a person comes to us and tells us her doctor said she has a chemical imbalance that is causing her depression, our first response is to enquire about precisely what medical tests the doctor gave to establish that fact. It is also significant to point out how vague the term "chemical imbalance" is in regards to the makeup of the human body. The truth is that no test is given to substantiate this diagnosis because in actual fact, science cannot accurately measure the functioning of serotonin.[25]

This is why people must be very careful in using anti-depressants because they are indeed mind-altering drugs. Doctors do not know why or how these anti-depressant drugs affect the serotonin levels, and there are some studies that suggest use of serotonin raising drugs can cause brain damage, especially in children. "Brain cell death, abnormal brain cell growth — either one can be rationalized as therapeutic by advocates of biological psychiatry and drugs. This kind of bizarre rationalization of drug-induced brain damage is commonplace in psychiatry but is not generally accepted in other fields of medicine where drug-induced damage is usually recognized for what it is."[26]

The plain and simple fact is that most of the drugs being prescribed now (Prozac, Zoloft, Paxil and Effexor to name a few) are too new to really tell exactly what long-term effects they will have. People used to think there were no problems with Prozac, but now there are lawsuits[27] being brought against the makers of it because it has caused very irrational behavior in people. Until many people use it for a long period of time (several years) we simply will not know what all it does. One need only look at the drug Phen-fen that has recently caused such an uproar and has been the object of several lawsuits because they finally connected it to heart valve problems. They do not know what these relatively new medicines will do in the long run.

We believe that there really is no reason for the use of an anti-depressant medication. If a person has a physical reason for the depression, then a medication specific for that physical reason should be taken. For instance, if a low thyroid function is causing the depression, then the person does not need an anti-depressant, but a thyroid medication. If a woman has hormonal problems that are causing the depression, then she needs to be taking hormonal medications and not an anti-depressant.

We are not at all suggesting that people should stop taking blood pressure medicine, thyroid medicine, heart medications, etc. These are for validated medical problems. If you have a physical problem and a doctor prescribes medicine for you, we are not at all saying that you should not take it. Medical problems are a valid reason for taking a medication.

The problem lies, though, with the fallacy that mental illnesses are physical, medical problems. No, they are not. This is a lie the media and the drug companies are trying their best to perpetuate. Why? Prozac in and of itself was responsible for 26 percent of the revenue of the drug company that makes it in 1999. Why are they working so hard to promote it? It's money in their pockets. Make up a disease and then provide the cure...and watch your bank account soar to new heights. Zoloft is making about 25.4% of their revenue, Paxil 24.9% and Effexor 11.1%. By the way, Paxil only became FDA approved in 1992 and Effexor in 1997. There has not been nearly enough time for these two drugs to be labeled as truly "harmless."[28]

Gary Greenburg says, "Of course, the use of any drug, especially one that tinkers with the brain's machinery, involves risk, the full extent of which can't be known until a large number of people have used it for many years."[29]

There is a serious danger factor inherent in the usage of anti-depressants. First, many doctors do not have the time to research fully the side-effects of these drugs. In fact, most of them rely on information from the drug company itself to show its effectiveness. Obviously, in the drug company's own monetary best interests, they are going to downplay the possible side-effects and tout it as the answer to everyone's problems.

Even in cases of severe depression that is not caused by a physical illness, we believe anti-depressants are not necessary. Good, solid biblical counseling is what is needed for these people, as well as a group of caring Christians to rally around them in love. Anti-depressants often make counseling more difficult to do because the person *feels* better and is no longer as driven by the pain they are feeling to get to the root of the problem. Temporary relief replaces struggling with the real issues and becomes the same as someone who gets drunk in order not to have to deal with their problems.

Anti-depressants merely cover up the real problems.[30]

Dealing With Symptoms and Not the Problem

As an illustration, think about walking into a doctor's office with a rubber band tightly wrapped around your index finger. You tell the doctor that you are having a good deal of pain in that finger and ask him for something to ease the pain. He writes you out a prescription for a painkiller and you walk out of the office.

What has the doctor really done for you? He has given you a way of alleviating the symptom of pain, but the cause for the pain still exists and, if left untreated, will result in the death of your finger. Yes, the medication will certainly ease the pain, but it does nothing for the problem except to compound it.

This is often what happens with anti-depressants. They relieve the pain one feels and make it appear that the depression is better. Yet the root cause of the depression has not changed. It is still there and can often get worse because it is not being attended to. Do anti-depressants make a person feel better? Yes, they do (as do any number of illegal drugs on the street these days also). But they are a false hope, a false sense of security, a deception of the senses that all is now well with that person.

If people you work with are already on an anti-depressant, you should advise them to ask their physician to get them off of it. We do not recommend stopping the medication without the help of their physician because some anti-depressants can cause a pendulum swing, and they will find themselves in a deeper depression for a short time while the medication works its way out of their system. A few of the medications will cause withdrawal symptoms that also compound the problems they are having.

If a doctor refuses to help them get off of an anti-depressant, we suggest they find another doctor who will understand their desire to live without the medication. Prescribing an anti-depressant is a quick and easy diagnosis for a doctor and is often more to their advantage than taking time to listen to the patient.

When you are counseling someone who is on an anti-depressant, it is wise not to make an issue of this matter though. As you deal with their relationship with God, He will lead them into making the choice to stop the medication in His timing. However, when people ask our opinions on the subject, we do not hesitate to say that we believe the problems can be dealt with completely without medications being involved.

When Legitimate Sadness Turns Into Depression

It is important at this point to make a distinction between sadness and depression. These two are not the same and you can have one without the other. When a loved one dies, we can be sad and that is a normal, natural reaction. This does not mean, however, that we will always be depressed when this happens. We can be sad at losing them without being depressed. The major difference between the two is that sadness is other-centered while depression is self-centered. Sadness is a legitimate grief over a loss of some kind, whether it be a person, a pet, a job, or a relationship. When we are sad, our focus is on the person, pet, job or relationship or whatever it is we have lost.

When sadness is brooded over, the feelings turn inward, and the focus becomes, "How will I ever survive without this?" This is when sadness begins to turn into depression. At this point the focus is no longer on our loss, but now it becomes ourselves. We look only to ourselves for the answers, and we see no way out so we sink deeper into the realm of depression.

For example, a woman came to us because she had been raped by her father when she was younger. The loss of her childhood innocence, the loss of her relationship with her father and the loss of her ability to trust are all legitimate things for her to grieve over. This sadness is part of the way we were made. But when the sadness turned inward, this woman began to see herself as *damaged goods*, with no way out of being that way but to kill herself. This is because the sadness, born out of legitimate grief, turned the focus inward to herself and that was soon all she could see.

Those who are caught up in depression will be like this. You will try to show them the many options they have, but they will shoot down every idea you can come up with. They will find excuses why they cannot get out of the situation or why they cannot do anything about the situation. This is where biblical counseling must come in. The basic doctrinal problem that causes this is that they are putting their faith in what their own power can do instead of in the God of the universe.

If the person you are talking with is not a Christian, the first step must always be to tell them about Jesus and the grace He offers to us, just as we are, without us changing one bit. BIBLE counseling can do little for those who are not believers (apart from offering them the life-changing experience of becoming born again) because we cannot bring them back to what they believe about God if they don't believe in God in the first place. We can listen to their problems, but in the long run, our only real solutions come from the healing of the Holy Spirit, and before they can experience true help, they must be drawn into a loving relationship with God.

The Three Questions

If the person is already a Christian, then there are some basic questions you can ask them to help them see where their focus is. These are based on an audio series by Bruce Wilkinson called, *The Testing of Your Faith*.[31] We highly recommend this resource for an aid in your biblical counseling. We believe you will find it invaluable as you help to expose the faulty beliefs about God that are keeping people from resting in His goodness.

Depression (other than that of physical origin, which we have already discussed) is always caused by some exterior situation. We become depressed because a situation is not pleasant and we are looking inwardly for the solution to it. When we know that our own power cannot change the situation, then we become depressed because we are looking to ourselves for the answers. Those who want to help people get away from their depression need to engage in the battle of tearing their eyes off of themselves as the source of answers and to help them return their focus to Jesus.

Since depression is based on a situation we feel powerless to change, when we are depressed we need to examine why we are so upset about feeling powerless if we truly do believe in an Almighty God who loves us unconditionally and is powerful enough to handle anything. In other words, it all boils down to what do we *really* believe about God. Do we believe what we say we believe?

Or do we only say the words without a deep confidence that what God claims to be is true?

Is God Really All-Knowing?

The first question to ask someone is, "Do you believe that God knows all that you are going through?"[32] God is indeed all-knowing and sees everything that happens to us.[33] If He is to be able to help us, we must first understand that He does indeed know exactly what we are going through. You as a counselor may not be able to understand what the person is feeling, but God certainly does. He knows how her husband is beating on her. He knows how unreasonable his boss is. He knows what awful things that other teen in school said to her yesterday. He knows each and every little detail that happens to each of us.

Is God Really All-Powerful?

Most people will agree with you that God is all-knowing. This one is not a very threatening question to begin with. The next question, however, begins to dig at the root of their beliefs. "Is God in ultimate control of what is happening to you?"[34] Does anything ever happen that God cannot control? We must remember that God is the Creator of all there is and as such, there is nothing that can happen in His creation that is not allowed by Him. He has the power to stop anything or to allow anything. He is in complete control of all that happens.

There will be some who, at this point, will admit that they do not really believe that God can handle the situation they are in. When they say this, we must always bring them back to the Bible. Numbers 11 gives us an illustration of the people of Israel who struggled with this when they were wandering in the wilderness. Because of their disbelief that God would provide for their needs, God responded by providing more than 60 bushels of quail per person (which probably would have been one to two million people – this would be 60 to 120 million bushels of quail given to them in two days time). After sharing this story with them, ask again, "So, if God could do that, then can He take care of the situation that is bothering you?"

Is God Really All-Loving?

From here we go to the next question. Once we establish that God is all-knowing and all-powerful, then we need to ask them, "Do you really believe that God loves you so much that He always has your ultimate best as the purpose of what you are going through?" When someone loves us, really loves us, they will want to do what is for our best. But for most of the people you work with, especially those who are depressed, this question will be the one to trip them up. It is easy to sing, "Jesus loves me, this I know, for the Bible tells me so," but it is an entirely different thing to truly believe that God loves you so much that He would never allow anything to happen to you that would not be for your ultimate good.

One of the most incredible stories in the Bible that points this out is the story of Joseph. Here was a boy who was taken from his family when he was still a teenager, betrayed by his brothers, taken to a foreign land as a slave, falsely accused of molesting his master's wife, and imprisoned unjustly for over two full years. Joseph was one who must have felt the genuine, legitimate sadness over his losses, but yet did not allow himself to turn inward for solutions. Joseph looked to God and had a confidence that God loved him so much that He would eventually work all of these bad things out for Joseph's best.

When Joseph revealed himself to his brothers, he told them, "But God sent me ahead of you to preserve for you a remnant on earth and to save your lives by a great deliverance. So then, it was not you who sent me here, but God." (Genesis 45:7-8) Joseph had spent his time, not looking at how he could get himself out of this awful situation, but looking for how God was going to use this situation for his best.

We see another affirmation of this in Genesis 50:19-20. Jacob had just died and Joseph's brothers were afraid their brother would use this opportunity to get revenge on them. The brothers expected Joseph to react as they would have, by turning these bad circumstances inward and letting them brood for years. Yet Joseph's reaction surprised them. Joseph had a firm belief that God was a loving God. He knew that God was always in control of all that had happened to him. And he knew that God had allowed these things to happen so the ultimate best would be the result for Joseph and his family. When his brothers asked him, Joseph said, "Don't be afraid. Am I in the place of God? You intended to harm me, but God intended it for good to accomplish what is now being done, the saving of many lives."

Being depressed is rather like standing four inches from the Great Wall of China. We can see only the wall, and it seems to go on forever in every direction. We lose heart because of the impossibility of getting past it. But God can see it from a different perspective. He sees the beginning; He sees the end; He sees the way out; and all of it is under His sovereign control. When we can know for sure that our God loves us this deeply, it gives us a peace in our being, a joy that permeates our behavior. This is the *secret* Paul talks about in Philippians 4:12. If God loves us so much, and He is always in control of things, and He knows what all we are going through, what is in our past and our future, and what is best for us, then whatever happens to us is something that is part of His wonderful plan for our ultimate best. How can we be distressed or anxious or depressed with a God like this caring for us?

As BIBLE counselors, this is the deep faith we want to encourage in those with whom we are working. Once they grasp this concept, the stress of the situation disappears and is replaced by His wonderful peace and joy, a deep confidence in the goodness of an omniscient, omnipotent God who loves us so much that He came to die on a cross so we could be freed from these things that would seek to overcome us.

Then we can say with Paul as in Romans 8:35, 37-39: "Who can separate us from the love of Christ? Shall trouble or hardship or persecution or famine or nakedness or danger or sword?...No, in all these things we are more than conquerors through Him who loved us. For I am convinced that neither death nor life, neither angels nor demons, neither the present nor the future, nor any powers, neither height nor depth, nor anything else in all creation, will be able to separate us from the love of God that is in Christ Jesus our Lord." In 1 John 4:18, we are told, "There is no fear in love. But perfect love drives out fear, because fear has to do with punishment. The man who fears is not made perfect in love." This is not talking about our own perfect love, but of God's perfect love for us. If we come to an understanding of God's love, we can see that we no longer need to fear anything. There is nothing that can keep us from His love doing what He has promised in Romans 8:28, to work everything out for our ultimate best. No longer do we fear because we are truly loved.

Chapter 5:

Suicidal Thoughts
◆◆◆

As depression progresses, it moves into suicidal thoughts. While not everyone who is depressed will be talking about suicide, the longer the depression lasts and the deeper it goes, the more often thoughts will turn this direction. The same techniques that are used with a depressed person can be used with a suicidal person, but there are also some additional factors that are involved.

At the root of the suicidal person's beliefs is that God has really messed up for some reason, whether it be that He is not really *able* to help them or He does not *want* to help them (meaning He does not love them) or He just goofed by creating them, and that they can do better by taking care of things in their lives. And since this is a situation that is impossible for them to solve on their own, their only choice becomes suicide because this is the only thing they really have the power over.[35] Essentially, suicide puts the person on the throne of his or her life and shoves God off into a corner.

One of the most frequently asked questions we will get from a suicidal person is, "If a Christian kills himself, will he still go to heaven?" Obviously the answer is yes.[36] We continue on, though, to tell them what suicide really is, saying that God messed up royally with their life and that they are saying they can do a better job. We then point out that this is not really the attitude of someone who has become a Christian and believes that God is all-knowing, all-powerful and all-loving.

It also is important to validate that suicidal thoughts grow out of a legitimate grief. It is our response to this grief that determines whether we become suicidal or not. For instance, a woman who is presently being abused by her husband has a legitimate reason for grief. The situation she is in is not at all what God wants for her, but because of the sin of her husband she is there. At this point, the woman has two options. She can turn outwardly to those around her and accept the help that they want to give her to get her out of this situation, or she can turn inwardly and try to find all the answers inside of herself. This second type of response is where the legitimate grief turns into depression and then suicidal thoughts. If she is looking only within herself, then she soon sees that she cannot, in and of herself, do anything to change the present situation. This causes the frustration and feeling of lack of control over things to bring her to where the only thing she is able to do, the only thing she has control over, is to end her own life.

When someone makes a suicidal statement, the counselor must evaluate that statement in view of past history and present situation. Since our counseling room is on Monday and Friday nights for two hours, we can almost guarantee that a couple of our regulars will suddenly become suicidal during those two hours on those nights. This type of suicidal talk is an attempt to get attention. Much talk about suicide is actually just that. If you think about it, it makes sense. People who are really bent on killing themselves do not contact others because they want to actually go through with it without interference. With such a person, the only intervention that can be done is by God Himself.

In cases where suicide is mentioned in order to get attention, we know it is a type of manipulation and, to avoid being manipulated, many times people may ignore it completely. The other extreme is to fall into responding in a way that feeds this manipulative behavior. Neither extreme is a godly way of responding to this cry for help. Dan Allender in his book, *The Wounded Heart*, indicates that true love takes a position in the middle of these two. "To love is to be more committed to the other than we are to the relationship, to be more concerned about his walk with God than the comfort or benefits of his walk with us."[37] As Christians, we are called to hold our brothers and sisters to godly behavior (God's standards, not our own) while showing them the compassion of understanding that will move them closer in their relationship with God.

A teenager who attempts suicide by swallowing the entire contents of a bottle of aspirin does so to gain the attention of her parents. Should the parents totally ignore this attempt? Or should they drop everything in order to mollify her desires? The godly answer lies in-between these two extremes. She should be confronted about her behavior, but not in order to "give in" to her demands, but to challenge her to look beyond herself for the solutions to her problems. This may cause her to be angry with her parents, but the commitment must be to move her closer to God and teach her a better way of solving her problems for herself.

The Bottomless Pit of Self-Contempt

For those we meet online, their suicidal talk is screaming out loud and clear, "Help me!" An interesting pattern that most suicidal people follow is putting themselves down (self-contempt). This becomes a type of unconscious (or conscious) game the suicidal person plays. Their thinking is, "If I say I am bad, they will tell me how good I am." Unfortunately, this becomes a bottomless pit and their desire for more nice words becomes insatiable. The nice words you say to them can never fill the painful hole in their hearts. The hole they are craving to fill is that they are loved unconditionally, just as they are, even though they have no worth to speak of. And this love comes only from God above. Until they firmly believe that God loves them, they will be struggling with suicidal thoughts.

Another reason for suicidal thoughts is as explained in the last chapter. The person[38] has come to the place where she can see no other way out of the pain, because she will not trust God and has only herself to look to for the solutions. She rejects any offers of hope, any possible ways out of the situation that is consuming her. These offers give her a degree of hope and when the hope begins to rise in her soul, she turns to self-contempt in order to divert the pain she knows she is going to feel in the future when the hope dies, as it has done so many times in the past. Self-contempt then becomes a distortion of the true view of the depravity of man, with pride being the distortion of the true view of the dignity of man.[39]

If self-contempt becomes severe enough, she will usually manifest it in a physical sense, such as cutting herself, burning herself, undermining her looks by overeating or purposely keeping herself from being attractive, undermining her health by anorexia or bulimia, and attempts to destroy herself by suicide. In hurting herself, she feels a type of penance for her "sins," showing God how much she hates herself and her sins, and so alleviates the guilt and shame that is associated with what is going on inside of her. The distortion is that often the shame and guilt are not legitimate but have been put upon her by her abuser or by the impossible situation she is in. Even if the shame and guilt is caused by her own ungodly reactions to the situation, she intensifies it and draws it inward instead of turning outward to God and allowing His grace to forgive and heal.

This is another example of how being unable to accept God's grace, His goodness to us without any effort on our part and His willingness to forgive our sins without requiring painful penance from us, can cause intense emotional pain in someone. Self-contempt is a form of pride that keeps us from truly experiencing the relief from our pains by choosing to do our own "works" to gain forgiveness instead of resting in the incredible grace of a loving God.

Chapter 6:

Helping the Sexually Abused

◆◆◆

As the disintegration of families grows, the cases of sexual abuse increases. Whether it is rape, incest or any other form of sexual abuse, the toll on the wounded soul is immense. God created us to be sexual beings and Satan, in his usual style, has done an excellent job of desecrating what God intended to be good.

Nowhere else in counseling is sharing the comfort we have received[40] more appreciated than working with those who have been sexually abused. It is difficult for one who has not experienced this to really understand how someone who has been sexually violated feels. Although it is not impossible to work with someone who has been through this if you have not, it requires a special understanding by the Holy Spirit to empathize with them.

There is a danger here, however, of creating or supporting a victim mentality in the person with whom you are working. While it is true that the person was a victim, to continue to live their life from a victim perspective is not the godly way of dealing with their past. We cannot control what others have done to us, but God *does* expect us to be responsible for our responses to those hurts.

Most likely one who has been sexually abused will be dealing with depression and possibly suicidal thoughts. The three questions are still a very important way of helping someone who has been sexually abused and will bring to a head the central questions all sexual abuse victims must at some point struggle with: Where was God when it happened and why did He not stop it?

The best thing you can do to help a sexual abuse victim is to help them deal with this question without any fear on your part. Unfortunately, for many victims, they are closed off by Christian friends who are not willing to, or more likely *cannot*, help them face these questions. We often fear to ask these questions of our own selves because we are afraid that we will expose these questions in our own hearts. For a solid understanding of who God is, however, we all must deal with the problem of evil in a world created by a good God.

From the beginning, the doubt Satan has wanted to put in our minds is that God really is not good and He is at the root of all these evil things that happen to people. Many of us feel the nagging of this question at the back of our minds, but few of us are honest enough with ourselves to face it full on. We are afraid that if we actually do face it, the doubts about God will grow into an uncontrollable forest fire that destroys our faith.

Yet it is the opposite that is true. God is not afraid of those who struggle with this issue because His reputation will stand up to this kind of scrutiny. In questioning like this, we are in good company. The one person in all of history who had a clear-cut purpose in life from the time of his birth was John the Baptist. His parents knew from before his birth that he was called by God to prepare the way for the Messiah.

But even John struggled with the question of God's purpose in his life as he spent his last days languishing in Herod's prison. In Matthew 11:2-6, we see John the Baptist questioning whether God knew what He was doing. Jesus' response is key in dealing with this question. "Go back and report to John what you hear and see: The blind receive sight, the lame walk, those who have leprosy are cured, the deaf hear, the dead are raised, and the good news is preached to the poor." (Matthew 11:4-5)

When we are struggling with the issue of God's goodness and His plan for us, we need to look at the good things, the miracles that He has done in the past and see that His character is indeed good and He will accomplish His purpose in us.

Sometimes those who are going through very difficult times in their lives need help to see the good things God has done for them. In the midst of our troubles, we often only see the bad situations around us, much as Peter, when he took his eyes off of Jesus, saw only the storm raging about him (Matthew 14:25-33). We are called to encourage each other in times like these to return our eyes to the One who calms the storm.

An illustration we sometimes use to help people see the situation a little clearer is to compare life to a Monopoly® game. Let us say we are involved in playing Monopoly® and every time you land on a space where you were required to pay money, I changed the rules so you did not have to pay out that amount of money. What would be the quality of the game if we kept changing the rules so they kept us from dealing with any of the bad consequences that were inherent in the game? It would really be no game at all if the rules continuously changed to keep us from being unhappy.

Life is similar to that. God set up a world with certain rules. Those rules included giving Mankind the ability to choose to do right and wrong, freedom to choose for our own selves. If we were not allowed to choose whether we would do right or wrong in the world, we would be mere robots, performing the tasks that were programmed into us. But since we have been given that choice, some will always choose to do their own will rather than the will of the Creator. While God does indeed have the power to intervene in those cases, if He did, He would be taking that free will from those people who want to choose evil, and this would be reducing them to robots, pre-programmed to do only good, incapable of doing evil.

Why was free will necessary to our creation? If you have ever been in love, you will know that only love that is given freely is true love. A love that is forced is not love at all. It is only because we have the freedom to choose whether or not to love that makes the love sweet. I love you because I have chosen to love you, not out of coercion, but out of my own free will. This is what is love.

God chose to create us so we could choose to love Him. Some of us do choose to love Him and others do not. God knew this would be the result of giving us the choice, but having choice was the only way to allow us to truly love.

Back to the Monopoly® illustration we can see that if I step in whenever bad consequences happen to you, I am not allowing you to play the game and thereby I would be taking your freedom to choose from you. God does not step in to stop evil each time it occurs because if He did, we would no longer have the freedom to do right or wrong, but only the "freedom" to do right, which would be no freedom at all.

Another point we need to remember when dealing with the issue of evil is that we forget that we ourselves are not blameless. The Bible tells us, "All have sinned and fall short of the glory of God." (Romans 3:23) If God were to step in and judge those who do evil, we must never forget that we would be included in that judgment as well. God does not see sin in levels of evil; all sin is equally sin in God's eyes in that it all equally destines us for judgment. If we demand God's judgment on evil, that will always include us too.[41]

We are not saying that a victim of sexual abuse is responsible for what happened to them (usually they are not at all), but God does indeed hold them responsible for how they will relate to people in the here and now. If we store up the bitterness towards the abuser, we hurt only ourselves and God is aware of this. In Ephesians 4:31 Paul tells us, "Get rid of all bitterness, rage and anger, brawling and slander, along with every form of malice." This is not an option, but a command.

The Truth About Forgiveness
God wants us to forgive others who commit offenses against us for two major reasons. First, He knows that if we hold such an offense in our heart, it will eat away at us and consume us from within. Holding on to an offense against us does absolutely nothing to the other person and only damages us.

Secondly, we are to forgive because we have been forgiven. We usually cling to an offense because the other person does not *deserve* to be forgiven. This is quite true. Especially in regards to sexual abuse we can see that abusers usually do not repent of their sin (although some do indeed, most do not). But we also have to remember that we ourselves did not *deserve* for God to forgive us. Have we forgotten where we were when God reached down to us? "But God demonstrates his own love for us in this: While we were still sinners, Christ died for us." (Romans 5:8) We were still sinners, enemies of God, yet Christ died for us even though we did not *deserve* it.

Those who find it hard to forgive others have a strong sense of self-righteous pride[42] because they did not stoop as low as the "offender" did. Although we may not have sexually abused someone, we have committed other sins against those we come in contact with. It may be the sin of withholding our being from others by being detached and hiding behind an emotional wall, unwilling to share any of ourselves with others for fear of being hurt.

We must help those who have been sexually abused to look to the present instead of focusing on the past. There is a scene in *The Lion King* movie where Rafiki, the monkey, hits Simba, the lion, on the head with his staff. Simba reacts as most of us would, wondering why Rafiki had done that. Rafiki replies, "It doesn't matter. It's in the past." Sexual abuse victims often need to be reminded of this simple truth. Yes, indeed, what they suffered was awful. God is grieved over what their abuser did to them. But to stay in the past will only cause them to relive those painful memories over and over instead of moving on and into the future God has for them.[43]

Too many times forgiveness is confused with forgetting. Although Hebrews 10:17 says, "Their sins and lawless acts I will remember no more," we as humans do not have the capacity to forget what others have done to us. We must also note that many times we are told to forgive others but "forgive and forget" is a human idea.

When we are talking about forgetting here, we mean erasing the event from our memory. God *does* want us to put the hurts of the past as much out of our mind as possible, but they *will* stay with us during this earthly life. It appears to be a matter of where our eyes are. In Isaiah 43:18, 19, we read, "Forget the former things; do not dwell on the past. See, I am doing a new thing! Now it springs up; do you not perceive it? I am making a way in the desert and streams in the wasteland." God wants us to keep from dwelling on the past and live with our eyes looking at what good He is doing right now.

As with those who are caught up in depression and suicidal thoughts, one who has suffered sexual abuse needs to have a more godly perspective of the situation. We need to see the abuser as one who desperately needs a relationship with God, without which they will spend an eternity in hell. We ought to be thanking God daily that we have been saved from a God-less eternity and pray for the soul of this one who has hurt us. We are all sinners and without God, we are on the same level as any other offender in this world. When we hang onto our own self-righteousness, we can never really experience God's grace in our hearts.

The Theft of Trust

One of the most devastating effects of sexual abuse is a loss of the desire to trust others. Most sexual abuse occurs within the context of a relationship. The abuser is often a relative or a friend. Because of this, the betrayal of the trust that has been built up in this relationship causes the abused to have difficulties trusting others, including God.

It is this distrust of God that must be addressed. If trust in God's goodness can be restored, trust in others will naturally follow. It is a rather quick process to tear down someone's trust in you, but it takes a long time to rebuild trust that has been broken.

Rebuilding trust requires one major factor: a good track record. Throughout the story of the Exodus and the wanderings of the Israelites, we see God giving them ways to remember His acts of goodness. The Passover tradition was established so once a year they would remember how God saved them and brought them out of Egypt. The Israelites were to create a stone altar on the side of the Jordan to remind their children of when God parted the Jordan so they could cross it on dry ground. In the New Testament we have been given communion to remind us in a tangible way of what Christ did for us on the cross.

Looking back and remembering what God has done for us is a very important factor in rebuilding trust. We need to be reminded of the times where God has been faithful and has done good to us. When we look at God's track record, we begin to see His continuing goodness and love towards us.

At this point it is essential to separate works done by God and works done by men. The abuser's actions cannot be, and should not be, attributed to God. God did not cause the sexual abuse to happen, but He certainly is in the business of taking those awful wounds that scar us all and changing them into incredible opportunities for our ultimate best.[44]

A man we talked to online had spent over ten years being angry at God because his wife and children had been killed by a drunk driver. He came into our room obviously angry at God and all who stood for Him. He asked, "Why did God allow this to happen to them?" We responded that it was because of sin that the accident occurred. The man became angrier yet. "What do you mean? My wife and kids sinned so God had them killed?" he growled. "No," we replied, "it was caused by the sin of the drunk driver." After a pause, he responded, "So you mean I've been angry for over ten years at God when it wasn't His fault at all, it was the drunk driver's?"

It is easy to blame God for the fault of Man. We must always be on guard for those who want to vilify God when the fault really lies on the choice of a sinful man or woman. God does not cause the evil in the world. Sinful men and women do so by the evil choices we make every day. Although sinful Mankind cannot be trusted, God has always proved Himself trustworthy, and He will always do what is for our ultimate best because He loves us.

It may be beneficial for the one who has been abused to keep a written record of the good things God has done for them. This allows them to refer to it when the doubts of God's goodness set in from time to time. Even though the person we are working with might grasp these principles immediately, it always takes a couple of periods of testing for it to become a part of them. We see God's pattern as teaching us first and then testing us to see if we have actually learned what He intended for us to learn. Our role is to be patient and encouraging through the trials so they will continue to grow strong in their faith.

As we see God's faithfulness being worked out in our own lives, we can help others to see His faithfulness in theirs. We encourage them to draw closer to God as we help them to deepen their faith in the God of the Bible, who indeed is all-knowing, all-powerful and all-loving. He is the only One who can heal the souls wounded by sexual abuse. No soul has been damaged too much for His healing hand, and we need to offer hope to those who feel like they are now *damaged goods* because of this type of violation. God has plans for them and He *will* work things out for their ultimate best.

Victims of Physical Abuse

Many of the same issues that sexual abuse victims have will be found in those who have been physically abused. Obviously in either type of abusive situation, if the abuse is currently going on, we must have access to resources that we can refer them to so they can be removed from the situation. Local police departments and social services can often give you this type of information. Your church also may be able to help you if you are working with someone in this situation. Sometimes removing the victim from the situation will give the abuser a wake-up call to get the help he or she needs.

We strongly suggest, in either of these abuse cases, that the local church leadership step in to help the one being abused. If the local church will intervene, it can save the victim from the wrath of the abuser. For instance, if a man is physically abusing his children, the church's leaders could work with the mother to provide a safe place for both her and the children, and then they could be the ones to confront the father. When done in this manner, the father may get angry at the leadership of the church, but he will rarely get physical with them as he might with his spouse and children. Usually one who is physically abusive will only hit people who are weaker than he is, knowing he can get away with it. This is a very loving way for the leadership of the church to step in and protect the wife and children.

The role of the local church is of utmost importance when helping people as they struggle with the problems of life. We will have more about this in a later chapter, but suffice it to say that the local church was never called to be a passive bystander as her people flounder alone with their troubles. Let us remember the words of Paul in Galatians 6:2, "Carry each other's burdens, and in this way you will fulfill the law of Christ."

Chapter 7:

Are Disorders Real?

◆◆◆

If you recall what we have given as the three marks of a cult, let us now take that and apply it to psychology. First of all, cultic thoughts and false teachings redefine God. Psychology redefines God by making Man into his own god and relegating God as cosmic myth that is fine to believe in as long as He does not make you feel guilty (because guilt is bad).

Psychology also replaces the Bible with their own texts, written by Freud, Jung, Rogers, Skinner, etc. These have been exalted to replace the wisdom of the Bible and, in fact, they ridicule those who hold to the Bible as a help with problems.

Thirdly, psychology has taken away the grace of God and replaced it with works, telling us that the answers to our own "salvation" lay within ourselves. We can save ourselves from our difficulties, according to them.

Psychology really does fit into the same category as the other cultic thoughts and false teachings we will be dealing with in this book. Because of this, we, as Christians, need to be on our guard against anything that comes from the psychological community as "truth." We should be skeptical of their opinions and their theories.

This is especially true in the area of what is classified as "disorders." Many laypeople are uninformed as to how something comes into the psychological community as being a "disorder." Psychologists and psychiatrists meet together and vote on whether these are valid illnesses that need to be included in the latest Diagnostic and Statistical Manual (DSM). The majority determines what is out of the norm and deserves to be classified as a mental "disorder."

> In previous decades homosexuality was always recognized as unnatural behavior. In 1974, however, on the basis of a vote by members of the American Psychiatric Association (5854 to 3810), homosexuality was changed from deviant/abnormal behavior to a 'sexual preference.' Finally it was removed from the diagnostic manuals altogether. This is not science.[45]

We have to agree with Dave Hunt. Science does not rely on majority vote to establish what is fact. But this is all Mankind has to resort to when they take God out of the picture. If there is no Bible to use as the standard of right and wrong, the only recourse we have is to go with our own flawed thinking.

In this, we must remember that when sin entered the world, our thinking processes were part of the corruption that occurred. We cannot trust what *we* think is right or wrong because we think from our own sinful desires. We do not normally think in terms of what pleases God, but instead our normal way of thinking is what will please ourselves. Homosexuality is no longer deviant behavior because our sin nature does not want to call it sin. We choose, instead, to rebel against what God has plainly said in His written word and rewrite it to satisfy our hedonistic wishes.

The beginnings of the DSM in 1952 listed 112 mental disorders. By 1994 the list increased to 374 disorders you may be diagnosed as having.[46] There is a disorder for any behavior you would like to identify if you just look hard enough. Dave Hunt, in *Occult Invasion*, quotes a sarcastic newspaper editor to illustrate how silly these disorders have become:

> Does your 10-year-old dislike doing her math homework? Better get her to the nearest couch because she's got No.

315.4, *Developmental Arithmetic Disorder*. Maybe you're a teenager who argues with his parents. Uh-oh. Better get some medication pronto because you've got No. 313.8, *Oppositional Defiant Disorder*....I am not making these things up. (That would be *Fictitious Disorder Syndrome*)....

I know there are some cynics out there who...wouldn't be caught dead on a psychiatrist's couch....Your unwillingness to seek professional help is itself a symptom of a serious mental problem. It's right here in the book: 15:81, *Noncompliance with Treatment Disorder.*[47]

As you can see, the term disorder can now be applied to anyone who has some behavior we find objectionable. We know of one lady whose pastor (not trained at all in psychology) diagnosed her as having a "personality disorder" because he could not get along with her. The term "disorder" has been thrown around so easily because of our own personal preferences.

Another reason we seek to have our problems diagnosed as a disorder is because it gives validation to what we are feeling — and it gives us a reason, other than sin, for our behavior. The current thinking is that if we have a disorder, then we are not responsible for the behavior caused by that disorder.

If we have a panic disorder, we have no responsibility to try to control it. If this were so, however, Philippians 4:6[48] is in error. It makes no sense for Paul to tell us not to do something (be anxious) if we have no control over it.

What is now called a "disorder" used to be called sin. Anger disorders, sin. Personality disorders, sin. Compulsive sex disorders, sin. Anti-social disorders, sin. Anxiety disorders, sin. All of these "disorders" are things that stem from sinful ways of responding to situations, not from biological, out-of-our-control medical conditions. Psychology would love to have you believe they really *are* medical conditions because then they can convince you that you will continue to need medication and counseling for the rest of your life. This is just another way of siphoning money from your pocket to theirs. As long as you believe the lie, you become just another reason they do it.

Multiple Personality Disorder (MPD)

Since the book and the movie *Sybil*[49] came out, there has been a drastic rise in the number of people suffering from MPD. Once again we need to look to the Bible to see how many people afflicted with MPD Jesus encountered.

The only time we see Jesus interacting with someone who was MPD was when the people were demon-possessed. Are we saying that *all* MPDs are demon-possessed? On the contrary! We believe that the majority of those who have been diagnosed as MPD are merely using it as a way of avoiding responsibility for the wrong behavior they do.

Dr. Gary Almy says, "The diagnosis of multiple personality has essentially been an American phenomenon, with little or no utilization by European psychiatrists. The dominant view worldwide is that multiple personality disorder is a product of suggestion in a troubled, susceptible patient, serving in some way to explain the patient's life.[50] From this we can see that MPD is not hardly diagnosed at all by European psychiatrists, but only by Americans. It does not make sense that a true mental illness would not be found in equal parts of the world's population. This would seem to indicate that it is merely a fad diagnosis, following on the heels of American media hype.

What is the best way to help someone who thinks they are MPD? We have found the most effective way is to tell them up front that we do not recognize any such thing as "alters" and that we refuse to talk to the person as if he or she really were the alter. With this understanding, we can then talk directly to the person and use the three questions to expose the lack of belief that God is powerful enough and loves them enough to give them the strength they need to deal with reality.

As we have said before, if the person is not a Christian, this should be our top-priority. If they do not believe in the God of the Bible to begin with, they will not be able to understand BIBLE counseling.

If you are talking with someone who is not a Christian and you observe distinct personality differences, there is a possibility you may be dealing with someone who is demonized. Although this is rare, it does exist. There is a balance to take, however, when it comes to demons. In the next chapter we will be discussing the idea of demonization and the philosophy of many popular deliverance ministries.

What About Bipolar Disorder?

Formerly called manic-depressive disorder, bipolar is diagnosed when someone has great swings between being manic (excited, elevated moods) and depression. Drugs are usually prescribed to balance out the person's mood. Yet once again, there is no biological evidence that this is a physical disorder.

Quite often what will happen is that a person in their "manic" state will believe themselves to be able to do anything. When something is done that is not appropriate, they will sink into the depressive state, and thereby build a wall around themselves to keep from facing their behavior during their "manic" state.

Helping someone who is bipolar is the same as helping someone who is depressed. The same principles will apply. We need to be reminded that we all have ups and downs in life. Those who can sink into the depths of depression might also swing to the other extreme from time to time. This is what causes the psychological community to diagnose it as a disorder.

Extremes of emotions often occur to those who are not being controlled by the Holy Spirit. Let us remember what the fruit of the Spirit is: "But the fruit of the Spirit is love, joy, peace, patience, kindness, goodness, faithfulness, gentleness and *self-control*." (Galatians 5:22-23, italics added)[51] Self-control does not mean we become emotionless, but that our emotions do not rule over us. We note again that if emotions are not subject to our control, then why does God include self-control as something we, as Christians, are to have? The closer we get to God and the more we allow the Holy Spirit to produce His fruit in our lives, the easier it will be for us to control our emotions. This is a sign of maturity in a Christian. As we strive to be more mature in our faith, our emotions will come more under our control and the ups and downs of life will balance out.

Chapter 8:

The Fraud of Deliverance Ministries

◆◆◆

Literally tens of thousands of deliverance ministries market their services on the Internet. People flock to deliverance services to find freedom from the demonic influences in their lives. Demons are being cast out right and left. But is all of this biblical or is it merely another wild goose chase used by Satan to keep our focus off of Jesus?

There are two thrusts to the popular deliverance ministries, one of a ministry to non-Christians and one to Christians. We are going to deal with their ministry to Christians first and then discuss how to work with a non-Christian who may be demonized.

A basic premise of deliverance ministries is that Christians need to be delivered from demonic influences. Their theory is that it is demons that are behind our inability to stop certain sins, and in order to be free from these sins, we need to cast out the demons that are causing them.

Next to psychology, deliverance ministries are often the place people turn when they are having difficulties in their lives today. Those who get involved in these types of ministries are usually new Christians or those who have little training or understanding of the

Bible. The ministries themselves are always earmarked by a strong reliance on the experiences of the "deliverance warriors" instead of a sound, biblical exegesis. We must always be willing to give up our own experiences if they contradict the biblical truth. Experiences should never be used to form our theology, and theology should never be viewed through the lenses of our experience. A study of the Bible can soon reveal the false foundation upon which these ministries are based, including the faulty foundational beliefs and the heavy reliance on experiences.

The first thing we must be certain of is from what exactly salvation saved us. Were we merely given "fire insurance" to save us from hell or was there something deeper that occurred when our soul moved from unsaved to saved? If we look at examples of conversion in the Bible, we see that the changes that occurred were dramatic and immediate, especially those who were demon-possessed. And in each of these cases, the change was permanent. We are never told of one instance where a healing was done more than once because its effect did not last.

Saying that our salvation was incomplete (we were not totally freed from the power of Satan) is saying the same thing Catholics do in regards to purgatory.[52] From this way of thinking, Jesus was surely misquoted on the cross because in reality He must have meant, "It is *almost* finished." Human nature *wants* desperately to add more to what Christ already finished on the cross. It is almost impossible for us to accept the pure and simple grace He offers us without our desire to add a human element to it.

Denying the Completion of Our Salvation

Deliverance ministries do just this. They deny the efficacy of Christ's work on the cross, one even saying that on top of this we need to have "seven steps to freedom" to be truly free. The proponents of deliverance ministries change John 8:36 from, "So if the Son sets you free, you will be free indeed," to "So since the Son sets you partially free, we can help you become free indeed." Will we trust Scripture when we read a truth such as this and place its authority over that of the men who are at the root of the deliverance ministries, or will we mistakenly trust them to have the answers

God "forgot" to give us in His written word?

If we have not been set free completely from the moment of our conversion, then Jesus was nothing more than a deluded liar who tricked people into believing in His power yet denied them the full effect, hoping they would find their own way through their own works to final, complete salvation. We must remember that Peter tells us, "His divine power has given us everything we need for life and godliness through our knowledge of him who called us by his own glory and goodness." If we are going to place our trust in this truth God has revealed to us in the Bible, this leaves no room for additions of teachings to what the Bible says.

Because of this stance, we must repudiate teachings about demons that try to convince us that a Christian can be demon-possessed from within. This basic, yet faulty, foundation of all deliverance ministries has led to a plethora of misinformation to flood even mainstream local churches.

Probably the most popular deliverance minister today among mainstream Christians is Neil Anderson. His is also probably the most dangerous of the deliverance teachings because it is not 100% false (although very few are 100%). His teachings are subtly true, yet false, and it takes a very discerning eye to see which is which. Pastor Steven J. Cole sums up Anderson's teachings quite well when he says, "Reading Neil Anderson's *Victory Over Darkness*[53] is like eating steak laced with arsenic. The steak tastes great and makes up the major portion, but the arsenic, imbedded throughout, will kill you."[54]

But if the majority of it is steak, does this mean these teachings really are dangerous? J.I. Packer, in speaking of another matter of truth being mixed with error (the Keswick view of sanctification), also reminds us of the danger of mixing these two into a lethal potion.

> It is not much of a recommendation when all you can say is that this teaching may help you if you do not take its details too seriously. It is utterly damning to have to say, as in this case I think we must, that if you do take its details seriously, it will tend not to help you but to destroy you. Manufacturers publicly recall cars that have been built with

faulty parts, because defective parts spell danger. One wishes that teachers and institutions that have in the past spread Keswick teaching would recognize the pastoral danger inherent in its defective parts and recall it in the same explicit way.[55]

Much of Anderson's teaching is quite biblical, yet he mixes this truth with portions of psychology and illogical Scriptural conclusions that seem to contradict his position as the chairman of the Practical Theology Department at Talbot School of Theology. It is amazing that one who has a Ph.D. in Theology should miss the basic theological flaws in the teachings by which he makes his living.

You might wonder why, if his flaws are so basic, others do not see them. This is because we have a society that is lazy at heart. We look at someone's credentials and assume from those that whatever that person says will be biblically accurate and can be trusted. We see quotes such as, "A calm, practical, workable plan from Scripture that results in freedom and victory for the child of God. Neil Anderson is one of the most experienced and dependable authorities in America today,"[56] on the back cover of *The Bondage Breaker* by normally doctrinally sound preachers such as Chuck Swindoll and take it on faith that what Dr. Anderson says must surely be truth.

Such is not the case, however. There is much truth there, yet it camouflages the tiny, yet deadly, bits of arsenic within the whole. Let us take a look at Anderson's "Seven Steps to Freedom" and examine them in light of the Bible. Again, we must always remember that experiences should *never* take precedence over the truth of God's written word. It is required of us to give up any and all (even our own) experiences if what they tell us is not confirmed by the word of God. Satan is quite deceptive and will give you whatever experiences it takes to lead you away from the God you think you are moving towards.

A Biblical Look at Anderson's Seven Steps to Freedom

Step one of the "Steps to Freedom" is to renounce your involvement in any and all demonic activities.[57] While it is an admirable and a necessary thing to determine no longer to follow in doing, which is renouncing, demonic activities, there is not one mention in this portion of confessing your involvement as sin before God. Throughout his works, Anderson is not fond of the word *sin* when it comes down to one of his counselees needing to confess it.[58] His concept that we are not sinners, but "believers are called saints — holy ones — who occasionally sin"[59] takes away the necessity for confession of our sins because the real problem is the demonic influence in our lives that *causes* us to sin.

Another problem with this first step is the definition of "involvement" that Anderson assumes. His idea of demonic involvement is that it can even come on us without our being aware of what we are doing. Here is an example he gives of how one can have demons attached to them. "One young woman I counseled had simply ridden along while her mother visited a psychic, and the daughter walked out with her own spirit guide."[60] If we follow along with his thinking, then we should remain closed up tightly in our church buildings among only Christians so we do not "pick up" a demon from someone we encounter. There is absolutely no Scriptural backing to this idea at all. Paul did not walk away with a spirit guide after meeting the girl who had a spirit of fortune telling in Acts 16. Even the girl's non-Christian owners showed no signs of "catching" this demonic spirit from her (if they would have, they would not have been so upset when the demon was cast out).

Anderson tells of another instance of someone unknowingly "catching" an evil spirit. "A former missionary related to me that, while serving in China, he attended a Buddhist funeral and innocently participated in the ritual by taking off his shoes, which is an act of worship in many Eastern religions. That night demons mocked him while he tried to do his devotions."[61] Once again, we remind you to look at the biblical precedent for this and not to the "experience" of a man. Where do we see anything even close to such an incident revealed to us in the Bible?

Step two of Anderson's formula is to readjust our thinking so it lines up with the truth of God. On the exterior, we have to agree with this one. This is what this entire book is about, exposing the lies that we believe about God and remaking them to line up with who God says He is in the Bible. However, as we continue to read Anderson's words, we see that there is a twisting of this truth as well. "Dear heavenly Father, I know that You desire truth in the inner self and that facing this truth is the way of liberation (John 8:32)."[62] In John 8:31-32, Jesus tells us, "If you hold to my teaching, you are really my disciples. Then you will know the truth, and the truth will set you free." What is the truth Jesus is speaking of here? Is it the truth of our "inner self?" Or is it the teachings about Him that are the truth we need to know?

This leads us to one of the most deceptive teachings of Anderson. His ministry is built around the little catch phrase that tells us victory is found when we "know who we are in Christ." At first glance, this sounds like a worthy goal, to know who we are now that we are in Christ, yet in reality, this is a very self-centered goal and is not Scriptural. This concept fits right in with the false teachings of psychology and the other cults we will be studying later in this book. It takes the emphasis off of Christ and puts it on the believer. It is not at all important for the believer to know who *he* or *she* is in Christ. The *only* thing that counts is *who Christ is in us*!

Anderson bases this idea on a piece of faulty logic. Because Matthew 28:18 tells us that Jesus has all authority in heaven and earth and Ephesians 2:6 says we are "seated with Christ in the heavenlies" and because I am a member of Christ's body (Ephesians 1:19-23), then I have exactly the same authority as Jesus had. Although the first three parts of this are true, the conclusion is not at all. Christ is the head of the Church[63] and, just as the different parts of our own body have different roles, so we have a different role in God's creation than Jesus does. The head is in control of the other members of the body. The fingers do not have the same authority to tell the feet what to do as the head does. So we do not have the same authority as Jesus did. After all, Jesus is God.

If we had the same authority, then we would be setting ourselves up to be little gods.[64] If we have the same authority, then even the wind and waves would have to obey us as they did with Christ, yet we do not see deliverance ministers encouraging their people to calm storms. We could raise people from the dead whenever we wished. We do not see this happening either. Why is this?

Because even the Pharisees saw that the authority Jesus had was unique, unequaled by anyone else. The authority Jesus has is very different from the authority we have. Who are we to audaciously claim equality in authority with the God who created us?

Since this is a foundational concept in Anderson's teachings, who we are in Christ, we see it throughout his works. The self-emphasis becomes much clearer when we see a listing of the statements he encourages Christians to read "aloud at least once each day for a month."[65] Each of the 65 statements begins with the word, "I." How can you read 65 "I-centered" statements 30 days in a row and yet still focus on God as you do so?[66] What we focus on will become the attitude that is incorporated into our lives. Not a God-centered theology, but an "I" centered one, exalting Man instead of God.

We are not saying that these statements are incorrect theologically, but the focus on the believer instead of on God is a twisting of what we were created to do. Instead of saying, as Anderson would have us do, "I have been given a Spirit of power, love and self-discipline,"[67] we should be saying, "*God* has given us a Spirit of power, love and self-discipline." Who *we* are will not change one thing in the course of eternity. God's character and who *He* is, however, will change *everything*. It is God we should be thinking of and not ourselves. This is the popular myth of self-esteem that is promoted by today's psychology as we have already discussed in our chapter on biblical self-esteem.

In step three of Anderson's path to freedom, he emphasizes how we need to forgive others who have offended us. Once again, we applaud this stance on the surface. When we hold onto a sin someone has committed against us, we are only hurting ourselves. This is why God tells us to forgive others. It also is a way of passing on the forgiveness we ourselves have received, although undeserved, from the gracious hand of God.

There are two people, however, that we disagree with Anderson about forgiving. The first is God and the second is ourselves. If we "forgive" God this would mean that God has truly committed an offense against us, which questions the character of the God of the Bible. If we really believe that God is all-loving and holy, how could we even suggest that He has sinned against us? In this we see the tables being turned and the creation exalting itself above the Creator. God does not need to explain any of His actions to us (for us to require Him to do so is born out of pure human pride). But because of what He has already revealed to us in His word, we know that His actions are always out of love because He *is* love itself. To question His motives is to question His character. There is no need for us to forgive God in any way, shape or form, but every reason for the God who created us to forgive us many times over. To think otherwise can only be called blasphemy.

The only true type of forgiving ourselves that is Scriptural would be when we accept Christ's payment for the sins we have done and give up the claim to use those sins against ourselves. This is actually not forgiving, but is a giving up of our pride and humbling our hearts to Christ. When we hold onto these sins inside of us, we refuse to accept the payment as paid in full and want to add our own self-abuse into the picture in order to add our two cents into the payment. Our pride keeps us from understanding that there is no longer anything to hold against ourselves because of Christ's finished work on the cross. To "forgive" ourselves would mean that the entire price has not been paid, and there is yet something we need to do in order to have complete payment.

Anderson's step four encourages us to confess our sin of rebellion. Again, by all appearances at a glance, this is a solidly biblical step. Rebellion is caused because we choose our own pleasure over pleasing God, which, at its root, is plain old pride rearing its head again. We should be willing to confess all of our sins, not just the sin of rebellion before God. Yet Anderson seems to take this confession as a "lucky charm" that will keep us from harm and that if we do this, "all will go well with you."[68] Confessing our sin does not ensure that things will always go our way, but it does ensure that we will feel no separation from God. Our reason for confessing our sin should not be for what we will receive from God, but out of our love and gratefulness to Him. We must not forget that all sins were already forgiven on the cross, sins past, sins present and sins future. Confession does not give us more forgiveness than we already have, but is an agreeing with God that we have sinned and a gratefulness for His grace and forgiveness He has already given us.

Step five is to confess your sin of pride. We agree that you should give up your pride, confess it before God and be prepared to choose to please God even when it goes against your pride. It just seems odd to us that there is a distinction between rebellion and pride since they both have the same root. Also, the goal of confessing sin is no longer because it is what God asks us to do, but instead it has become a way of keeping the demons from getting to us, again, like a magic talisman. The focus again goes to ourselves and our own reasons instead of God's reasons and out of worship of Him.

In step six, Anderson calls the pattern of "sin-confess-sin-confess" as a "trap"[69] that keeps people in bondage. However, isn't this what God calls us to do? When we sin, we are to confess that we have done it. The "trap" is not confessing our sin after we do it, but in not being willing to give up our own pleasures in order to choose to please God instead. Confession of our sin does not trap us, but it frees us from the feeling of separation from God. Shifting blame to other sources for our sins is the trap we must avoid.

Anderson's suggestion here is to go to James 5:16 and confess our sins one to another. Accountability is definitely a good way of dealing with a sin that is difficult for you to resist. Praying with another person and knowing that you will have to "report" to them on your behavior can be a positive (and biblical) way of dealing with problems. The thing you must remember in this, though, is that these specific sins that catch us grow out of our own fleshly desires and are not demonically inspired. Satan may send temptations our way, but it is our own flesh that causes us to give in. We do not give up these sins only because there is a part of us that is not willing to give up our own desires in order to choose to please God instead.[70]

The summary of his seven steps in *The Bondage Breaker* gives merely an overview of Anderson's theology. On the exterior, many of the steps appear biblically sound. But when you read through the rest of Anderson's material, you can see what he means by any particular step. This step six is one of those. Confessing and repenting of your sins is what we are called to do biblically, however, we see that in all the "experiences" he gives us examples of in his books, in practicality this means we are to rebuke demons who are causing us to be caught in these sins. This is where we see the arsenic being added to the steak and it calls us to extreme caution to sift carefully through all we read and hear.

Generational Curses

The final step is clearly not a biblical one, although he tries to use a verse from the Bible to justify it. In this step we are told we need to renounce the sins of our ancestors because their sins open doors for demons to attach themselves to us. Generational curses have become quite a popular thing in the deliverance ministry circuit and also among the word faith people.[71]

The entire hubbub has grown out of a misunderstanding of Exodus 20:4-6. "You shall not make for yourself an idol in the form of anything in heaven above or on the earth beneath or in the waters below. You shall not bow down to them or worship them; for I, the LORD your God, am a jealous God, punishing the children for the sin of the fathers to the third and fourth generation of those who hate me, but showing love to a thousand generations of those who love me and keep my commandments." From this passage, with an emphasis on verse 5, many have determined that there exist "generational curses" where if your father sinned, then you will be cursed because of his sins. Because of this, you must not only renounce all of your own sins to be safe, but also that of every relative of yours who might have let a demon into the family.

But, as with all Scripture, we must take it in context within the passage and within the Bible as a whole. Does this mean that you can be punished for the sin your father committed? How can we reconcile this thinking with the following passage from Ezekiel?

> He will not die for his father's sin; he will surely live. But his father will die for his own sin, because he practiced extortion, robbed his brother and did what was wrong among his people.
>
> Yet you ask, 'Why does the son not share the guilt of his father?' Since the son has done what is just and right and has been careful to keep all my decrees, he will surely live. The soul who sins is the one who will die. The son will not share the guilt of the father, nor will the father share the

guilt of the son. The righteousness of the righteous man will be credited to him, and the wickedness of the wicked will be charged against him. (Ezekiel 18:17-20)

If we buy into the concept of generational curses, then this passage directly contradicts it and the Bible is in error. However, we know that the Bible is not in error so it must be the concept men devised that is in error.

This passage in Ezekiel actually sheds light on the passage in Exodus. The reason Exodus talks about the children down to the third or fourth generation being cursed because of the sins of the father can be easily seen in our society today. Ungodly parents (those who hate God) raise their children in ungodly ways and those children in turn raise their children in ungodly ways. This cycle is only stopped when the son does "what is just and right" and he keeps God's decrees. This person is no longer one who hates God, but one who loves God and will then enjoy the benefits of God's favor to thousands of their generations.

Sin is the generational curse we are *all* born with. Breaking this generational curse does not require us to renounce demons or pray certain prayers. All we need to do in order to break this generational curse is to accept Jesus Christ as our Lord and Savior and to follow God and His ways.

The Three Basic Flaws of Deliverance Ministries

All deliverance ministries revolve around three basic beliefs: the authority of the believer, the ability for Christians to be indwelt by demons and the practice of commanding and binding demons. Unfortunately, all three of these beliefs are not logical conclusions to what the Bible has to say.

These conclusions have come about through the "experiences" of people who supposedly have a good deal of practice in deliverance ministries, yet there are no biblical foundations for any of the three. Those who have not had these same experiences are labeled as ignorant of the truth of demons and written off as Christians who are not tied into God's power and therefore cannot understand such spiritual things.

Church history, however, refutes this. These deliverance principles were not used by the Reformers yet God still worked in mighty ways in their lives. It cannot be questioned that Martin Luther and the others who spoke against the religious errors of the time were deeply connected to the power of God. Instead of honoring those who tout credentials based on experience, we should be exalting those who practice solid, biblical exegesis.

A foundational question we must ask is, "Does the believer have the same authority as Jesus?" Deliverance ministries assume the answer to this is yes. We have already discussed this earlier in this chapter, but a review of the arguments for and against would be *apropos* here. Anderson's position on this is clear. "And as long as we fail to perceive our access to Christ's authority over the kingdom of darkness, we will fail to exercise that authority in our lives, and we will live in bondage."[72]

It is obvious from Anderson's proof text in Ephesians 1:18-23 (and other places in the Bible) that the Father has indeed given Christ all authority in heaven and earth. "That power is like the working of his mighty strength, which he exerted in Christ when he raised him from the dead and seated him at his right hand in the heavenly realms, far above all rule and authority, power and dominion, and every title that can be given, not only in the present age but also in the one to come." (Ephesians 1:19-21)

The faulty theology comes in the next step, the conferring of this authority directly to the believer. Steven Fernandez, a professor of theology at the Grace School of Theology and Ministry, exposes the flaw in Anderson's illogical leap that bestows on us the same authority as Christ has. "It does not follow that the believer is equal in authority to Christ, nor does it follow that the believer is to confront demons as Christ did. Christ's authority is unique. He is the Lord of glory. Every knee will bow to Him (Philippians 2:11), not to believers. Christ will judge the living and the dead (1 Peter 4:5), not us....We are under the umbrella of Christ's authority. We benefit from it, and in that sense we share it. However, the direct display of it over nature and the demonic realm was His unique prerogative."[73]

Can a Christian Be Demon-Possessed?

Although any particular ministry may not use or approve of the term "demon-possessed" in regards to Christians, they all believe in the concept that a demon can live inside of a believer. Their belief on this is summarized by the late Merrill Unger when he wrote: "But who dares assert that a demon spirit will not invade the life of a believer in which the Holy Spirit has been grieved by serious and persistent sin and quenched by flagrant disobedience? The demon enters, it is true, as a squatter and not as an owner or a guest or as one who has a right there."[74]

However, a look at the incidences of demonization in the Bible does not confirm this stance. The idea of demons indwelling humans occurs in the Bible under three terms: demonized, having a demon and having an unclean spirit. By reading these accounts with their parallels in all the Gospels and the incidences in Acts, you will see that in each of the cases where these terms were used, the demon spirit was indwelling and in control of the person in question. None of these people had previously met Jesus and this was before the cross so the Holy Spirit had not yet been given to believers. Because of these two things, we know that none of these indwelt persons were believers.

The moment we accept Christ, the Holy Spirit (God Himself) comes to live inside of us. If our salvation is indeed once for ever, as discussed in our chapter on the basics of Christianity, then the Holy Spirit takes up His residence permanently. How can we think that the Holy God would share His residence with demons? Peter tells us in 1 Peter 2:9, "But you are a chosen people, a royal priesthood, a holy nation, a people belonging to God, that you may declare the praises of him who called you out of darkness into his wonderful light." If we have been called out of the darkness and into light, as a child is born from the darkness of the womb into the light of life, how can we have darkness come back to dwell in us?

There is a clear separation that occurs when someone becomes a believer. "But thanks be to God that, though you used to be slaves to sin, you wholeheartedly obeyed the form of teaching to which you were entrusted. You have been set free from sin and have become slaves to righteousness." Notice here that the setting free is complete and has already been accomplished. We no longer have any obligation to sin and therefore no obligation to demonic spirits.

If we *do* have the capacity to be subjected to the indwelling of a demonic spirit, then Jesus Christ is not sovereign and the Holy Spirit we have inside of us is merely a sham. We are not ping pong balls in a celestial game going on between God and Satan, with Satan scoring from time to time on God. No, if we have been delivered at all, we have been delivered *from all*, or we have been delivered from nothing. To question God's power to save us from what would be an invasion of His temple[75] is to question the power of the Almighty or even worse, to question His love for us. If He cannot protect us, He is an impotent god. If He chooses not to save us, He is a cruel God who does not care if we go back under the heavy hand of the enemy and who needs Man to step in and deliver us from this evil.

This is why we continue to press the three questions: Do you really believe God is all-knowing? Do you really believe God is all-powerful? Do you really believe God is all-loving? If we truly believe this is who God is, then we cannot maintain a belief in the lies of demonic possession of Christians.

What *can* demons do to a believer? Well, after the book of Acts, we see no other encounters with demons. And, more importantly, we do not see any teachings *about* demons. We are told to stand firm and resist the devil, but we have no commands to "bind" or "command" demons to do anything.

One verse where James gives us instructions about how to deal with the devil is, "Submit yourselves, then, to God. Resist the devil, and he will flee from you." (James 4:7) Does resisting the devil mean that we are to bind him? Does this mean we are to command him? Does this mean we are to rebuke him? Nowhere in this verse do we see anything about binding, commanding or rebuking the devil. We are told only to resist him.

What further advice does James give us about exactly how we are to do this resisting? "Come near to God and he will come near to you. Wash your hands, you sinners, and purify your hearts, you double-minded. Grieve, mourn and wail. Change your laughter to mourning and your joy to gloom. Humble yourselves before the

Lord, and he will lift you up." (James 4:8-10)

In 1 Peter 5:8-9 we see the same pattern given. "Be self-controlled and alert. Your enemy the devil prowls around like a roaring lion looking for someone to devour. Resist him, standing firm in the faith, because you know that your brothers throughout the world are undergoing the same kind of sufferings." Peter's method for resisting the devil is to stand firm in the faith. We do not see him giving steps to freedom. We do not see him giving prayers of renunciation. We do not see him telling us to renounce generational curses.

In fact, if you look at this passage closely, along with that in Ephesians 6 about the armor of the Lord, it becomes clear that our role in regards to Satan is not one of offense, but of defense. We have to agree with one who participated in a "Freedom in Christ" seminar (Anderson's teaching seminar) when he said, "Nowhere in scripture [sic] does God say to Satan, 'your adversary, the Christian spiritual warrior, prowls about like a roaring lion, seeking a demon to devour'. Yet this is exactly the mindset that characterizes contemporary deliverance ministers, people Neil Anderson affectionately calls his 'colleagues'. [sic]"[76]

If all this binding is truly what needs to be done, why do the problems soon return? And why is it we cannot see the obvious evidence of the efficacy of these deliverance ministries by the reduction in the number of demonic cases? The above mentioned observer of a "Freedom in Christ" seminar has a point when he says, "And by the way, who keeps letting them loose?"[77] Binding, commanding and rebuking demons are not biblical concepts and once again, have sprung from the fertile imaginations and "experiences" of today's deliverance ministers.

If the entire foundation of the deliverance ministries is based on anti-biblical thinking, then how can the ministries be doing what they claim to be? They have no authority to be claiming such demonic influences in Christians, and they have no biblical leg to stand on in regards to the binding of demons they do.

We must continue to measure the truth we believe by the unchangeable standard of the written word of God. Experience-based "knowledge" that does not line up to the Bible always questions the goodness of God who has indeed provided us with "everything we need for life and godliness through our knowledge of him who called us by his own glory and goodness." (2 Peter 1:3) Let us rely on what He has provided and not on any experiences that might mislead us.

Demons and the Non-Christian

So where does this leave us with non-Christians who are being demonized? Do deliverance ministries have a role to play in their freedom? For the reasons expressed above, we do not believe they should seek out a deliverance minister to cast out those demons.

Let us look at a passage that deliverance ministers like to use a portion of as part of their liturgy over a person they claim has a demon and as a support for the purpose of their ministries. In 2 Corinthians 10:4 we read, "The weapons we fight with are not the weapons of the world. On the contrary, they have divine power to demolish strongholds." This verse is used by deliverance ministers to show that we are fighting demons, and we need to demolish their strongholds on us. However, this is another example of taking a verse out of context in order to prove your belief.

If we examine the entire passage, the overall meaning and even the definition of these strongholds becomes clear. "For though we live in the world, we do not wage war as the world does. The weapons we fight with are not the weapons of the world. On the contrary, they have divine power to demolish strongholds. We demolish arguments and every pretension that sets itself up against the knowledge of God, and we take captive every thought to make it obedient to Christ." (2 Corinthians 10:3-5)

As you can see, the strongholds are defined in the very next verse as arguments and pretensions that go against the knowledge of God. This would be any belief or teaching that goes against knowing God as the root. It is when we get to know God better that we demolish these strongholds, and we take our thoughts captive and make them obedient to Christ.

Because of this, we believe the way to free an unbeliever from demonic oppression/possession, etc., is to introduce them to the good news of our risen Savior. In learning who Christ is and what He has done for us, the strongholds of arguments and pretensions will be demolished. Through acceptance of His finished work on the cross, they will be set free by the only One who has that power, Jesus Christ Himself.

Why Are Deliverance Ministries Flourishing?

Deliverance ministries have become quite popular lately, especially on the Internet, for various reasons. One of the main reasons is because we have a microwave mentality in our society today. It is much more appealing to us to go to a deliverance minister and *poof* our problems with lying are suddenly gone because he has cast out that demon that was causing us to lie. Is this really what happens though? Is the demon really gone and is the sin of lying gone?

In reality, the pattern goes much more like this. A man goes to a deliverance minister because he has a problem with lying. He has read a couple of the popular deliverance books out there and decided that surely it is a demon causing him to lie like this. The deliverance minister agrees and takes the man through the seven steps to freedom or something similar, and then the man and minister go through a deliverance session. The man walks out of the session, thrilled at being freed from lying.

For a time, the man has no problem with lying, but then it happens. He tells one lie and then another. He wonders what has happened. Has the demon returned? He starts to feel anxious at the thought of the demon coming back into him. The deliverance minister welcomes the man back, explaining to him that he surely must have given the demon a foothold to come back in. Because of this, it is not surprising to have, not only the original demon return, but for it to bring along another demon. In fact, the deliverance minister takes the man to Matthew 12:43-45[78] and explains how it is possible to be seven times worse off if he is not very careful. The deliverance minister again casts out the first demon (of lying) and also the new demon (of anxiety over the first demon coming back in) and the man goes home.

Although there is an immediate sense of relief once more, the feeling is not the same as the first time because the deliverance minister's words are in the back of his mind. If the demon came back this time, and brought another one with it, then it could come back again. The man returns to life, renewing his resolve to stop lying, vowing to himself that he will not lie again.

Soon, the man lies again and the anxiety rushes back over him, accompanied by fear at being overrun by an entire hoard of demons. He rushes back to the deliverance minister. The deliverance minister again scolds him and reminds him of all the other demons he might be allowing to have control of his life. And the cycle continues on and on until the man is much worse off than when he started the process. Ironically, the demons this man is plagued with were put in his mind by the very man who was claiming to free him.

As you can see, one reason the deliverance ministries are flourishing is that they perpetuate their own clientele by causing the very problem they claim to cure. When a person comes to us claiming to have a demon, we ask them how they have come to that conclusion. Almost without fail it will be because someone has told them they did or they have read it in a book. The power of suggestion is very strong.

It is so very important to direct people to the Bible to see their problems through God's eyes and not the eyes of a deliverance minister and his flawed theology. We must teach people to stand up and take responsibility for their own sins and not play the blame-game, as in Flip Wilson's famous quote: "The devil made me do it."

It might help to remember that armor, as in the armor of God in Ephesians 6, is for an external battle, not an internal one. The demonic forces are indeed battling against Christians, but they are relegated only to an exterior fight. They do not work from inside us. What works from inside us? Our own flesh. Our flesh is much like the "inside man" in a crime. There is no way the outside man can do the job alone, and he cannot come in so it is the inside man who seals the deal. When our own flesh gives in to temptation, we fall into the demonic trap. This has nothing to do with demons inside of us, but merely with our own lack of resistance to the temptation.

In the spiritual battles we have, we need to remember these basics and take responsibility for our own failures. Paul tells us in 1 Corinthians 10:13 that God always guarantees us a way of handling our temptations so we can be successful. Since this is biblical truth, if we fail, there is no one else to blame but ourselves. The sooner we realize this and confess our weakness to our Heavenly Father, the sooner we will be back on track, with a new resolve to withstand that temptation in the future.

Cult Check

In evaluating deliverance ministries under our three marks of a cult, it might be surprising to many to see how accurately our marks apply to them. Because the deliverance ministers claim that we are not completely freed by Christ's work on the cross, we can easily see how they have made their ministry into something that requires the person to live a perfectly sinless life in order to be truly freed from their sins. This is nothing less than a doctrine of works, basing our salvation on what *we* do and not on what Christ has already done.

The authority and knowledge for their ministries comes from the experiences and writings of self-proclaimed deliverance ministers. These experiences take precedence over what information we have on the topic from the Bible. If you remove all portions that refer to the minister's experience, most deliverance writings would be very meager indeed. There are several ministers who have no problem in declaring that their knowledge of demons has come from the demons themselves.[79] This is precisely what Paul meant when he talked about "things taught by demons" in 1 Timothy 4:1. In this verse, he says that because of these things taught by demons, many will abandon the faith they were taught when they were young and will follow after these things. Why would it be to Satan's advantage to promote deliverance ministries? As we have seen earlier, it becomes a hopelessly circular trap that Christians can get into and thereby become so focused on themselves that they are no earthly good to the kingdom of God.

Do deliverance ministries challenge the very being of God? Yes, indeed. If what Christ did on the cross was not enough to save us, then we require a deliverance minister to step in and finish the job. As you can see, this raises up the man over Christ.

So what is the solution to sins that try to entrap us, sins that we become "addicted" to? In the next chapter, we show the biblical solution to sins we find hard to resist.

Chapter 9:

The Great Addiction

❖❖❖

Addictions are one of the touchiest areas to deal with when working with people. On the one hand, they desperately want help to fight the addiction, yet on the other hand, they hesitate opening themselves to the fact that there is a deficiency in an area of their lives that they are embarrassed to have exposed.

We all have areas of our lives that we feel weak in, and it is those areas that we are most likely to try to hide from public ridicule. This is what happens to people who are caught up in an addiction of any kind. It becomes a tender spot that we are eager to protect by hiding it from others.

People become addicted to many things, food, drugs, alcohol, smoking, a perfect body, exercise, owning things, and pornography to mention a few. Although addictions may have different surrounding circumstances or effects, they all have the same basic root. When it boils down to it, an addiction is caused because we are choosing our own pleasure over pleasing God.

To make certain we have the same thing in mind when we are talking about addictions, let us give you our definition of it. An addiction is a life-dominating behavior in which we feel compelled to engage. The behavior by itself may or may not be a sin, but our attitude towards it most certainly is. We allow it to rule over us. We do not believe, however, that addictions are caused by uncontrollable compulsions that we cannot change. They are composed of a series of choices we make to feed our own desires.

Although we might *feel* as if these addictions control us and that there is nothing we can do to change them, this is not the truth we find in the Bible. We read in 1 Corinthians 6:9-11, "Do you not know that the wicked will not inherit the kingdom of God? Do not be deceived: Neither the sexually immoral nor idolaters nor adulterers nor male prostitutes nor homosexual offenders nor thieves nor the greedy nor drunkards nor slanderers nor swindlers will inherit the kingdom of God. And that is what some of you were. But you were washed, you were sanctified, you were justified in the name of the Lord Jesus Christ and by the Spirit of our God." If sexual addictions, homosexuality, or alcoholism cannot be changed, how can this verse be explained? How is it these people *used to be* these things but are no longer?

While it is true on a level that we, in and of ourselves, do not have what it takes to stop sinning, through the work of Christ on the cross and the indwelling of the Holy Spirit inside of us, we have access to His power that supercedes any other hold on us. The reason addictive sins have such a hold on us is because there is a part of us that wants to cling onto it. In that sin, we find a type of comfort, enjoyment, and most likely a sense of controlling at least one thing in our otherwise out of control lives.

Addicted to Control

Most people who become addicted to a specific sin are really addicted to control. They are not willing that anyone, be it society, friends, family, or even God, dictate to them what they can consume, who they can sleep with, what they can look at, where they can go or any other aspect of their lives. Many who are bulimic or anorexic or who overeat find food is the only thing in their lives they truly can control and they do so either by overeating, undereating or overeating and purging.

For a Christian, wanting to control others or ourselves in this way stands in direct opposition to being controlled by the Holy Spirit. We who are Christians have been freed from slavery to sin.

We are no longer obligated to live under the control of our sinful desires. Paul tells us about the obligation we *do* have in Romans 8:12-15: "Therefore, brothers, we have an obligation—but it is not to the sinful nature, to live according to it. For if you live according to the sinful nature, you will die; but if by the Spirit you put to death the misdeeds of the body, you will live, because those who are led by the Spirit of God are sons of God. For you did not receive a spirit that makes you a slave again to fear, but you received the Spirit of sonship. And by him we cry, '*Abba,* Father.'"

Does this mean that if we continue sinning we have lost our salvation? No, this is not at all what it means when it says, "For if you live according to the sinful nature, you will die." In the truly regenerated heart, there will be a desire to do what is right, even if there are times that desire is overwhelmed by our own sinful desires. However, if we are complacent in our sin, satisfied living in it, our consciences untweaked by any move of the Holy Spirit, then we must question if the Holy Spirit does indeed dwell in us or not (whether our conversion was real or merely words we repeated after someone).

One of the purposes of God giving us the Holy Spirit in our lives is to convict us of our sins against God.[80] If we do not hear His voice in the way of guilt and shame when we sin, then we must ask ourselves whether we have refused to listen to Him or if He does not dwell within us to begin with. He *will* convict Christians of their sin; whether we listen or not is our choice.

We are not going to deal here with those who feel comfortable in their sin and see no reason for change. If this is the case, we must assume an unregenerate heart. It is our responsibility to question those who claim to be Christians but are unwilling to make any changes in their lives because of it. One of the major differences between BIBLE counseling and other forms of biblical counseling is that when someone presents themselves to us as being a Christian, we do not take that at face value. Most biblical counselors will assume that anyone who considers himself a Christian has a proper understanding of what that means. Working on the Internet as we do, we assume exactly the opposite. Most of those who come to us for help have a wrong view of who God is and that is where their problem lies.

If someone does not want to turn from an obvious sin and does not feel that what they are doing is wrong, we would work with them as with an unbeliever, presenting the gospel to them. The others, however, who are Christians and who know what they are doing is wrong, have not come to the point yet where they are willing to give up their addiction to do things God's way instead. At this point, we must depend on the perfect timing of the Holy Spirit and not rush in to condemn them of their sin, demanding instant change.

Much of the biblical counseling that is out there now is so behavior-based that it forgets where the real battle needs to take place: in the heart. For some, God changes their desires immediately upon conversion. For others, it takes longer because the issue is not one of behavior, but one of the heart.

In regards to addictions, we could probably write an entire book on the subject, and it would sound as sterile and aloof as many clinical books on the topic. We've decided instead to be more transparent with the subject and offer you a view "from the inside" of an addiction. Some of what you read might seem to you a bit silly if you have never been caught in the addiction of overeating, but we believe if you look closely, you will see parallels with all the other addictive sins that make people both miserable and delighted at the same time.

The Reality of Addictive Sin, Deb's Story
4/7/01 Saturday

Today is day 3. Day 3 of what you might ask? Three days ago I humbled my heart before God and confessed to Him my sinful eating habits. I eat when I'm not hungry because I'm bored. I eat things that have way too many calories in them just because they taste good. I binge on favorite foods just to feel that orgy of taste in my mouth, totally ignoring the pain in my stomach because I've eaten far more than my stomach can hold.

What has happened in these three days? Well, I'm going to set this down on paper so maybe I can use it to help others some day. If I don't, well, then, I guess I'll have something to remember this by.

I've done so many diets, starved myself, limited myself so much that I decided I couldn't do that again. Besides, since none of them were working, obviously they weren't getting at the root of my problem. If the depression I used to suffer from was caused by my being frustrated because I was not in control of my life, perhaps the eating problem was the same. After all, I know that I often ate things that were bad for me just because I wanted to. I would lose a few pounds and then gain back more because it scared me to be out of control of my body in such a way. Weird. The more weight I gained, the more out of control I really was. And yet, while I felt that on one level, on another level I was more in control of my life because I was eating what and when I wanted to.

So, the time came. The book Doug and I are writing has a chapter on addictions. Since he was writing on the false teachings, I was the chosen one to work on the more counseling oriented chapters...which meant, addictions. Ever since last summer I have been wracking my brain to try to figure out what to write in the chapter of a book about how to biblically deal with addictions, all the while wanting to hide my own addiction to food. Oh, not that it can be hidden when you weigh 245 and are only 5'3" tall. It's pretty obvious to everyone around you.

Sure, I would have liked to have excused it or claimed heredity, but at the back of my mind, the matter wasn't settled at all. Open Arms believes that the problems we are faced with are doctrinally oriented. If this is really true, if I really believed what I was using to counsel others, then my overeating must also be because I am not believing God to be who He is and me to be who I am, a wretched sinner, choosing my own way over His.

I took the matter up with Doug one night and he, being a dear who didn't want to hurt my feelings, told me that yes, addictions really do come down to our choosing our own self-satisfaction over what God has told us is right but that change would come in time. But I think the time has now come, three days ago.

After talking with Doug, I felt drawn to go before God and confess to Him that my eating habits were not pleasing to Him. I admitted how I overeat instead of trusting in His provision. I look for comfort in food instead of looking for comfort in Him. I choose to satisfy my own selfish desires rather than do what is best for the kingdom of God. There were so many people I'd helped to take the speck out of their eyes that it was now time for me to take the plank out of my own eye by confessing my sin to our holy and perfect God.

When it came time for breakfast the next morning, something was different. I was a bit rushed and normally would have stopped at McDonald's for a quick breakfast on the go, but instead I found myself reaching for the yogurt in the frig. When I packed my lunch, I "felt" like eating a salad and some brown rice. I took less than I normally do without even realizing it. I was hungry at noon but not hungry throughout the day.

I thought to myself, "This is just a fluke. I'm just not hungry much today for some reason. I bet I'll be really hungry after school because I haven't had much today." I was a bit concerned because it was the end of the week and the cupboards were kind of sparse so I needed to stop at the grocery store to pick a few things up on my way home. Well, any woman who does the grocery shopping in her house will tell you the first cardinal rule to shopping: Never go to the grocery when you are hungry.

But the end of school came that day and my stomach was satisfied. I began to wonder if I was getting sick! I am usually famished by the end of the school day and often carry yogurt or some kind of snack (chocolate usually!) to tide me over till supper. Again, I was skeptical. Thinking to myself as I walked into Kroger's, "Yep, this won't last long when I start seeing the food in here. I'll be plenty hungry when I start walking down the aisles." But it didn't happen. In my mind, instead of walking past items and asking myself, "What do I want to eat?" I asked myself, "Would this be pleasing to God if I eat it?"

This was getting really weird by now. My grocery cart was filled with vegetables, fruits, lean cuts of meat and healthy cereals, everything I knew in my mind was good for me, but what I'd passed by on before because it didn't taste as good as other things. Hmmmm. I figured this was just because it was so on my mind to begin eating healthier.

It's now day three of this, and the same things have been happening. When faced with an eating temptation (like those Cadbury Caramel Eggs, *yum*!), the first thing to cross my mind was, "Will this be pleasing to God if I eat it?" It was almost as if God was saying, "Trust me in this, honey. If you worry more about pleasing Me than about pleasing yourself, you will never be disappointed in the results."

So, this is where I am now. I'm not going to show anyone this writing until I am certain this is from God and not something within myself. But I know one thing for sure...confessing your sin is always something that pleases God so I don't think I can go wrong with it. Am I still skeptical? I sure am. It's such a simple answer! Is this really how God wants me to deal with my addiction to food? I guess it all makes sense. When we get our eyes off of ourselves and put them squarely on His face, He will give us the desires of our hearts, since the desires of our hearts are to do whatever it takes to please Him. It does seem to be consistent with how God works – the last will be first, those who gain their lives will lose them and those who lose their lives for His sake will gain them. If I take my eyes off of my own self and my own desires and put them on Him, I can't go wrong spiritually.

I keep thinking of Philippians 4:13. "I can do all things through Him who gives me strength." And I guess the only real way to do that is to be more concerned about pleasing Him than pleasing myself.

Oh, and the scales this morning? 241. May I always choose to please Him over myself!

To be continued.....

4/8/01 Sunday

Ouch, Lord! You've drawn me into this because I humbled my heart to you, but that heart I thought was humble keeps rising up proudly over and over again. The scale yesterday sent me into another bout of pride about (of all things!) my humility! I am so sorry, Lord, that I have such a proud heart. I know that all I have comes only from you and it is only through your grace that I am anything. It's so painful to have to face the sin inside of me, and it seems like the more I admit it to you, the more of it inside me you show me. I guess it is true what they say: the closer you get to our Holy God, the more sinful you will see yourself as. Have mercy on me, Father, for I am but dust! Pour out myself so there is more room for you.

I was wondering earlier today why this was going as it has. I mean, I've gone to God before and asked for His help to lose weight. Why should I expect this time to be any different? Well, God gave me the answer. (In times like this, you must understand that I am not saying God verbally spoke to me. I am saying that He impressed these things on my heart. I believe they are from Him, but I am not going to declare, "Thus saith the Lord" as some do because I am fallible and often make mistakes. One of my greatest fears is putting words in the Almighty's mouth when they are not from Him. One should not proclaim himself a prophet unless they are very certain that it is God who gave them the words. If there is a lack of truth in what I say I believe was from Him, then it lies not in the Sovereign God above, but in this inadequate human vessel.)

The reason was all in a matter of motive. It was as if God was telling me that all the other times my motive was to lose weight. This time, however, He reminded me, my motive was different. Before, I was seeking *my* goal (i.e., to lose weight). This time I am seeking *His* goal for my life (i.e., to live in humble obedience to His voice, no matter what my body might be telling me).

So, God taught me this in the morning and gave me a pop quiz over it at noon. I was sitting in church and got so much hungrier than I have been in the past 4 days. It was pretty intense! I was overwhelmed by weakness and a horrible headache that made it almost impossible to think. Well, you must understand that the church I go to is a 30-minute drive from my home and since it is rather out in the country, there are not a lot of places of any kind between here and there. However, there is a Burger King about ten minutes from home. I asked God what I should do. Should I eat at BK or should I try to tough it out till I was home? After all, ten more minutes wasn't going to kill me...but then it wasn't just 10 minutes. By the time I fixed something to eat, it would be at least another 20 minutes – and the headache was getting worse, making it hard to drive because of its intensity (those who are addicted to food will understand me here, those who aren't, well, an extra 10 minutes one way or the other doesn't seem to make any sense to you, and this is all silliness...but those who are addicted as I am, they will understand and it is for them I am writing this). I asked God what would be the most pleasing to Him for me to do?

I weighed the options. If I waited till I got home, I could make something healthy, salad, vegetables, a lean cut of meat. If I stopped at BK, I wouldn't eat healthy (I'm just not a fan of fast food places' salads) and it would really add the ol' calories to my day. Why wasn't God answering me this time? Why wouldn't He tell me what would be most pleasing to Him?

Finally, He responded. "Deb," He reminded me, "this is not an issue of what foods you can or cannot eat or how many calories are involved. Make no mistake, my dear, it is purely a question of the heart. Are you willing to humble your heart to me?" Again, there was my pride popping up. Or maybe it was really my vanity this time. Less calories=less weight, right? But here I was, changing my motivation back to myself instead of just wanting to please God. It really doesn't matter to God whether I eat a cheeseburger and fries or if I eat salad and vegetables. After all, He has provided it all. What He's concerned about is my motivation for doing so, my reason for anything I do. The eating and drinking is not the problem. The problem is whether everything I do is done because I love God and want to please Him with everything I do or not. And you know what? A burger and fries tastes *really* good when served with humble pie. :o)

4/9/01 Monday

It's really interesting to examine motives on something. It amazes me how this whole addiction thing is not an isolated part of my being, but rather is making changes in all of my life. In training myself to ask myself whether or not something I'm about to put in my mouth is pleasing to God, I have to apply such a thing to the other parts of my life as well. Is my performance at work pleasing to God? Is the way I use my free time pleasing to God? Whew! This submitting to His will over mine sure is hard work!

Just about the time I think I am getting the knack of this submission thing, someone brings in brownies and banana nut bread! So, here's the choice. What is most pleasing to Him? And that's the easy question. Now, for the hard one. Will I choose to do it? The first brownie, not bad. The second? Totally for my own selfish desires. Sigh. Confess and try to do better next time.

I think there is one really important factor here that made the rest of the day easier. So many people when they fail feel like they have to "pay" for their sin by beating themselves up. That is a lesson God has been teaching me for a very long time. Self-contempt keeps me from allowing God to be the one to have paid for my sins and puts me in the place of my own "savior." God does not require us to "pay" for our sins; He's already done that. My responsibility is to confess the sin, which means to admit my guilt before Him. Do I need to ask Him for forgiveness each time? I don't believe so. To me that is rather like my father giving me a car and then for me to continue asking him for it. The car has already been given to me just as the forgiveness has already been given 2000 years ago on the cross.

What does God expect from me then? Gratitude. And love. You know, the more I am getting into things, the more I am seeing it as really a matter of gratitude. Am I grateful for what I am and what I have? Or do I want more, more food, more love, more whatever? Will I be satisfied with what God has provided or will I deny that He has provided all I really need and turn instead to myself, believing my desires are not really satisfied by what He has provided?

I have hesitated even writing these things down because it forces me to think more about myself than I sometimes think I should. But it also forces me to think about the incredible grace of my loving Lord. How wonderful He is to grant me His love and forgiveness especially when I have such a rebellious heart.

4/11/01 Wednesday

I didn't write yesterday mainly out of fatigue, but also because there were not any pressing things to deal with. And perhaps it is this uneventful-ness that is what is most remarkable. When I was on a diet, whichever one it might have been, I became obsessed with food and my days revolved around my meals, snacks, or whatever. But these past few days have been normal days. I have not been any more or less focused on my meals and instead of the frantic obsessed mode I normally go into, I am filled with a deep peace and calm assurance that this is the right path.

I did step on the scale this morning (239) but I'm not sure I'll be doing that much more. I don't think that is in keeping with why I am doing this. If it is really that I am doing this to focus on pleasing God and not to lose weight, then I have no need of scales. It's not the numbers on the scale that concerns God, but the attitude of my heart, and so that should be what concerns me as well.

Here's what I think is kind of interesting about all of this. One might think this kind of process that I am going through might turn someone legalistic, trying to keep the "law," but just the contrary is true. When I tried to diet, I felt under a bondage. Yet here I am, feeling freer than I've ever felt. I don't feel any type of bondage to food or to a diet or to anyone or anything. I am not bound to the law of obeying God, but I choose to obey out of my love and gratefulness to Him. Because of this, I feel free!

The idea of my eating habits was that I was going to be in control of them and nobody was going to tell me what to eat or when to eat or how much. I was going to be my own boss. And that included God. One would think that giving all of this over to God would be to rip that control from me and make me a type of "victim" (or at minimum a puppet) to God who would dictate my every move. If that were so, why do I feel like the little boy who watched Jesus take his five loaves and two small fishes and feed five thousand people with them? It's all so much different than focusing on myself! Praise be to God who grants us His grace and then gives back to us even more than we could ever ask or imagine!

I need to take a moment here to explain a few things for those who might be reading this and who do not know me personally. You might be thinking that this is an average time of year for me, however, this is not so. Last Friday was my fifth anniversary, or well, *would* have been my fifth anniversary. This Monday was my ex-husband's birthday and today is my birthday. We had planned it that way so we could share all of our joyful times together within just a few days.

A year and a half ago the divorce was final. Why did we get divorced? Ironically because he had an addiction – to pornography.[81] Do I think how I am handling my addiction to food would have helped him? Yes, I really do believe that. Although he'd claimed to be a Christian, he'd only said the words. He was not able to humble his heart and really submit to God. He couldn't bear to give up his own desires and choose to focus on God instead.

He chose his own pleasure over anyone else's, including God's and mine, and ended up looking to another woman for happiness. I pray that someday God will lead him to understand exactly what his heart is searching for and how only God can fill that hole he seeks to fill with pornography.

The reason I shared this is that I think it's important for you to know that out of all the weeks of the year, this past one would probably be the most trying for me. And yet, through it all, I have had a deep, abiding peace because I have found the rest, the Sabbath-rest, spoken of in Hebrews 4:9-11. "There remains, then, a Sabbath-rest for the people of God; for anyone who enters God's rest also rests from his own work, just as God did from his. Let us, therefore, make every effort to enter that rest, so that no one will fall by following their example of disobedience." That rest comes when we humble our hearts, admit our helplessness, and fall on the mercy and grace of our loving Lord who gave His life for us!

4/12/01 Thursday

For some reason today I have been thinking about the term gluttony. I know that many classify it as a sin, but the Bible really doesn't speak of it. In the New International Version, it is mentioned only once in a verse in Proverbs. So, is gluttony really a sin? I am convinced that it is not the actual eating God sees as sinful, but the attitude behind it. God always looks to the heart when He sees us. He sees our intentions, the deep motivations that drive us – and He knows whether we eat to live or live to eat.

This morning on the drive to school, God impressed Philippians 3:18-21 on my mind. "For, as I have often told you before and now say again even with tears, many live as enemies of the cross of Christ. Their destiny is destruction, their god is their stomach, and their glory is in their shame. Their mind is on earthly things. But our citizenship is in heaven. And we eagerly await a Savior from there, the Lord Jesus Christ, who, by the power that enables him to bring everything under his control, will transform our lowly bodies so that they will be like his glorious body." The phrase, "their god is their stomach" slapped me right in the face!

I couldn't believe it! Was God telling me that I had been making food my god??? I was appalled! Indignant! Offended at the very suggestion! Me? No way! Not me! I loved God and would never do that to Him...or so I thought. After a few minutes of incensed tirade, my spirit began slowly to grow quiet, reminding me of the men with the stones slowly dropping from their hands as they slipped away after Jesus had said, "Let the one without sin cast the first stone." A shame washed over me, guilt for what I knew deep down was true. I had allowed food to become a god to me; it ruled my waking hours; it commanded me where to go; it ordered me when to eat; it demanded my allegiance.

As I looked further into this passage, I saw that allowing my stomach to be the god of my life that was pulling all the strings, I was actually putting myself in opposition to the true God who I wanted to love. I was setting my mind on earthly things and forgetting where my citizenship truly is. Once again I had no choice but to throw myself on the mercy of my loving God and confess my sinfulness at allowing my stomach to take precedence over Him. And as always, He grace-fully picked me up and urged me to continue my journey.

I can't really emphasize enough the difference between self-contempt and humbly confessing your sins. Self-contempt keeps us from experiencing the grace of God that covers over our sins and declares us righteous because of our faith in Him. The two can't exist together. As long as you hold on to your right to contemptuously degrade yourself instead of accepting God's forgiveness, you will not be able to experience His incredible grace.

It could be that some who are reading this don't really have an understanding of what grace is. I don't think I really understood it until just a few years ago. To understand what grace really is, you have to first believe with all your heart that you are a sinner. In today's world where everyone wants to "feel good" about themselves, the idea of being a wretched sinner is strongly discouraged by the "mental health professionals." But Open Arms believes that this is precisely why people are more mentally unhealthy than ever before in history, and I think what I am going through right now is proof that God's way is so much better than anything a man could think up.

4/13/01 Friday

I know there may be skeptics out there who have read what I have put down so far, but I am telling you that there has been a major change in my eating. Today I went out for lunch with my mom and could actually see the difference. Instead of devouring everything on my plate quickly, eagerly looking at the dessert menu before my mom was even half done, I ate some but then I surprised myself when I pushed my plate away after eating only half of it. I didn't think about doing it; I just did it. I guess I was full and didn't feel the need to eat more.

It really amazes me at how this is working. You are probably thinking that my eating habits and diet are on my mind all the time because I'm talking about them here. This is not true, though. I have not really thought much about it at all, and my life has gone on pretty much like usual. The only real changes have been in my heart. In submitting my will to His, He has given me a joy that I just can't hide. My heart is lighter and the peace inside is utterly incredible. I feel so humbly confident, not in my own self or my own abilities, but in my wonderful Lord who is the only true source of strength.

4/14/01 Saturday

I'd like to clarify something in case I've been obscure about one thing so far. Although I may be choosing my foods a bit more carefully, I am not in any way whatsoever feeling deprived. I am eating much the same foods as I have before, including desserts, but the amount I have been eating for this past week or so has drastically decreased. In other words, I am feeling satisfied by much less than I used to need to feel only moderately satisfied. This is the miracle of God. He is the one behind it, not I.

Okay, so, I stepped on the scales again this morning and saw 237. That was a nice sight to see. I asked God if that was my vanity creeping in, to want to see the numbers go down, and He impressed on me that it wasn't as long as I was keeping things in perspective. I was reminded of a quote I once read by C.S. Lewis, "The one who has God and nothing else has the same as the one who has God and has everything else." As long as I remember that the only thing that matters is the state of my heart before God, the numbers are a bonus that I am seeing. It is not the numbers I am focused on, but the God who loves me. If I see no change in the numbers, I will still be satisfied with this because it has caused my heart to fall more into alignment with my God's will. Nothing else matters.

This whole thing is amazing me still, though. I know for certain that God is all-powerful. I know He has the ability to make the pounds melt away. But I also am well aware that He is not going to force us to stop sinning. Will this work for anyone? Yes, but only if they decide to truly humble themselves before our holy and perfect God and confess their sin of choosing their own pleasure over pleasing God. This is the key that will free people from their addictions…no other way will give them the type of freedom I have experienced for over a week now. Absolutely nothing can truly free someone from the bondage of living for ourselves — only confession of our sins and willingness to submit our hearts under the authority of God Almighty. May this be a lesson I always remember!

4/21/01 Saturday

You might have noticed that it's been a week since I wrote. One might assume that this is because there has been nothing out of the ordinary to write about, but that is not the case. A large portion of me has wanted to write, but my schedule has just not permitted it.

But I do have to confess that a small portion of me was glad to have the excuse not to write. Of course, that is the portion of me that has been fueled by pride and vanity, knowing that in writing what this week has held I will be exposing myself and my fallen nature even further than I have had to so far. Yet this is what God is calling me to do so I guess it's time to swallow my pride and just do it.

Some of the week has indeed been uneventful, but of course, not all of the week. On Tuesday God and I had a bit of a falling out. Well, I guess it wasn't really God AND me – it was really just me. I am coming to the conclusion that this conquering addiction thing is a joint effort between God and myself. He's made a lot of changes in me since I started putting pleasing Him before pleasing myself. However, it appears He wants me to do my part as well. He's made my stomach feel full faster; He's reduced my cravings for things that are bad for me; and He's given my self-control quite a boost. But He's not done in my life yet.

Tuesday after school, I was hungry. This, most likely, was because I'd been busy on the weekend and not thought ahead to the week so I hadn't gone to the grocery store to get things for my lunch for the week. Tuesday came and grades were due and I was in a hurry so I grabbed a quick and too light breakfast, with a similar lunch as well. I kicked myself for not having prepared for the day by providing for my body's needs (more on that in a bit), but that didn't change my situation. Here I was, after school, and my tummy felt like it hadn't eaten in years.

I have a fifteen minute drive home from school and the entire fifteen minutes were me complaining to God how hungry I was and how I had to go with my mother to the chiropractor so I wouldn't be able to eat for another hour and a half and how I really felt He needed to let me have something to tide me over. (Isn't it funny when we start feeling like we have to tell God what is best for us? Like He doesn't already know!) By the time the gas station came up, my mind had been made up...and not by God. I had to stop because I needed to gas up my car; that much was fact. What wasn't fact was that I felt I "needed" this brownie and a pop. I pleaded with God. I reminded Him of how hungry I was. I told Him how good I'd been for the past week or so. I recounted the little I'd had for breakfast and lunch and told Him surely this would justify my eating this brownie and the pop. The answer He gave me was no. Again, He reminded me that it wasn't a matter of *what* I was eating, but whether I was going to choose my own pleasure over pleasing Him by obedience. This is the God who created the world out of nothing! This is the God who parted the Red Sea! This is the God who rose from the dead! Did I really think He wasn't able to provide for me?

Well, I made my choice. I chose my own pleasure over pleasing Him. Yes, the brownie still tasted good. Yes, the pop still went down fine. But it lay in my stomach like a rock, continuously pointing to the state of my spirit. I confessed my sin. I confessed, not a sin of eating a brownie, but the sin of a haughty spirit, putting my own desires before what God has told me was right.

Wednesday presented a similar challenge. Once again I was hungry at school because I'd not prepared well. I had only had a small breakfast because the staff was going to have pizza for lunch. Lunch was later than normal and I felt that the only way I was going to make it was to find something, somewhere to eat to ease the pangs in my stomach and the awful headache I had.

This helped me to start realizing something about my part in this whole thing. God does indeed help us when we call to Him, but we should not expect Him to do things we are perfectly capable of. Jesus provided for the 5,000 because there was no food available for them. If Maurice's catering service would have been there to feed that group, Jesus wouldn't have had to do the miracle. God doesn't do miracles when we have the ability to do it ourselves. That is superfluous. God's power is only manifested in doing what we are totally incapable of doing. The people of Israel could never have parted the Red Sea. In fact, this is what makes a miracle really a miracle...that we cannot do it ourselves.

And that is what God is working on in my life. He is providing me with the miracle of doing the things in my life that I cannot do on my own. On my own, I cannot walk down the candy aisle at Kroger's without getting something sweet. This is where God has stepped in to work in my life.

Yet what about my part? It is *my* part *not* to go down the candy aisle. I think a lot of times people who are caught up in an addiction, whether it be eating, pornography, smoking, working, whatever, are often not wise. We often put our own selves in positions where the temptation is and then get upset with God that He didn't provide a way out. For instance, as I mentioned before, smart grocery shoppers know not to go grocery shopping when they are hungry. It causes you to buy many things on impulse that you wouldn't have bought otherwise. MY part is to make certain that I don't walk into a grocery store when I am hungry.

My part of this last week? I should have shopped over the weekend to make certain I had good ingredients for the meals I would need this week. When I didn't do that, I basically disrespected my body. Bodies need food to work properly. You don't expect a car to run without gas and you can't expect your body to work without food. God has given me this body as a gift. I need to make certain I please Him with it by treating it respectfully. In not providing the proper meals for my body's needs, I was ignoring it and by doing so, I was really being disrespectful to God as well, since He was the one who gave me the gift.

I will be perfectly honest with you. The scale has gone up and down this week, ending this morning at the same place it was this time last week, 237. Part of me was disappointed, but I had to keep reminding myself that this whole thing is not about what the scale says. It is all about my spiritual condition. God is teaching me and testing me. Will I be humble and willing to accept His instruction? God expects me to be a good steward of what He has provided me with, and frankly, I've messed up big time this past week. My pride just keeps popping up at the most inopportune times. Sometimes it seems that the more I confess my sin of pride, the more of it I see to confess. I guess it's just good that my God's grace covers those imperfections of mine, rather like a cast covers the broken bones in a leg until it has time to heal and become what it should have been. May His grace cover me until I become the person He wants me to be!

4/22/01 Sunday

I'm not quite sure how (or perhaps why) I didn't include this in yesterday's writing. This was probably *the* most important event this past week in my life. I had intended on it being the major subject of my writing yesterday, but when I got into things, I completely forgot about it. Could be that my pride didn't want to have to take yet another blow. Oh, well, grin and bear it. :o)

Wednesday I went to the dentist. That's not at all an unusual thing for a person to do. Since I had to teach all day, I scheduled the appointment for as soon after school as I could, 3:30, because I also had a doctor's appointment that afternoon at 4:45 in a town that was 20 minutes away. The dentist had to put in a filling so he numbed the half of my mouth he had been working on. He did a great job in quickly and efficiently completing the filling in enough time for me to reach my doctor's appointment on time.

By the time I got home from the doctor's, it was 5:30 and, as I said yesterday, because I had not planned my week well grocery shopping-wise, both breakfast and lunch had been substandard and pretty much a matter of "what can I grab quickly out of the cupboard." (Something I think I need to insert here for those who may not know me personally. A little over a year ago, I caught the flu – or at least that's what I thought it was. For several weeks I was so fatigued that I could not be up for more than two to three hours at a time. Much of the fatigue has still lingered, although now I can make an entire day at school before I collapse with fatigue. This is why the mistake I made of both appointments on the same day was not a good thing for me. Normally I have to rest after school before I can do any other activity and weekends are limited to one major activity on Saturday and one on Sunday, such as grocery shopping or doing laundry. It has been a difficult year, yet one in which the Lord has taught me many things. However, I'm more than ready to be done with this illness!)

Because of my fatigue, I knew that although I was hungry, the time and energy it would take to fix supper was just more than I could deal with that night. I decided to stop and get a Subway sandwich on my way home from the doctor's. I felt like God was telling me to just lay down for a bit before I ate anything, but I was pretty hungry and the sandwich was sitting there, beckoning my name. Once again, I ignored what I believe God was trying to tell me and I disobeyed. Although half of my mouth was numb, I was trying so very hard to be cautious about it while I chewed with the other side. I really felt I was doing a pretty good job of it…that is, until the numbness started wearing off.

Oh, my goodness! I had chewed my bottom lip to pieces and hadn't even felt it because it was numb! As the numbness wore off, the lip swelled bigger and bigger and the abrasions on the inside became more and more painful. I put ice on it as much as I could and rinsed it carefully with antiseptic, feeling foolish at what a dumb thing I'd done! I'd sacrificed the well-being of my bottom lip, all for a sandwich.

The next morning I woke and ran to the mirror, but the swelling had not decreased at all during the night. I had to go to school and face my students, looking like I'd been in a brawl! Once again, my pride was exposed and my disobedience as well. I am so glad God's a patient teacher. I think after trying to teach someone a lesson as many times as God has been trying to teach me about humbling myself I'd give up if they hadn't learned by now! I'm grateful He hasn't given up on me!

And so, for the past few days, my painful, swollen lip has been a constant reminder to me that God knows what He's doing and we just need to listen to Him. When we start doing things our own way, we're sure to get ourselves into trouble...even when we think we're being *really* careful. It only goes to show us that we can never really be sure of the consequences of our actions. Spiritually, we are all "numb" because of our sinful nature. We really don't know what we are doing to ourselves, how we are hurting ourselves or others by what we do. This is why we have to rely 100% on what God has told us to do, whether it is what we want to do or not. God says not to lie for a reason. God tells us not to covet what our neighbors have for a reason. Whether we can see the reason or not, we always have to follow Him.

After all, this is what real faith is...following Him when we can't see a reason. If we only followed His commands when we could see the how's and why's, well, then, we wouldn't have faith. Faith comes from believing what God says even when it doesn't make sense. I sure hope I can start getting some of this through my thick head and heart. Sometimes these lessons are kind of painful!

The Biblical Solution, 1 Corinthians 10:13

In dealing with addictions, there are a few things we must remember. First, God is all-knowing. This means He knows what our past has been like. He knows what things we are most likely to be tempted by. He knows what our "breaking point" is. He knows what is the best thing to strengthen us for what we will need to face in our future. And He loves us so much that He will always do what is for our ultimate best.

Once we are confident of these things, we can face the challenges of turning our heart away from our own pleasures and back to our God who knows what is best. A foundational verse to help us through any temptation is 1 Corinthians 10:13, "No temptation has seized you except what is common to man. And God is faithful; he will not let you be tempted beyond what you can bear. But when you are tempted, he will also provide a way out so that you can stand up under it." An in-depth look at this verse can give us the strength and endurance we need to hold fast to what is right, even when we do not feel like doing so.

The first phrase, "No temptation has seized you except what is common to man," gives us some important basic information about temptation and about ourselves. The word "temptation" is also often rendered as "testing," "trials" or "proving." We are tempted when our basic beliefs in God are tested to see whether we will choose our own pleasure or choose pleasing God. We must remember that whatever temptation we are facing, others in history have also faced the same thing and have made it through. This gives us encouragement because we know for sure we are not alone in our struggle.

The next phrase is only four words, "And God is faithful," but what powerful words they are! In calling Him faithful, we see how God is committed to us. In medieval times there was a generally accepted responsibility the nobility had to take care of the serfs who worked for them. This *noblesse oblige* obligated them (at least the ones who were noble at heart) to protect those who were under their authority. We see this *noblesse oblige* in this phrase, "and God is faithful." God is obligated, out of His love for us and His character, to take the very best care of us.

"He will not let you be tempted beyond what you can bear." This is God's commitment to us. Will He allow us to be tempted? Yes. Will it *ever* be more than we can resist? No! Since God is all-knowing, He has no false ideas of what we can or cannot handle. He sees through our whining into the heart of the matter and goes past what we *think* we can handle to the reality of the thing. Prize-winning athletes are the ones who go beyond what they *feel* they can do and push themselves to realize their true capabilities.

The concept of "I can't handle anymore!" is not a valid reason for us to give into temptations. God never gives us a test He doesn't expect us to pass. The words, "I can't," should really be "I don't wanna." If we can't handle it, then God is an unloving liar. But the reality is that God *does* love us and He has promised to do whatever it takes to make us the best we can be.[82] If we believe otherwise, we are listening to lies.

Does becoming a Christian mean that we no longer have to struggle with temptations? Certainly not, or people would turn to the Lord only because of this and not out of love for Him and gratefulness for His mercy to us. The next phrase tells us clearly that we should expect to be tempted: "But when you are tempted." Being tempted is actually part of the sanctification process we are going through in this life. The pattern God often uses is to teach us something and then to give us a "pop quiz" over it. Teaching then testing is the same pattern God used as the Israelites wandered through the desert after leaving Egypt.

This is why many of us see our lives as roller coasters, going from the extremes of calm to storms. If we can change our perspective from seeing the storms in life as hindrances to our Christian life to seeing them as opportunities to show God that we have learned what He has been teaching us, it takes much of the fury from the storms of life. When we see them as God's quizzes, we can then realize that teachers do not give tests for the purpose of flunking students, but to determine how much knowledge they have retained. And God, being the perfect Teacher, will never test us over things we have not been taught.

So, knowing that temptations are going to come, what does God promise to do when they do come before us? "He will also provide a way out so that you can stand up under it." At first glance, this phrase might seem contradictory, but it shows us two ways that God will see us through the temptation.

Sometimes God provides us with a plain and simple "way out" so we can get away from the temptation in front of us. Joseph took this "way out" when he fled from Potiphar's wife. To be honest, most of us fall to temptations because we refuse to take the way God provides for us to get away. We often blind ourselves to the "way out" God gives us because we are too focused on satisfying our own pleasure.

David saw Bathsheba — this was the temptation. Seeing her was not the sin, however. It was when he continued to look that sin began developing in him. He must have spent time imagining what it would be like to be with her because he soon sent someone to get her and bring her to him. David had the perfect excuse not to give into this temptation. She was not even present at the time the sin began in his heart. Yet David did not take this "way out" and instead took action that would cause the death of Uriah and the illicit child.[83]

Many of us set ourselves up to fail when it comes to temptations. We purposely go to places that will be extreme temptations for us. We spend time with people who will lead us into doing things we should not. We surround ourselves with things that will only egg us on to submit to the temptation. An alcoholic who frequents bars "just for the company" is setting himself up for failure. A man addicted to pornography who continues to buy *Playboy* merely for the "articles" is considered quite foolish. We know ourselves better than any other person in this world, and we must take responsibility for not setting ourselves up for failure in situations like this. If we think we cannot handle it and there is a way for us to physically remove ourselves from it, we should by all means do so.[84] This is the "way out" God is giving us…let's take it!

However, sometimes temptations come and we have no way of removing ourselves from them. In cases like this, God gives us the grace we need to "so that you can stand up under it." Whatever strength we need to endure a temptation we cannot avoid will be there. It is a promise from God we can count on, 100%, all the time.

Expect the Downs and Don't Be Discouraged

Whatever addiction it is that you are caught in, whatever it is in your own life where you choose satisfying your own desires over what will please God, as we strive to humble our hearts and bring our lives into obedience to Him, we need to expect failures. If we did not fail, then we would be perfect people, and we know this is not going to happen in this life. How we handle our failures says more about our character than handling our successes.

Heartfelt confession before God produces a strong desire to repent from the sin and to do all we can to refrain from falling into it again. As we have discussed before, abusing ourselves in penance for our sin is in reality a lack of confidence in the efficacy of Christ's sacrifice on the cross. The sin we commit has already been paid for. To say that we need to add our penance of self-contempt to it is to add our own works to the grace we have been given.

As we maintain this faithfulness of sincere confession and repentance, the downs will become less frequent and not as deep and, through this process, we will build our spiritual strength to stand firm in the future. When we sin, we need to be ready to confess our lack of confidence in God's faithfulness and to train ourselves through our mistakes to trust the One who is indeed trustworthy.

Chapter 10:

Till Death Do We Fight

❖❖❖

Dealing with our own sinfulness in and of itself can often be a frustrating and difficult experience. Multiplying that by two, as in marriage, compounds the problem immensely. Yet it is within the marriage relationship that we have the best opportunity to live out our Christian life with all the realities that entails.

While Christianity is an interior relationship with God, it is only validated as we live our life in regards to those around us. Because of this, we will include several sections in this chapter. Not only will we deal with marriage relationships, but also with other relational situations such as how to relate to others if you are single and what to do about homosexuality.

A Christian-Christian Marriage

In talking about marriages, there are three types of marriages we might encounter. Whether both partners are Christians, non-Christians or one of each will make a difference in how to help them in their marriage.

Ideally, those who come to you will both be Christians. Marriage problems between two Christian spouses are the easiest to help because they both respect the authority of the Bible, hopefully. When a couple is having difficulty, and they identify themselves as both Christian, do not assume this is necessarily true. As we have said before, many who *think* they are Christians base this on words they have said or works they have done and not on a change in their heart. Examining their beliefs about God is the first place to start in any counseling situation.

It is important to have a solid foundational understanding of their beliefs about God before you launch into helping them in other areas. Once our beliefs about God line up with the Bible, then we have a basis on which to work. If those we are helping do not accept the authority of the Bible or of God to give instruction in their lives, telling them what the Bible says and insisting they follow what God has commanded becomes nonsensical if the commitment to the authority of God's word is not there.

Once we know that both people are Christians, we can begin to shed light on the problems they are facing. Marital problems essentially fall into one of two camps. The root cause is either self-centeredness on the part of one or usually both of the spouses or it is because of misunderstandings, indicating a problem with communication.

To expose selfishness, it is good to bring the couple back to the biblical purpose for marriage. Jay Adams gives us a straightforward statement of God's purpose for two people to marry. "What is the purpose of marriage? What, after all else is stripped away, can be said to be its essence? The answer to that question is set forth by God Himself in Genesis 2:18: 'The Lord God said: It is not good for the man to be alone....' The purpose of marriage is to meet man's need for companionship. Marriage was designed to defeat loneliness. Companionship is, therefore, the essence of marriage."[85]

The familiar vows a married couple takes, dating back to before the 1500's, are vows to be committed to that person for better or for worse, in sickness and in health, for richer for poorer, till death parts them — in other words, a promise of companionship for life no matter what the circumstances. Companionship means that we put the happiness and enjoyment of the other person over our own desires. In an ideal marriage, the husband would always seek to satisfy the wife's needs for companionship, and the wife would always seek to satisfy the husband's needs. If this happens, both spouses will have all their companionship needs satisfactorily met and the couple finds it easy to live in harmony.

But in reality, we all have at least moments, if not days, weeks or months, of selfishness where our spouse's needs are reduced to a far second to our own. The marriages that are in dire straits are the ones where this selfishness has taken over and has become the way of life for the couple. Exposing cases of selfishness will be the factor that causes change in a marriage.

Although both spouses usually share in this selfishness, sometimes one is more predominantly so than the other. This can often be seen even in their attitudes about seeking help from another Christian. The one who is more committed to the relationship than to their own comfort in asking for help will be the one who is less self-centered. Unwillingness to attend counseling with the spouse or a stubborn refusal to see anything wrong with their own actions in the marriage are obvious clues to a problem with self-centeredness.

As Christian brothers and sisters, God places us in marriages so we can learn to grow more Christ-like. In no other relationship on earth is the proverb, "As iron sharpens iron, so one man sharpens another,"[86] more true than marriage. It is also where the truest form of love should be played out. We must remember where the focus of love should be: "To love is to be more committed to the other than we are to the relationship, to be more concerned about his walk with God than the comfort or benefits of his walk with us."[87] Since we were created to please God, this is the goal we should strive for and what we should help our mates work towards as well.

Most Christian-Christian marriages will respond positively to being reminded of the original purpose of their marriage in God's eyes. Helping them to be aware of their own selfishness will also guide them into a more solid footing in their relationship.

Dealing With the Little Foxes

Not all marital problems, however, are based on selfishness. Some spring out of pure misunderstandings of, or lack of communication with, the other spouse. One wife may be frustrated because her husband will spend Sunday afternoons watching football games, which she considers a waste of time. She wonders why he does not enjoy the same type of Sunday afternoons her family used to enjoy when she was young where relatives were invited in for an afternoon of talking and being together.

This misunderstanding of expectations may start out as a slight annoyance, but can soon build to a major conflict if she does not discuss it with her husband. In the Song of Solomon 2:15 we read about these "little foxes": "Catch for us the foxes, the little foxes that ruin the vineyards, our vineyards that are in bloom." The foxes would hide in the vineyards until the blooms went off and the tender grapes began to grow and then help themselves to these delicacies, destroying the entire crop before they could be harvested. Little foxes then are small problems or sins that lie dormant until they come out to destroy the relationships we have. One little fox can often be easily dealt with, but little foxes will add up and can ruin the relationships we have by nibbling away at our perception of what is happening. Little foxes that we ignore will end up destroying our entire vineyard and will grow to be big foxes that become quite dangerous.

Minor annoyances that begin to grow should be faced head on by the couple. Each spouse should be willing to openly discuss these annoyances in order to keep them from growing larger and becoming more destructive. For many couples, however, they will keep things inside of them, seething, until they finally explode, spewing anger and frustration all over the unsuspecting spouse.

Much of the role of the BIBLE counselor in helping a couple like this will be to teach them how to discuss these annoyances and misunderstandings in a lovingly godly way. As sinful human beings, our first response in most situations will be to react in a way that reflects our sinful nature. In 1 Timothy 4:7-8, Paul acknowledges this need to train ourselves in a godly way, contrary to the nature we were born with: "Train yourself to be godly. For physical training is of some value, but godliness has value for all things, holding promise for both the present life and the life to come."

Children learn by imitating what they see. Many adults today grew up in a household where they never saw a biblical marriage modeled before them. This, coupled with a breakdown of God's intended training system,[88] has left many without knowledge of what exactly a biblical marriage should be like. Unfortunately, many watch marriages on TV and consider this the standard by which they should gauge their own. We must patiently instruct these couples in what the Bible says about God's intention for marriage.[89]

A Christian — Non-Christian Marriage

Moving into the realm of a marriage of a Christian with a non-Christian, the problems are compounded somewhat because the non-Christian will not feel bound to following the guidelines for marriage as set forth in the Bible. Obviously, a BIBLE counselor's hands can be a bit more tied in what can be done as long as one spouse does not acknowledge the lordship of Christ. Our major goal in helping this couple should be to lead the non-Christian into a relationship with Jesus. This does not mean we refuse to help them until this happens, but it does limit what the Holy Spirit will do in their lives.

There are times the non-Christian will be happy to point out the Christian's faults and expect that spouse to live up to what the Bible says, yet they themselves feel absolutely no obligation to uphold their part of a biblical marriage. It should be pointed out that if one spouse's vows are considered binding, the other spouse's are binding as well.

Depending on the willingness of the non-Christian spouse, working on the selfishness issue may be appropriate. However, if the non-Christian does not see the necessity to rid themselves of selfishness, this will be difficult to do. In such a situation, you must remind the believing spouse that God does not hold them responsible for how their spouse treats them, but only for their own response to that treatment.

This is important because God does not put conditions on how we respond to those who mistreat us. We are still required to do what is right, no matter whether the other person does or not. Wives are told to respect their husbands, and husbands are commanded to love their wives,[90] irregardless of their spouse's behavior. Following through with this if the other spouse is hard to respect or difficult to love can, at times, be a daunting task, but one that God fully expects us to accomplish. God will never give us a command to follow without giving the strength to do so.

Yet, how can one be loving to someone who is behaving in an unlovable way? How can a wife respect a husband who does things that are not worthy of her respect? Love is often much easier to define biblically than respect is because 1 Corinthians 13 gives a well-known description of the behavior of love. Respect, on the other hand, is not so clearly defined in Scripture. However, the principles of treating someone in a loving or respectful way are in essence the same. We can love the unlovable by treating them in a loving way, talking to them with loving words and viewing them through the eyes of the Savior. Wives who are treated as if they are cherished by their husbands will most likely respond in a positive manner to this display of love.

Respecting a husband who is not behaving in a respectable fashion requires the same from a godly wife. In front of their children, she must choose her words carefully so they show only a respect for her husband. In cases of men who are abusive or are seriously unrespectable, a Christian wife should remember that it is the position of husband that she is called to respect, even if she has lost respect for the man himself. God has allowed this man to be placed in the role of husband in her life and the role itself deserves respect. To illustrate this, one has only to look at the office of President of the United States to see how this plays out. One may respect the position of Bill Clinton as having held this authoritative office, yet at the same time one might not have respect for his behavior while there.

Women who are in abusive situations need to watch carefully what they say about their spouse, as a testimony to both their children and to those around them, but respecting her husband does not mean she must continue to put up with being a punching bag. We will discuss abusive relationships later in this chapter, but we want to make certain it is understood that a wife's respect for her husband does not mean she must tolerate abusive behavior.

The Non-Christian — Non-Christian Marriage

In cases where both spouses are non-Christians, there most likely is some respect for Christian values or they would not be seeking BIBLE counseling. Our primary duty once again is to foster a relationship with Christ in both spouses. This goal should take precedence over focusing on their behavior because the eternal fate of their souls is at stake.

We believe it is more effective to counsel a couple who is living together before marriage in their relationship with Christ *before* dealing with their sin of living together. We must remember that we cannot expect those who have not committed themselves to Christ to commit themselves to His commands. The change needs to come first in the heart. Once the heart has changed, the Holy Spirit will bring about the change in their behavior.

If we concentrate on their behavior at this point, they will see Christianity as merely a set of legalistic laws that are meant to keep them from living a happy life. This is not the message of grace that we are to be conveying. It is the gospel of grace that transforms lives, not the burden of legalism.

The Bride and Groom: Shadow of Things to Come

In marriage counseling, it can help the couple, whether Christians or not, to see God's original purpose for establishing the marriage relationship. We have already said that marriage was intended to provide Mankind with companionship. Companionship, however, can be accomplished through means other than a marriage relationship (i.e., living together, dating, friendship). There are two levels at which we see God's purpose for marriage, which are much like marriage itself, at the same time one yet two separate. We were created to have relationship with God and can achieve that through the finished work of Christ on the cross. Through marriage, we can not only have the companionship we need, but also comprehend more clearly the relationship we can have with God. The concept of marriage was given to us as a living illustration of our relationship with Christ. If we look at the traditional Jewish ceremony, we can see the similarity between a bride and groom and the Church's relationship with Christ.

In former times, there were two distinct ceremonies that took place, the betrothal ceremony and the marriage ceremony. Although the elements of these have been melded together in the modern Jewish ceremony, the original ritual was in two separate parts.

The betrothal was a time where a payment was made to secure

the bride. The price was often a ring, given to the bride by the groom, to show that legally she now belonged to him. From this time on, the bride and groom were considered legally bound to each other. The ring sealed the covenant between the bride and the groom, assuring her of the promise of the groom's return for her in due time to complete the marriage. The groom used the time to prepare the home the couple would move into.

When the groom's father was satisfied that the house was ready to receive the bride (the father's consent kept an eager groom from too hastily building their future home), the father would then send the son to retrieve his bride and bring her back to their new home. The groom would secretly take his bride back to their new home and then the celebration would begin. Traditionally, there would be seven days of feasting, the same number of days as there were after Jacob's marriage to Leah before he was able to marry Rachel.

The marriage itself is composed of three parts. The first is the giving of the ring to seal the covenant. Because the desires of the bride are as respected as that of the groom, this must be a mutual agreement. If the bride does not accept the ring, the marriage will not be valid. This is a type of Christians being given the Holy Spirit as a seal of the eminent return of our groom.[91] The moment we accept the price Jesus Christ paid for us, He sets His "seal of ownership" on us and marks us as being His.

The second part of the Jewish marriage process is the Ketubah or the marriage contract. Understanding that real love is something you do and not just something you feel, the Jews believe that marriage should be based on a legal and moral agreement. The Ketubah spells out exactly how the husband pledges to work for and provide for his bride. It is interesting to note that traditionally the Ketubah was only concerned with the husband's obligations to his wife and mentioned nothing of her obligations to him. In this we see that after God gave the Holy Spirit to us, He gave us His written word, declaring the promises He has made to love us, protect us, and provide for our needs. The Bible is our Ketubah, reminding us of the promises of our groom.

The final part of the Jewish marriage ceremony today is when the bride and groom leave the crowd of their friends and family for a short time, to be alone together, signifying their intimacy with each other. In former times, this was when the groom would come to physically take his bride away into their new home. We see this as a symbol of Christ's return for His Bride, where He will pull us away from all others, to be with us alone for a short time before the celebration begins.

When we understand this symbolism, we get a fresh perspective on the reason we have been given marriage. It also becomes easier to see how our own role as husband or wife was intended to be. The husband has been called to love his wife in the same way as Christ loves the Church. God has called the wife to respect her husband and honor him in the same way as the Church has been called to honor Christ. The marriage relationship has been given to us as a living example of our relationship with Jesus Christ.

Spousal Abuse

To deal with only the positive aspects of marriage in such a counseling training manual as this and ignore the darker sides of marital problems would not at all be a just representation of what a BIBLE counselor will face in their counseling sessions. Although we have been called to remain in a marriage covenant until death parts us, there are times when God allows divorce. In the Old Testament we see three requirements that a man was obligated to provide for his wife: food, clothing and marital rights.[92] In the New Testament we see Jesus reminding us that adultery was worthy of divorce.[93] There have been many books written on the subject of divorce in a biblical context which we have included in Appendix G. But how does God feel about a man who abuses his wife?[94]

Many who counsel women in abusive relationships advise the woman that if her husband has not committed adultery, she is required to stay with him no matter what he might do to her. Those who counsel this way often quote Malachi 2:16, and tell the woman that God hates divorce. She is then left devastated, wondering if it will take her death to free her from this nightmare of a marriage. She wonders how God can possibly be loving and yet condemn her to live her life in daily terror.

What this type of counsel ignores is the context of the entire passage in Malachi 2. God is condemning the men of Israel for their relationships to their wives.

> Another thing you do: You flood the LORD's altar with tears. You weep and wail because he no longer pays attention to your offerings or accepts them with pleasure from your hands. You ask, "Why?" It is because the LORD is acting as the witness between you and the wife of your youth, because you have broken faith with her, though she is your partner, the wife of your marriage covenant.
>
> Has not the LORD made them one? In flesh and spirit they are his. And why one? Because he was seeking godly offspring. So guard yourself in your spirit, and do not break faith with the wife of your youth.
>
> "I hate divorce," says the LORD God of Israel, "and I hate a man's covering himself with violence as well as with his garment," says the LORD Almighty.
>
> So guard yourself in your spirit, and do not break faith.

How did these husbands "break faith" with their wives? Verse 16 gives us the clue. God does indeed say, "I hate divorce," which many are quick to quote, but we must also look at the ending of the statement. "And I hate a man's covering himself with violence as well as with his garment." Since this is in the context of a husband and wife relationship, we can take this to mean that God equally hates divorce and a man who uses violence against his wife.

Because of this passage, we believe it is important for anyone who wants to get involved in BIBLE counseling to think through their stance on this before it comes up during counseling. To maintain the sanctity of marriage is important, but so is the sanctity of human life.

In regards to a physically abusive situation, we believe it is the wife's responsibility as a law-abiding citizen (which we are called to be[95]) to report this behavior to the police. We know this is difficult for many women, especially those who have been told that the wife must always obey the husband no matter what he does to her. But to allow him to continue his behavior is not the most loving thing to do.

We are not being loving to let someone keep doing a sinful behavior. The most loving thing sometimes is to confront that behavior and help them stop it. Since confronting directly can be dangerous for an abused woman, she needs to rely on others who are in authority to protect her. This will happen when she reports his abusive behavior to the police or, within the context of the local church, the elders step up to protect her by being the buffer between her and the spouse by reporting it for her (with her consent, of course).

This is a vital step to encourage the woman to take especially if she has been raped by her husband.[96] Most women will hesitate to take this step because of her love for him, but she will have a difficult time feeling safe in her marriage after a violent violation by her husband. We know that this can be an embarrassing and frightful thing for one who has already had to suffer through the rape. She will often be hesitant because she does not want to have to retell it again and again during court proceedings, but especially in particularly violent or sadistic incidences, she should be encouraged to make a police report. A counselor needs to be especially cautious and sensitive to the woman's wishes in this; it will be her ultimate choice whether she wants to report it or not. Helping her to see it as we have explained above may give her the strength she needs to bring the police into things.

When confronted with police action against his sin, the abuser will choose one of two avenues, sincere repentance or angry denial. If he chooses sincere repentance, the church leaders can help him learn what appropriate behavior towards his wife should be and give guidance for putting that into practice. A short time of separation for the protection of the wife will give the husband the motivation to work at understanding his role as husband.

Sadly, though, many abusers will choose angry denial as their reaction to police intervention. It is here that the elders of the local church (or a women's shelter if there is no local church to take this responsibility) need to step in as the woman's protection. She needs to be sequestered, out of reach of her angry husband, and the husband should be confronted by the elders of the church. If there is no repentance, the legal process should be allowed to run its course.

In such a situation, we must assume the unrepentant husband is a non-Christian.[97] By his own actions, he has chosen to leave her (by doing what was illegal and being taken away by the police). Because of this, she is no longer bound to him as 1 Corinthians 7:15 says, "But if the unbeliever leaves, let him do so. A believing man or woman is not bound in such circumstances; God has called us to live in peace." If the abuser has made the choice to do illegal actions (the abuse), then he has voluntarily, by way of the choice he made, left his wife and she is no longer bound by their marriage.

It is most likely that a woman would not be ready to follow this procedure after only one or two bouts of abuse. Most women who have finally decided that they will no longer put up with the abuse will only decide to do so after giving their husband an inordinate amount of chances for change. The most difficult part of helping a physically abused woman is getting her to see that she does not deserve the abuse and that it is not the way a husband is supposed to treat his wife.

Women, however, always want to believe the best in the man they love and will have hope that he will change even if it is clearly a hopeless case to the outside observer. Be patient with her and understand that it may take her a couple of times of separation from the abuser before she can see him for what he is. Abusers do not change easily or quickly, even though they usually have silver tongues that try to convince their wives otherwise. The woman should be reminded to believe his actions rather than his words.

Living Single in the 21st Century

Although there is a great emphasis in the Church today on ministering to families, there is an increasing, yet often unmet, need to minister to singles. Many churches have excellent family growth programs, marriage retreats, and children's activities, but are lacking in the area of activities for singles.

The needs of singles are both distinctively different and exactly the same as that of a married person. All of us have certain basic needs and desires for things such as fellowship, love, understanding, and relationship. In counseling with a married person (or a couple), the relationship is what we focus on and how that relationship can be used to bring each spouse into a closer relationship to Christ.

Single people, however, have a different focus in life. Much of the difficulty in marriages today comes from problems that started in the person's singleness. If a person did not practice self-control in regards to their sexuality before they were married, a ring on their finger will not guarantee self-control in this area afterwards. If a person allowed himself to be self-absorbed as a single, he will carry that self-absorption over into his married life.

We encounter a large portion of singles online because they are looking for connections with other people. We believe this is because of the lack of many churches to provide for the needs of these singles. For most Christian singles, they feel frustrated by the lack of opportunities for meeting and interacting with other singles. Some throw themselves into their work; some resort to the bar scene; and others stay sadly secluded at home, giving up hope for relationships with others.

When we are speaking of singles, we are speaking mostly of adult singles, those in their 30's or older. Younger singles most likely still have a good foundation of their friends around who are also still single. Older singles, however, have seen most of their friends marry and have lost many of the connections they used to have.

Single Without Children

Singles with children, although they might have less time for making friends, will find themselves involved with more people than those singles who do not have children. Children, by the very nature of raising them, will help keep a single parent involved with other adults. They will have opportunities to meet others at PTO meetings, sports activities and other such events of which their child is part.

Single Christians without children, on the other hand, will find it more difficult to have a similar level of involvement. If the single has never been married, there will be a stigma that they are not as mature as married people or other such falsities. It is unfortunate, but many unmarried women face the rumor mills' accusations of lesbianism or are labeled as "husband-stealers" and are jealously snubbed by married women their age. Even though society is more accepting of singleness in males, there is still a trend to choose a married man for a position of authority rather than one who is single.

Being single nowadays presents the challenge of fulfilling our need for companionship in a godly way that does not include a spouse. Because of the high profile sex has in our society, this challenge has become increasingly difficult. Unfortunately, with less and less pastors willing to preach against sexual immorality and the media promoting it, many single adult Christians are falling into the trap of relegating sex to merely an act and not a covenant between a man and a woman.

It has become almost laughable for us to expect a single person to maintain their virginity outside of marriage, and with good reason. The Church does not give much support to those who want to live a godly lifestyle. There is very little said to encourage them in this honorable goal. It has become more acceptable to be a woman with children out of wedlock than to be a virginal single woman who has none.

It is important for married people to be sympathetic to the singles in their church. We have heard more than one story of a couple who divorced and then immediately lost their married friends. This is a sad thing to see happen. The answer, though, is not to create divorce recovery groups where people persist in keeping their divorces alive through the retelling, but for local churches to have a number of married couples and other singles who are willing to offer companionship to these divorced people.

Adult singles are in reality one of the greatest untapped resources for the local church. They have more time and usually more financial availability than married couples. Enlisting their help in activities around the church can benefit everyone and help to fulfill their need for companionship.

If you are doing BIBLE counseling within your own local church, you can encourage the leadership of your church to make programs available to the adult single Christians with whom you are working. Some churches have their hearts in the right place when they form a single adult ministry, but then insist on putting a married couple in charge of it. Besides causing these adult singles to feel like they are not adult enough to manage a ministry, the married couple, often married in their early 20's and having never really experienced singleness, do not in actuality understand the needs of adult singles.

These are things a church must consider before beginning a singles' ministry. Because of a lack of support for godly behavior in singles and a lack of confidence in their ministry abilities, many singles leave the church and do not return until after they have children or a spouse. This is evident by looking at the proportion of singles in the community and that of the singles in the Church. With the increasing amount of singles today, this is a ministry the Church needs to make a priority. The wounds of divorce or of singleness can be healed by active involvement in the local church.

Paul gives a special honor to those who remain single[98] and it would do well for the Church to take notice of his words. Let us not shelve adult singles until, or unless, they get married, but let us open the door for them to deepen their commitment to Christ through serving Him.

Homosexuality

We have included homosexuality in this section because when marriage and singleness are not handled in a godly fashion, the result is sometimes homosexuality. Homosexuality becomes the choice of a person who has a distorted sense of sexuality as God created it. This distortion of biblical manhood or womanhood can grow out of abuse or out of a poor knowledge of the biblical reasons for sex.

Abuse can often cause a fear of the opposite sex and this fosters a feeling of being more comfortable with those of the same sex. Normal sexual relations can often bring back memories of the past abuse and sex becomes connected with fear instead of pleasure.

There is also a great movement in our society towards making homosexuality a valid lifestyle. Elementary-aged children are being taught to accept parents who are gay with the same or even more respect than heterosexual couples. Popular TV shows represent a far higher percentage of gays than is a true representation of society. Being gay will soon be lauded for being the best solution to the problem of overpopulation. Young people who do not have godly parents to teach them the biblical role of male and female are easily duped by the media's exaltation of homosexuality.

Yet God's command stands firm. "Do not lie with a man as one lies with a woman; that is detestable." (Leviticus 18:22)[99] This does not give us the right to be abusive to homosexuals any more than it gives us a right to be abusive to adulterers or liars or thieves or even ourselves. God does not see sin in levels of degrees, but all as abominations before His holiness. And all sin was paid for on the cross 2000 years ago.

Is Homosexuality a Genetic Disorder?

As much as science would like to prove that homosexuality is not a choice, but merely a result of one's genetic make up, they have not been able to do so. We, as Christians, can be solidly sure that this is not the case because in order to believe this way, we would need to deny the God of the Bible. If God has told us not to do something (and we have already shown that He has in regards to homosexuality) and yet it is something that is physically impossible for us to do, then the God of the Bible is a liar and a fraud.

But we know that this cannot be true. God is not a cruel sadistic fiend who delights in watching us try to do things He already knows are impossible for us. If homosexuality were something we had no control over, then God would not be loving to command us not to do it.

Homosexuality is indeed in our genes, just as all sin has been passed down to us through our forefathers. We all have in us the desire for sinful behavior and so, in this way, saying it is genetic is quite true. We cannot stop sinning without the power of Jesus Christ. It is the same with homosexuality. A true change will only come about when the Holy Spirit takes control of the person's heart.

We can see homosexuality as the distortion of God's plan for human relationships. God intended for us to be either single (and celibate, the two were always meant to go together) or married. Homosexuality, however, goes against both of these because there usually is appearance of singleness yet with multiple sexual partners.

In choosing a partner of the same sex, a person goes against what should be the basic focus of sex, the pleasure of the other spouse. (Of course, many heterosexual couples have gone against this focus as well.) Because of how men and women were put together, sexual satisfaction comes from two completely different ways.

A woman finds her satisfaction in the intimacy surrounding the actual physical act of sex. This is why women place more emphasis on being held and on the relationship with the man they are with than on the sex itself. Men, on the other hand, find their satisfaction in the physical act of sex rather than in holding their spouse.

Many women will get involved in lesbianism because they are dying to have someone hold them. Men will get involved in a homosexual relationship for the pure sexual release. We are not saying there is no mixing of these two, however, the majority of the sexual interaction is to satisfy their own desires rather than the satisfying of the other person's desires. It is much easier to satisfy someone who has the same needs as you because it is, in essence, like satisfying yourself.

God's intention, however, was for two very different people who would be satisfied in two very different ways to learn how to please someone else. In learning to please a spouse who has a different way of being satisfied and a different goal in the sexual relationship, we learn the ultimate unselfishness. And in learning the ultimate unselfishness, we find the ultimate fulfillment of our own sexual desires.

The irony is that when we are so focused on our own satisfaction over that of our spouse, there is often a drive inside us that is not completely satisfied by this type of sex. This is how many men can be drawn into the pornography trap, by seeking only their own sexual satisfaction instead of that of their wife. The root once again in the relationship is self-centeredness.

In working with those who are living as homosexuals, it is important to remember what we have stated before. The change must be a change of the heart before they are ready to make a change of behavior. If they are not Christians, their hearts most likely are aching to meet the God who loves them unconditionally, not for what they can do for Him.

If you are working with someone who is a Christian yet is still involved in a homosexual lifestyle, the person will need to understand that God is trustworthy and will provide them with the strength they need to do what He asks them to do. Most of those struggling with homosexuality that we have worked with have had an incorrect understanding of God's unconditional love for them.

Another thing that they will need to understand is how serious our sinfulness is before God. In the world we live in, sin has been reduced to a minor irritation that can often be shrugged off and cured by a hasty, "I'm sorry." This is not the view God has of sin. God took sin so seriously that He gave His life to pay the price for it. Having a better understanding of how God views sin will help us to see why, out of love for Him, we need to choose to obey Him.

Working with someone who is caught up in homosexuality is no different than dealing with any other sin. As we deal with their concept of who God is, the Holy Spirit will convict them of their behavior. The more they know about God, the more their desire to please Him will take over and their behavior will come into line with it.

Chapter 11:

Integrating BIBLE Counseling Into the Local Church

◆◆◆

Although BIBLE counseling is a one-on-one type of counseling, it is most effective when integrated into the local church. The ministry God has led us into is to work with people online, however, the real need for this type of counseling is in the local church.

As we have said before, BIBLE counseling is not something that is meant to be reserved only to "professionals" or the ministers of the church. In fact, it is the everyday layperson who will be there for their neighbor when they need a shoulder to cry on, who will help their friend who is suicidal, and who will talk to the Jehovah's Witnesses at their door. A church that has given its members the skill of looking to the Bible for their counseling needs will find the members growing to love and care for each other in a way that parallels Paul's command to the Colossians: "Let the word of Christ dwell in you richly as you teach and admonish one another with all wisdom, and as you sing psalms, hymns and spiritual songs with gratitude in your hearts to God. And whatever you do, whether in word or deed, do it all in the name of the Lord Jesus, giving thanks to God the Father through him." (Colossians 3:16-17)

To encourage mutual counseling in a church, it is important to build a training ministry to pass BIBLE counseling knowledge onto the individual members of a congregation. We expect our public schools to have detailed curriculum guides in order to responsibly educate our children, yet most churches educate their members on a hit and miss basis. We must take the matter of education in the Church very seriously. Sunday School classes should be staffed by those who understand the difference the Bible can make in their lives, instead of merely by a warm body.

If teachers are trained how to biblically counsel themselves and others, then in their teaching, they will pass these skills on to their students of all ages. As a result, the church will train up the kind of member who is "a workman who does not need to be ashamed and who correctly handles the word of truth." (2 Timothy 2:15)

It is unfortunate that many pastors have bought into the myths of psychology and abdicate their biblical responsibility to shepherd their flocks, herding their wounded sheep off to a "professional." And yet others are inundated by having to shoulder their burden of counseling along with all the other responsibilities they have. The answer to both of these situations is to train, train, train.

The majority of those in the pew have a difficult time seeing how the Bible can be applied specifically to their lives. They carry their Bibles to church on Sunday and follow along with the pastor's sermon, but they have little or no understanding of the role of the Bible to change their lives. If a church will begin with a nucleus of BIBLE counselors who have been trained to reach out to other members of the congregation, this nucleus will soon grow to include a growing and self-perpetuating circle of maturing disciples.

The training seminars we do are geared towards those laypersons who feel led to a ministry of helping other Christians grow. We are actually not giving Christians anything new in what we say. We are not teaching a "new" technique that the Church cannot survive without. Our teaching is just a reminder to go back to our roots, to the words God has given us for "life and godliness through our knowledge of him who called us by his own glory and goodness." (2 Peter 1:3)

The local church has an important role to play in this type of counseling. The leaders themselves need to be trained in how to counsel others from the Scriptures and some of them should be gifted to teach others how to do this as well. There will be times when the elders of the church will need to step into situations that require their help.

As we touched on when we talked about spousal abuse, the leadership of the church sometimes will need to take the responsibility to step in and act as a buffer in order to protect one of their members. With the amount of spousal abuse that goes on, the chances are very good that your church will have at least one situation like this in the next five years, and probably more depending on the area you are in.

It is vital that your church have an established plan on how to help in crisis situations before the crises occur. Any church today that is honest with itself will need to deal with sexual abuse, child abuse, spousal abuse, physical abuse, suicidal people, and many other crises over time. Shepherding sheep includes the whole ball of wax, healthy or sick, good times and bad, and a good shepherd will make certain he is prepared to take care of the sick ones when it happens.

Because of the magnitude of time it takes to care for sick sheep, the staff of a church cannot and should not attempt it alone. God knows the needs of your church. We must trust that He will raise up people with just this gift of counseling who will be able to use their gift and, at the same time, free up the pastor to devote more of his time to studying and preaching the word of God.

The Cost of Counseling

Personally, it is our firm conviction that biblical counseling should be free to all. After all, we do not see Jesus charging people to be healed, and the apostle Paul made a point of saying he did not charge for preaching the gospel.[100] Instead we are commanded, "Freely you have received, freely give." (Matthew 10:8) In view of this, if you are looking to make a full-time occupation out of counseling, we would like to suggest an alternative to charging clients for your services.

If you attend a large church, it would be good to set up a counseling ministry under the umbrella of your church. Make sure that the elders who will be overseeing it have a good understanding of what BIBLE counseling is so they can make informed decisions as to how the ministry should be structured. Since you are under the guidance of your church, you should be compensated by the church for your time spent in counseling. In essence, you would be in a paid position by the church. The church then can refer their members to you without cost to the members themselves and can raise money for the counseling ministry much as they would for any other ministry of the church.

If you attend a small church, the task is more difficult. Most small churches cannot afford to hire another full-time person other than their pastor. In such a situation, you can talk to the ministers in two or three like-minded churches and arrange for each church to sponsor you for a certain number of counseling hours as a service to the members of their church. It is wise to spell out exactly what is expected both in regards to your compensation and the expectations of each congregation.

However you decide to set up a counseling ministry, foster a good rapport with the leadership of your church. There will be times when you will need their advice. Legally, you will need a lawyer to oversee the unique challenges of a biblical counseling ministry and to give you the guidelines for your own personal state. A few states limit the use of the word "counselor" to only those who are licensed by the state, but most allow it as long as you do not claim to be a psychotherapist or that you are licensed.

If you are going to be working completely under the auspices of your local church, they will most likely be able to guide you in the structure of the ministry. You will find more about this in our Appendices H and I where we deal with some legalities of BIBLE counseling.

Part 2:

The Gospel and Its Defense

Chapter 12:

The Basics of Christianity

◆◆◆

If we were to sum up the basics of Christianity in one sentence, it would be this: God came down to man to do for man what man could not do for himself. That brief statement is what distinguishes Christianity from all other religious[101] thought in the world. All religious thought is man-made and is man's pursuit to try to obtain his own godhood through his own good deeds. Another way of putting it is religion is trying to obtain one's salvation by one's own self-efforts.

When Satan tempted Man with the lie that he could become his own god, and Man believed this lie, he immediately became self-focused. In fact, this was the original sin: rebellion towards God. It is rooted in pride of self and is, in reality, plain selfishness. All proceeding sins are a result of this original sin, but it is the gospel of Christ that strikes right at the heart of Man's pride and selfishness.

It is said that the way to catch a monkey is to place a banana in a gourd that has a small neck on it. The monkey will put in its paw and grab the banana and then be trapped because the closed fist will not fit through the neck of the gourd. The monkey will sit for hours, tightly grasping the banana, trapped by its own greed, and hunters can easily come up and kill the monkey. This is like many who hear the gospel of Christ. They hold tight to their own pride, unwilling to let go of it, even to save their own souls. The majority who hear the simple gospel reject it because they are not willing to give up their pride in order to grasp God's grace.

The gospel of Christ and the plan of salvation are actually very simplistic and are not difficult to understand. Acceptance of the gospel, however, is another issue. What makes the gospel difficult to accept is because it requires humility and an acknowledgment that we are not gods in and of ourselves but that we need a Savior from our own sins of rebellion against the God of the Bible. It is the pride of Man that rejects and refuses to accept the simplicity of the free gift of salvation by grace through faith in Christ Jesus.

There is only one thing required for salvation and that is faith in God. Yet many want to minimize this phrase and make it into something other than what it is. True faith in God means repentance from dead works, works on our own part to try to make ourselves worthy.[102] Repentance is turning from the sin of self-sufficiency (pride) in trying to obtain salvation by our own works of righteousness. This is what the Bible calls "dead works" or the "works of the law." Paul says of this, "Since they did not know the righteousness that comes from God and sought to establish their own, they did not submit to God's righteousness." (Romans 10:3) When we repent, we turn from the direction of self-destruction and alienation from God and turn towards God, being reconciled with Him and obtaining eternal life.

Faith is the same as belief. When one says they have faith in Jesus, what is being said is they believe Jesus when He said, "I am the way and the truth and the life. No one comes to the Father except through me." (John 14:6)

Four Spiritual Laws

Almost everyone is familiar with the "Four Spiritual Laws" leading to salvation.[103] They give a good, concise basis for the gospel and revolve around four essential concepts of the gospel message. The following is a summary of what those basics are.

First, the main foundation of the gospel is God's love. John 3:16 is well-known by many, but really understood in the hearts of only a few. "For God so loved the world, that he gave his only begotten

Son, that whosoever believeth in him should not perish, but have everlasting life." (KJV) Knowing that God loves us is vital, but this truth needs to be viewed in context with the fact that our sin has caused a chasm between God and Man, that Man is unable to cross.

Paul reminds us that, "for all have sinned and fall short of the glory of God." (Romans 3:23) We are all in the same boat, separated from God's love and holiness by our sinfulness. We need a solution that will bring us back into relationship with our Creator.

Our own solution of good works falls far short of what needs to be done to bridge the gap between God and Man so God has provided us with the only answer to solve the problem. "But God demonstrates his own love for us in this: While we were still sinners, Christ died for us." (Romans 5:8)

Presented with God's solution to our problem, we are invited to respond with acceptance, not relying on any of our own works, but only on the gracious gift of a loving God. "For it is by grace you have been saved, through faith—and this not from yourselves, it is the gift of God— not by works, so that no one can boast." (Ephesians 2:8-9)

What is faith then? Faith is to believe God does love us because He demonstrated His love towards us. Faith is to believe Jesus is the only way to salvation. Faith is to believe His sacrifice is sufficient and complete. Faith is to believe that we are saved, not by what we can or must do, but to believe we are saved only because of God's love, mercy and grace. All of this requires dying to self and trusting only in the finished works of Jesus. We must believe it is complete truth when He declared, "It is finished." (John 19:30)

The entire salvation process is made available to all and is totally independent from anything that man can, or even *could*, do. Salvation is entirely the work of God and of God alone. This is why salvation is a free gift by the grace of God, through faith (belief) in Jesus. There is nothing Man can add to what God had already provided, and therefore, we can boast of nothing. All that Man can and must do is to respond to the calling of the Holy Spirit and receive the free gift of salvation. Or, if Man chooses, he can ignore the calling of the Holy Spirit and reject the free gift of salvation, thereby attempting to provide his own salvation apart from God.

What Happens At the Moment Of Salvation?

At the moment of our salvation, we are filled and sealed by the Holy Spirit. "And you also were included in Christ when you heard the word of truth, the gospel of your salvation. Having believed, you were marked in him with a seal, the promised Holy Spirit, who is a deposit guaranteeing our inheritance until the redemption of those who are God's possession—to the praise of his glory." (Ephesians 1:13)

At this time, His righteousness is imputed (credited) to us. "Yet he [Abraham] did not waver through unbelief regarding the promise of God, but was strengthened in his faith and gave glory to God, being fully persuaded that God had power to do what he had promised. This is why 'it was credited to him as righteousness.' The words 'it was credited to him' were written not for him alone, but also for us, to whom God will credit righteousness—for us who believe in him who raised Jesus our Lord from the dead. He was delivered over to death for our sins and was raised to life for our justification." (Romans 4:20-25)

Also at this time, we are justified. "Therefore, since we have been justified through faith, we have peace with God through our Lord Jesus Christ." (Romans 5:1) Through our faith we are pronounced by God to be blameless.

Redemption also becomes ours at the moment we have faith in God. "He [Jesus] did not enter by means of the blood of goats and calves; but he entered the Most Holy Place once for all by his own blood, having obtained eternal redemption." (Hebrews 9:12) The debt we owed has been paid in full for us.

At our salvation, we are also sanctified or made perfect. "Because by one sacrifice he has made perfect forever those who are being made holy." (Hebrews 10:14)

And, of course, at the moment of our salvation, we have eternal life; "I give them eternal life, and they shall never perish; no one can snatch them out of my hand." (John 10:28) Eternal life is not merely something in the future, but is given when we first believe.

What Happens After We Receive Salvation?

After having received eternal life, we enter into the sanctification process by growing in grace. What we mean by growing in grace is to strive daily to be conformed to the image of Christ. "Do not conform any longer to the pattern of this world, but be transformed by the renewing of your mind. Then you will be able to test and approve what God's will is—his good, pleasing and perfect will." (Romans 12:2)

The word sanctification means "set apart-ness." When we received Jesus as Lord and Savior, we were set apart, passing from death unto life. The sanctification process is a continuation of being set apart, being made holy. Sanctification, however, will not be complete until we shed this mortal body and receive our glorified body when we will be forever present with the Lord.

The Bible describes the sanctification process as putting off the old man and putting on the new man. "Surely you heard of him and were taught in him in accordance with the truth that is in Jesus. You were taught, with regard to your former way of life, to put off your old self, which is being corrupted by its deceitful desires; to be made new in the attitude of your minds; and to put on the new self, created to be like God in true righteousness and holiness." (Ephesians 4:21-24)

The foundation of our faith is Jesus and how we build upon that foundation is what will determine our eternal rewards. That which was done in the flesh will count for nothing and only that which is done in the spirit will remain. Paul describes it this way in 1 Corinthians 3:10-15:

> By the grace God has given me, I laid a foundation as an expert builder, and someone else is building on it. But each one should be careful how he builds. For no one can lay any foundation other than the one already laid, which is Jesus Christ. If any man builds on this foundation using gold, silver, costly stones, wood, hay or straw, his work will be shown for what it is, because the Day will bring it to light. It will be revealed with fire, and the fire will test the quality of each man's work. If what he has built survives, he will receive his reward. If it is burned up, he will suffer loss; he himself will be saved, but only as one escaping through the flames.

Wood, hay and stubble are representative of the works of the flesh that will be burned up when tested by fire. Gold, silver and precious stones are representative of the works of the Spirit that will stand the test of the fire of God.

Summary of Grace Versus Works

As long as Man believes he can add something to the finished work of Christ, he is believing there remains within himself some good or redeeming quality. Pride is what keeps us clinging to the idea that we can earn or maintain our salvation, but this view of our own works really diminishes who Christ is. To not fully understand the reason for his sacrifice is to not have fully seen the depravity of our nature and the depths of the ugliness of our sins. Until one sees how totally lost and sinful they are, they cannot understand the magnitude of the grace of God.

Mingling works with grace will always exalt man and diminish Christ because to rely on our own works of righteousness is being ignorant of the righteousness of Christ and is to trust in self instead of Christ. We see Christ's work as being deficient in some way and needing our own works in order to be complete.

The laws were given for one purpose and one purpose only, to convict Man of his sins and to bring him to the understanding of his need for a savior. The work of keeping the Law is the attempt to sidestep the only means and provision for salvation. It is believing we can earn our salvation by our own works of righteousness, and thereby we become the redeeming gods in and of ourselves.

The Law was given to show Man how sinful he is, to expose his transgressions and the futility of his own works to pay for those sins. Because of this, living under the Law becomes a miserable state, always striving to reach something we can never attain. It is a curse to have to live under such a state.[104] This is exactly the curse from which Christ has come to redeem us, the curse of trying to keep the Law when we cannot do so. Remember, the purpose of the Law was to convict Man of his sins. The more one attempts to live by the Law, the more he is constantly reminded of his sins and the less he can ever know if he is sinless enough to make the grade. For one to continue in this direction is to believe it is possible, on our own, to become sinless.

A works-orientated salvation message, taught by many legalistic churches, will lead in one of only two directions. The first direction will be made up of those who truly believe they are well on the road to perfection. Those with this attitude are extremely prideful in their accomplishments and their self-righteousness. However, the result of this type of religious pride is a judgmental and critical nature, void of love, mercy and compassion. It is the spirit of Pharisaism, which we have dealt with in a previous chapter.

The second direction is made up of those who know in their heart they cannot measure up to the righteousness of Christ and the demands of the church. These are the ones who sit silently suffering with a sense of hopelessness and despair. They are trapped through the fear, guilt and intimidation of the members and leadership of the church they attend. Although they are being told they must do these works in order to be saved, they are very aware of their inability to be all they need to be for this type of salvation. These are the ones who will either put on an outward front of righteousness and slowly die in despair inside, or they will turn their back on the church, proclaiming it to be full of hypocrites, and refuse any longer to serve such a cruel God who requires us to do what it is impossible for us to do.

The Importance of Doctrine in BIBLE Counseling

It amazes us that many biblical counselors do not see doctrine as an essential factor of their counseling. The type of counseling they do does not deal with basic doctrinal issues, but only with the behavior of the person coming to them for counseling. In fact, even the works of the popular founder of nouthetic counseling, Jay Adams,[105] deal very little with exploring or questioning doctrine in their counseling.[106] Many of the other biblical counseling proponents follow suit, rarely questioning the basic beliefs the person has about God. Although there are some things of value that can be gleaned from their books, where the problem really lies is that these authors go on the presupposition that those who are being counseled have the proper view of God. When a person comes to them, claiming to be a Christian, they assume the person's beliefs about

God are correct and, by doing so, sidestep doctrinal matters completely. This is understandable because it is often more or less of a generic kind of counseling, appealing to all denominations.

Our belief, however, is that how one counsels reflects one's beliefs. Therefore, a wrong belief results in an improper method of counseling. This is why we place a strong emphasis on sound doctrine. Even though most who come for counseling may not believe *doctrine* plays any role in their problem, it is really at the root of all we do, say and are as Christians. We must remember that the word doctrine means "teaching" and there is absolutely nothing more important than teachings about God. These are the foundation of who we are and must be examined to make certain they line up with what the Bible calls "sound doctrine." The keystone to sound doctrine is found in Ephesians 2:8-9, "For it is by grace you have been saved, through faith—and this not from yourselves, it is the gift of God— not by works, so that no one can boast."

There are only two views within Christianity, and everyone stands on either one or the other; there is no middle ground. One is a works-based gospel and all the various forms in which it causes confusion and division, or the gospel taught by Christ and affirmed by the apostles that salvation is a gift of God and that it is by faith we are saved by the grace of God and not of works of our righteousness.[107] Salvation comes through believing the finished work of Christ on the cross is sufficient[108] and that His righteousness has been imputed to us.[109] It is about this gospel that the reformers of the sixteenth century first stated, "Christ alone" plus nothing else.

This statement by the reformers was the reaffirmation of what the apostles knew to be true. It was the common salvation that was given to the saints for which we are to exhort others to contend.[110] All of this gospel spells *eternal security*[111] for the believer. We believe that much of what is at the root of depression and suicide is the hopelessness and despair that comes about through the fear of death. If this is what is common to a world that is without hope and is living in a state of hopelessness and despair, then why do so many Christians suffer with the same hopelessness and despair as does the world?

If a Christian has these same fears as the rest of the world, then this would indicate there may be a wrong view of who God is and a wrong view of what the gospel (good news) of Christ is all about. We suspect for many the "good news" was turned into "bad news" when grace was mingled with works for salvation. The fear of the loss of salvation creates the same fears and sense of hopelessness and despair as those who are lost.

Jesus came to *save* the sinner, not to bring condemnation.[112] Jesus came to bring freedom from the works of the Law, not to add to the laws and make it more impossible to obtain salvation by our works of righteousness. The false gospel of mingling grace and works creates fear and condemnation and produces the opposite effect, leading away from holiness rather than to it, because it is still self-focused instead of God-focused.

The good news was the good news to the apostles that set them free and it is still the same good news that sets the captives free today. Works-based salvation causes all kinds of anxiety, fears and hopelessness that can also cause many physical problems as well. Doctors are becoming more aware of the connection between stress and physical illness, and there are few things more stressful for a Christian than to be fearful of losing their salvation. Many Christians struggle with trying to gain or to maintain their salvation through their works of righteousness. This causes all kinds of despair because they can never be sure if they are sinless enough to be accepted by God or of being assured if their works of righteousness have made the muster of being good enough for salvation. *Proper doctrine* is the only thing that is the answer for many struggles that face Christians today and this is not taught in much of "Christian counseling" that operates more on the level of psychology than it does on true biblical counseling.

A few with whom we have counseled have stated, "I wish I could believe in eternal security because it sure sounds wonderful, but I just can't take the chance that it is wrong." We truly do not believe they understand how boastful and prideful that statement is. What is being said is, "I cannot believe that the sacrifice of Jesus was complete and sufficient. Jesus paid only a partial payment that I must now complete with my own works of righteousness." They have chosen to continue on in the despair and hopelessness of their own self-righteousness rather than humble themselves and acknowledge that they are lost in their sins and *need* God's eternal grace and *have* to have a *Savior*.[113]

This is not the case with all who suffer with depression from false teachings, however. Some are genuinely frightened to believe any other way without being aware that it is a works-based salvation that is built upon pride. They are genuinely trying to please God and believe this is what is required of them. Either way, though, the end result is a lifetime of struggles and fears from which Jesus came to set the captives free.[114] Proper sound doctrine is the answer.

The study of false doctrine is very much recommended for one who is a Christian counselor so one can spot false teachings, which will enable them to help the person who may believe what they have been taught is correct. This is important for two reasons. It helps to distinguish between those who are in need of being born again, and those who are born-again Christians, but who are following a false teaching that is at the root of anxiety and hopelessness. In Appendix F we list several good websites for studying current false teachings and in Appendix G we give a listing of many good books that deal with cults. A study of this is not for the purpose of debate or to win an argument, but is to become knowledgeable so as to know how best to approach and help lost souls come into salvation or to give hope and comfort to the damaged souls of born-again Christians who have received false teachings.

To illustrate the benefit of being knowledgeable of other beliefs, most notably of the pseudo-Christian beliefs, which are the most dangerous and deceptive because they mingle truth with falsehood and give the appearance of Christianity, let us look at an example of this.

A young lady comes to us who was suffering from bouts of severe depression and suicidal thoughts. She tells us that she used to be a Christian, but found it not to be fulfilling and is now a Wiccan. She states that Wicca also does not fulfill her heart's longing but that it was better than Christianity. The first response one might have would be to ask her why she had abandoned Christianity and if she knows Jesus. She answers affirming everything you may say to her but keeps rejecting what you are telling her about God by stating, "I've heard all of that before and I already know what you are saying. I don't want any more of that lie."

In digging a little deeper, we find she used to be a Pentecostal. Most counselors would assume she was a member of an AOG church (or of some other Pentecostal church body that may be doctrinally sound in many regards). This assumption would cause the counselor to be hesitant to question her beliefs and would, unfortunately, result in the conversation going around and around in circles with no resolution.

Since we have encountered hundreds of people online who claim to be Christians but have no real understanding of the Jesus of the Bible, we encouraged the counselor who was working with her to ask the lady by private message in the chat room[115] if she was a Oneness Pentecostal.[116] The counselor then asked her this and she affirmed that this had indeed been the group with which she used to be involved. With this knowledge, it was then apparent that her rejection of Christianity was not a rejection of what is historical, fundamental Christianity, but of a distorted, legalistic version of it. She was completely unaware that she had been taught another Jesus, another gospel and another spirit than the one taught by the apostles.[117] She had not rejected Christianity; she rejected what she *thought* was Christianity, and this was then the perfect opportunity to present the good news of the gospel of Jesus Christ to her. Without the knowledge of what Oneness Pentecostalism teaches, it would have been a continuation of hit and miss counseling that would never have reached the root of her depression and suicidal thoughts.

This is why it is important to know the beliefs of others when counseling and to also have a good solid understanding of the word of God. *SOUND DOCTRINE IS IMPORTANT* and is a *must* for proper biblical counseling. "All Scripture is God-breathed and is useful for teaching, rebuking, correcting and training in righteousness, so that the man of God may be thoroughly equipped for every good work." (2 Timothy 3:16-17) "He must hold firmly to the trustworthy message as it has been taught, so that he can encourage others by sound doctrine and refute those who oppose it." (Titus 1:9)

"Do your best to present yourself to God as one approved, a workman who does not need to be ashamed and who correctly handles the word of truth." (2 Timothy 2:15)

Do Not Presume

When counseling, do not presume the one you are counseling with is born-again. Even if what they say sounds correct, do not be fearful of offending them by asking what their beliefs are and what church they attend. Many times this knowledge alone is what will give one the insight to know exactly what the problem may be and set the course for the direction of the conversation.

There is a lie infiltrating the Church body today. That lie is that doctrine is divisive and unimportant and that love and unity is more important than truth. The truth is, however, the reason so many are suffering is because the truth has been withheld from them through false doctrines. This is not love at all. The Bible teaches unity of the faith, not the unity of faiths and acceptance of false teachings. We are told to speak the *truth* in love and that is what true Bible counseling is.

Ephesians 4:13-15 reminds us of the importance of the truth of sound doctrine. "Until we all reach unity in the faith and in the knowledge of the Son of God and become mature, attaining to the whole measure of the fullness of Christ. Then we will no longer be infants, tossed back and forth by the waves, and blown here and there by every wind of teaching and by the cunning and craftiness of men in their deceitful scheming. Instead, speaking the truth in love, we will in all things grow up into him who is the Head, that is, Christ." It is the truth that helps us to grow and the truth is only found in the words of sound doctrine. Bear in mind that this is not a denominational issue, but purely a doctrinal one.

Legalism, both within and without the church, distorts the three basics of historical Christianity that we have mentioned previously. It distorts the Trinity by declaring Jesus as insufficient to complete the payment for our salvation. It distorts the Scripture by preaching another gospel based on Man's own works, and it distorts grace by adding our own efforts to what Christ has already done, nullifying the grace of God.

We need to keep these in mind as we continue our study of false teachings. We will see this deadly thread throughout their teachings. These three marks of false teachings are always prevalent, and it is the truth of sound doctrine that will set those free who have received these false teachings.

Chapter 13:

Going on the Defensive

❖❖❖

The Bible alone has the words of eternal life within its contents. This is not to mean the words themselves have any redeeming qualities, but it speaks of the One who is our Redeemer. Not only does the Bible explain how eternal life is obtained; it is our road map that will guide us through this life. Paul strongly reminded Timothy of the importance of the Scriptures. "But as for you, continue in what you have learned and have become convinced of, because you know those from whom you learned it, and how from infancy you have known the holy Scriptures, which are able to make you wise for salvation through faith in Christ Jesus. All Scripture is God-breathed and is useful for teaching, rebuking, correcting and training in righteousness, so that the man of God may be thoroughly equipped for every good work." (2 Timothy 3: 14-17)

We have had some ask, "Why doesn't God speak to us today like He did in the Old Testament days?" The fact is that God *does* speak to us today through His written word and through His Holy Spirit. As we read the Bible, the Holy Spirit speaks to our hearts and gives us understanding. In John 16:13-15 we are told, "But when he, the Spirit of truth, comes, he will guide you into all truth. He will not speak on his own; he will speak only what he hears, and he will tell you what is yet to come. He will bring glory to me by taking from what is mine and making it known to you. All that belongs to the Father is mine. That is why I said the Spirit will take from what is mine and make it known to you."

With the Holy Spirit indwelling us, the only Teacher we need can speak directly to our spirit. "We have not received the spirit of the world but the Spirit who is from God, that we may understand what God has freely given us. This is what we speak, not in words taught us by human wisdom but in words taught by the Spirit, expressing spiritual truths in spiritual words. The man without the Spirit does not accept the things that come from the Spirit of God, for they are foolishness to him, and he cannot understand them, because they are spiritually discerned." (1Corinthians 2:12-14)

One thing we must remember is that God did not speak to everyone in the Old Testament; He spoke only to His prophets. "In the past God spoke to our forefathers through the prophets at many times and in various ways, but in these last days he has spoken to us by his Son, whom he appointed heir of all things, and through whom he made the universe." (Hebrews 1:1-2) The times have changed and no longer do we have the prophets who were the pipeline to God. We do not have the same need for them since we, as Christians, are indwelt by God Himself in the person of the Holy Spirit.

Could you imagine the added confusion today if we did not have the Bible to see what God has already said? The world has already plunged into a state of confusion like no other time in history, and if we did not have one specific standard as our guide, then anybody could claim they heard from God in ongoing revelation knowledge. There would be no way of knowing if what was said was really from God or not. In fact, come to think of it, many are already doing this and few check what is said against the written word. Many are being lead astray for the sake of unity at the expense of truth. Doctrine, which merely means "teachings," is of very little importance to many and in fact, it is thought of as being divisive. Those who *do* adhere to sound doctrine are often accused of being mean, hateful and not acting "Christ-like."

The Bible does indeed need to be defended. It is being attacked from all sides like no other time in history. In former times, the Bible has been burned to try to stop its influence. Instead of burning the Bibles today, the attack is even more effective, and they do this through intellectual intimidation. The impression is being given that those who *do* believe in the Bible are considered to be intellectual dimwits who believe in an old, outdated book full of contradictions, lies, fairy tales and myths.

In response to those who make such charges we must ask, "Why is there such hatred generated and so much effort and energy expended in trying to discredit a book that you are convinced is nothing more than a book of contradictions, lies, myths and fairy tales? We would not have such hatred and waste our time trying to discredit Mother Goose Nursery Rhymes because we know it to be nothing but fairy tales."

The fact is that in his heart man knows the Bible is the written word of God, and the hatred isn't towards the Bible itself, but towards the God of the Bible. Many have this false idea that if they can discredit the Bible, then somehow this discredits God and brings God down to or below the level of Man.

The one single thing that has caused more damage in recent modern history to discredit the Bible and Christianity is evolution.[118] Make absolutely no mistake that at the heart of evolution was and is the goal of attacking fundamental Christianity. If the first three chapters of Genesis can be discounted, then that leaves the door wide open for the rest of the Bible to be discounted as well. If the Bible is wrong on the creation account, then the rest of the Bible can also be discounted. This is exactly what atheistic evolutionists have hoped would happen, and it has been very effective in obtaining that goal.

For those who may be interested in answering the critics who challenge the authenticity and reliability of the Bible, we highly recommend Josh McDowell's *A Ready Defense*.[119] The evidence of the reliability and the authenticity of the Bible contained in his book is a compilation of material gathered from many experts in their particular field as well as Josh McDowell's own expertise in the field of Christian apologetics.

There is absolutely no other historical writing that even comes close to withstanding the extreme scrutiny the Bible has been subjected to, and yet many still reject it. If we use the exact same rules to determine literary integrity and historical accuracy with the Bible as we do for other sources, the Bible far exceeds any other text in every test it is given. But there are many who still wish to deny its claims. In fact, it seems as if any source may be considered valid, as long as it is not the Bible. Napoleon summed up the situation fairly well when he stated, "Man will believe anything as long as it isn't in the Bible." The fact that the Bible can indeed stand up to such investigation and, if considered fairly, overwhelmingly outmatch even the closest opponent is a strong evidence that the origins of the Bible are not of man, but that it really is the written word of God.

Not only is the Bible unsurpassed in literary integrity, historical accuracy and the support of archeological evidence that attests to its reliability and authenticity, but the Bible alone has the evidence of 100% accuracy of the fulfillment of prophesies that could only come through Divine foreknowledge. It is quite significant to note that a perfect record in regards to the fulfillment of prophecies that were made long before they came about has never been accomplished in any other work, religious or otherwise.

A study of the reliability of the Bible may be beneficial to bring the skeptic to salvation in the Lord Jesus because many skeptics are unaware of these mounds of support for the Bible's reliability. More importantly, though, we believe this knowledge will be even more beneficial to the believer as an aid to erasing any lingering or arising doubts about his faith. We need not fear intellectual questions about our faith because God has given us the proof we need, if our minds are willing to accept it.

Complexity Versus Simplicity

One of the main questions we have been asked by non-believers is, "How can I know which religion is right?" Another question that is akin to this one, but which is asked by professing Christians is, "How can I know which church is right?" If one attempts to go into a long discourse to explain the different beliefs one at a time, all that will result is adding more confusion to an already confused person. With the literally thousands of various religious thoughts available in the world, it would take many weeks of non-stop discussion and chances are, nothing would be resolved in the person's mind.

This is where complexity versus simplicity comes into play. Complexity only serves to bring more confusion into a situation, whereas simplicity brings understanding. The Pharisees built a wall of protection around the Law by adding so many traditions that the purpose of the Law was hidden. This prevented others from seeing the intended simplicity of the Law God gave. The simple intended purpose of the Law was for sinful Man to be made aware of his lost condition and recognize his need for a savior.

Satan knew he could not remove the truth of the simplicity of the gospel. Rather than focus his energies on trying to keep people from the gospel itself, he pulled out his same old trick that worked so well with the Pharisees. He built a wall of traditions around the Law, obscuring the simplicity of the gospel in order to make it complex. The Apostle Paul addressed this in 2 Corinthians 11:3, "But I fear, lest by any means, as the serpent beguiled Eve through his subtlety, so your minds should be corrupted from the *simplicity* that is in Christ." (KJV, emphasis added) Paul reaffirmed the simplicity of the gospel in the next verse, "For if someone comes to you and preaches a Jesus other than the Jesus we preached, or if you receive a different spirit from the one you received, or a different gospel from the one you accepted, you put up with it easily enough."

The simplicity of the gospel has always been, and still is, simple. The simple gospel is: "For God so loved the world that he gave his one and only Son, that whoever believes in him shall not perish but have eternal life. For God did not send his Son into the world to condemn the world, but to save the world through him." (John 3:16-17) And from Ephesians 2:8-9, we see, "For it is by grace you have been saved, through faith—and this not from yourselves, it is the gift of God— not by works, so that no one can boast."

Complex Answers Are Not Always the Solution

There is a supposedly true story about a truck driver that gives us a great illustration of complexity versus simplicity. Sometimes we overlook the simple solutions to life because we are expecting those solutions to be much more complicated.

A truck driver, who had a load of merchandise that was at the maximum height allowed by law, was traveling down the highway. In the process of watching signs for the exit he would take, he failed to read the sign that gave the height of the next overpass as being just a few inches shorter than the load he was carrying. He also failed to see the sign that gave an alternate route for any trucks that may exceed the height posted. With a forceful jolt, the truck driver soon found his rig hopelessly wedged under the bridge.

With traffic backed up for miles, horns blaring and people yelling, the highway patrol frantically tried to figure out how to clear the truck from under the bridge. All attempts to dislodge the truck with tow trucks, pulleys, wedges and grease all had failed, and the crowd standing around scratched their heads, trying to figure out this dilemma. One suggestion after another was attempted and then rejected as it did not work.

A small boy, riding across the overpass on his bicycle, stopped to listen to the conversation. The boy took in the situation and said innocently, "I know how you can get that truck out." The adults ignored him, obviously, because what would a little child know about something so complex? Anger mounted, with finger pointing and accusations flying around as to who was at fault, while the boy persisting in saying he knew how to get the truck out.

Finally, one of the officers responded with a tone of irritation, "Okay, what is your suggestion?"

The little boy responded, "It's easy. Just let the air out of the tires." Red-faced, the adults promptly did this, and it lowered the truck enough to where it could be pulled out from under the bridge.

Simplicity was the key to unlocking the secret to a seemingly complex and hopeless situation — and it is in the same way with spiritual matters. Simplicity is the answer to what appears to be a hopeless situation where there are no definitive answers to the complexities of religious thought. To see the entire picture and try to figure it out can appear to be complex, but by looking at the simplicity (like letting the air out of the tires) the confusion can be easily cleared up. This is why we emphasize the three major things that are prevalent in all false beliefs: a denial of the Trinity, a questioning the authority of the Scriptures and a denial of salvation by grace. With a thorough understanding of these three things, the smoke of confusion can easily be cleared.

The original purpose of this book was to equip members in the Body of Christ to effectively apply Scriptures to the many complex issues facing Christians and to offer answers concerning their needs. However, it became obvious in time that one cannot be a counselor without the application of sound doctrine. This application of sound doctrine is, in actuality, evangelization. Even though this is called counseling, what we really are doing is evangelizing by presenting the gospel of Christ on a very personal one-on-one, practical setting.

In counseling with literally thousands, this one recurring theme has sprung up over and over again. The lack of biblical knowledge of who God is keeps cropping up as the one single major problem we have encountered in those we work with online. Because we have studied cults, false religions and unbiblical teachings for many years, we are keen to recognize and identify false teachings in the words spoken or typed by the one we counsel. With this knowledge, we can point them in the right direction. It gives us great delight to see how God makes the changes in their lives after they hear the simple, sound teaching of the gospel. This type of counseling goes beyond the mere application of Scriptures. It dares to question the false beliefs they may be harboring that are at the root of their struggles and confusion.

Many claim the Bible is their only source for biblical counseling, but applying Scripture verses without sound doctrine at the heart will have little or no long-term effect if the one who is being counseled has the wrong perception of who God is. For one to say he is a biblical counselor is no guarantee he is presenting sound doctrine when using the Bible as his only guide. After all, all of the major cults make the same claim of using the Bible, yet their understanding of the Scriptures is distorted to where it is anti-Christian, or more aptly stated, anti-Christ.

Many who consider themselves "mainline Protestants" or "fundamental Christians" will not balk at this statement when it is applied to the more obvious cults such as Mormons, Jehovah's Witnesses, or the Unification Church, but if it is suggested that many of the same beliefs of these groups have infiltrated much of the mainline Protestant churches, they become offended instead of looking at the evidence. Satan has been so subtle with his lies that it is like a little bit of yeast that has grown to the point of being on the threshold of permeating the entire loaf.

Some try to make a distinction by saying, "Yes, but theirs is a prostitution and a perversion of the real thing." But we must ask ourselves, how valid *is* that argument? In order to answer this question, it is necessary to define what we mean by the two terms *legalism* and *liberalism*.

Legalism and Liberalism

Legalism is any attempt to obtain or maintain salvation through the works of the Law. Legalism is the belief that through strict adherence to the laws, Man can become righteous through his own works. His righteousness then comes from himself, through his own efforts.

Legalism is not the admonition to adhere to sound doctrine, exhorting, correcting and training in righteousness. Legalism is not the desire to daily strive towards being conformed to the image of Christ.

Liberalism is the disregard of sound doctrine and is, in reality, doing what is right in one's own eyes. This can also include elevating experience to where it takes precedence over the written word of God.

Liberalism is not the belief of salvation by grace and belief in the eternal security of the believer. We do indeed have liberty in Christ Jesus, and we are to stand fast and not be entangled again with the yoke of bondage of legalism.[120]

Jesus used the illustration of dough and yeast for a good reason. It takes very little yeast to affect a large loaf of bread, and the interesting thing about yeast is that it does not merely remain the same, but it grows. Left long enough in a suitable environment, yeast continues to grow until it consumes the entire loaf. Using Jesus' illustration of dough being representative of grace and yeast being representative of works, how much yeast then does it require before the entire loaf is considered permeated? Does it take 50% dough and 50% yeast? Is it 75% dough and 25% yeast? Or is it 90% dough and 10% yeast? Or how about 99% dough and 1% yeast? In actuality, the 99% dough with the 1% yeast is the most dangerous because it is the most difficult to detect. Although it is a meager one percent, it can no longer be considered unleavened bread and that tiny amount of yeast will eventually saturate the entire loaf.[121]

Keeping that illustration in mind and realizing that the dough is representative of the gospel of grace and the yeast is representative of works, how much mingling of grace and works does it require before it is no longer salvation by grace?

The Yeast of Man's Works

Yeast is representative of Man's own works of righteousness added to the finished works of Christ to gain or to maintain his salvation. As long as Man desires to cling onto any percentage of the false idea that his works of righteousness are needed to complete his salvation is in effect saying the work of Christ on the cross was not sufficient. If the sacrifice of Christ was not sufficient, then what is it *we* are able to complete that God was unable to complete? To even cling onto one percent of our own works is still saying that our works are one percent more righteous than the righteousness of Christ.

That one percent is to deny salvation by grace alone. It will continue to grow until we believe it is by our own works of righteousness we are earning our salvation. This takes the focus off of Christ and places the burden of salvation back upon ourselves. Whether one wishes to acknowledge that this belief diminishes who Christ is or not does not change the fact that this is exactly what it does do. To believe His sacrifice was not sufficient is to believe His sacrifice was not complete or acceptable to the Father. In turn, this is to question His holiness and righteousness. In essence, it makes Him less than an all-powerful, all-knowing, all-loving and holy God and circumvents the purpose and the reason for His sacrifice.

Where confusion comes in is when we attempt to redefine what grace is. This opens the door for all kinds of heretical teachings of mingling grace with works. It takes us from this one simple message of salvation by grace and not by works to a myriad of variations of adding our own works that leaves us stranded in an endless mass of confusion. In the same way the variations of adding traditions to the Law is endless because it is merely another mixture of grace and works that only adds to the confusion. The answer to this confusion is to remember the simplicity of the gospel, the simple gospel of salvation by grace and not by works. It is only when we add works to the equation that we find complexity and confusion. We find simplicity by the rejection of all the variations of mingling grace with works.

Looking back over what we just said about adding any amount of works to our salvation, we have the three points that are evident in every false teaching. (1) The Trinity was brought into question by reducing Jesus to being less than God and a less-than-sufficient sacrifice for our sins. (2) The authority of the Scriptures has been challenged and questioned because the Bible clearly says that Jesus' sacrifice *was* a sufficient payment. (3) There is a denial of salvation by grace, which is replaced by a doctrine of works.

Liberalism: The Flip Side of the Same Coin

In both legalism and liberalism, the message of salvation by grace and not of works is rejected. The Legalist will say of the Liberal that the evidence of his loose lifestyle is the result of the message of grace that gives the Liberal a license to sin. On the surface, this may sound fairly accurate, but this is not so when we keep in mind that pride is at the root of Man's rebellion. Within both the legalist and liberal camps, they are both saying they do not need the grace of God and are sufficient within themselves. It is the flip side of the same coin of pride in self.

What needs to be asked of the legalist is whether the thought of salvation by grace frightens him and if the only thing that keeps him from sinning is the Law. Or is his motive to not sin based upon the love and gratitude of the great sacrifice that God paid for the purchase of our souls?

Grace flies in the face of the root of all sin, pride in self, and is an affront to sinful Man who clings to the idea that there is some good thing within us. To use the very word grace is to say that Man is sinful and that there is no good thing in us. We have to have God's grace for salvation to even be made available to us.

To focus on the Law and sin is to remain focused upon ourselves. It prevents man from trusting in the sufficiency of the sacrifice of

Christ for the sin of Mankind. Notice that John the Baptist did not say Jesus would take away the sins (plural) of the world, but he said, "Look, the Lamb of God, who takes away the sin of the world!" (John 1:29) Note that he used the word "sin" (singular). What would be the one single sin of which all Man is guilty? Would it not be a rebellion that is rooted in pride, being our own gods and having no need of God's grace?

The confusion dissipates when we discuss belief in the simplicity of salvation by grace and not of works. It is this simple message that is in complete opposition to all religions and religious thought in the entire world. This simple message is exclusive to Christianity and Christianity alone. To recognize salvation by grace is to recognize our sinful nature and presents the true nature of the love of the God of the Bible. "But God demonstrates his own love for us in this: While we were still sinners [rebels, in rebellion against God], Christ died for us. Since we have now been justified by his blood, how much more shall we be saved from God's wrath through him! For if, when we were God's enemies, we were reconciled to him through the death of his Son, how much more, having been reconciled, shall we be saved through his life! Not only is this so, but we also rejoice in God through our Lord Jesus Christ, through whom we have now received reconciliation." (Romans 5:8-11)

A religion void of the full understanding of grace distorts the true nature of God. A God with limited or no grace is viewed as an angry God whom we spend our entire life trying to make happy and must appease in order to earn His favor and His love. A gospel without grace perverts and destroys the entire meaning and purpose of His substitutional death upon the cross. Without grace, his death is not viewed as a voluntary act of love but is viewed as an involuntary blood sacrifice to appease a wrathful God who still remains reluctant to open the gates of heaven. A gospel without grace views the sinless life of Christ as the example of the sinless life we must obtain before we are accepted by the Father before being allowed access into heaven.

This view would account for Christians being unable to come to and to trust God with their lives and would account for many to trust in themselves instead. How many Christians are needlessly struggling to obtain something they already have in Christ Jesus: forgiveness, acceptance and eternal life? How many outside of Christ reject the gospel message because it has been presented as a gospel of works? The presentation of the simplicity of the gospel of grace is the solution. God intended His gospel to be simple, easy enough for a little child to understand. Let us be ever so cautious not to muck it up with our own desire to add more to what He has already done. This is the truly good news the world needs to hear.

Chapter 14:

The Root of All Cults

♦♦♦

At the root of all cults and false teachings is the belief that Mankind is inherently good, but we sometimes do bad things. The solution to Man's problems, according to them, is to recognize this goodness within ourselves and become as God. In other words, Man becomes his own savior. For example, Buddhism describes God as the reality of existence, Jesus as a wise man, and Man through his awareness of existence (enlightenment) may become one with Buddha in obtaining the state of Nirvana (that means becoming one with or melting into this power or energy called God).

New Age thought describes God as a Universal Law or an impersonal energy or force, and Jesus as a great man who realized His oneness with God. In their philosophy, Man is one essence with God. This is why we saw the classic lines by Shirley Maclaine in the movie *Out on a Limb*, "I am god. I am god."

The Unification Church, Sun Myung Moon's organization, describes God as a divine energy, Jesus as a special creation of God, and Man as God incarnate, or one with God. For the Unitarian Universalist, God is described as however one wants to view Him or it. In this belief, keeping right along the same route as other cults, Jesus was merely a good man. Man is the highest point of evolutionary wisdom (which should be quite a sobering thought!) and some believe in Man's potential divinity.[122]

The concept of God might sound wide and varied throughout all cults, but if one looks carefully, there are three basic threads you will find. As we examine these teachings of other religions, we can see that many of them define God as unknowable and impersonal. Jesus is reduced to the level of merely a man, and Man is equal to or elevated above Him. Again, these are very common marks of cults. Denial of Jesus being God is in contradiction to the doctrine of the Trinity. None of these recognize the Bible as the ultimate authority in matters of faith, and all of them are based on Man's good works for their "salvation," however they may define that.

Occult Practices

Any system of belief where the biblical God is not at the heart of the teaching really becomes simply a matter of understanding that if it is not of God, then it is of Satan. The word *occult* comes from the word, "hidden." Those who are involved in the occult believe they have found some knowledge that has been hidden from the general populace. Spiritually speaking, however, occult involvement means having thoughts (at the very least being *influenced* by demonic forces to the worse case of being *controlled* by demonic forces) that are in opposition to the things of God. Because of the fallen nature of Man, our own thoughts do plenty of damage just on their own without any demonic influence. Mankind has a propensity towards evil and, depending upon the amount of occult involvement, he will be influenced or controlled to that degree by demonic forces.

Examples of Occult Involvement

The occult is infiltrating many areas of our lives. Some of the practices are obvious while others are more obscure and have become more "accepted" in our society. Being aware of them will help us steer clear of their effects as well as enable us to help others who are ensnared by them. Occult practices would include things such as the following.

Visualization. This is done when we envision a desired result in our "mind's eye," and if we will keep that vision in our mind, the desired result will happen. Such practices are common in

Hinduism forms of worship, Voodoo and most of the practices of the primitive religions such as the North American Indian and many African religions.

Psychic meditation. This means to develop one's intuition, clairvoyance, seeking psychic powers for the practice of foretelling the future or reading the thoughts of others. It can also include going on "feelings" in determining what is truth.

Mystical practices such as altered states of consciousness. This would be such as being placed in a trance or the practice of hypnosis for the purpose of seeking guidance from mystical powers. This would also include "divination" (or channeling), which is seeking "familiar spirits" as our personal spiritual guides.

Magic. The practice of seeking spiritual powers to bring to pass a desired result through ritual practices of magical formulas that would include the use of inanimate objects or repetitive chants of "magical" words.

The practice of any of these things is to call upon or rely upon unknown powers or beings to attempt to exalt yourself to become like God. Some desire to use such powers to control and manipulate others for their own personal gain. What is appealing with all of these things is that it gives the appearance of giving some sort of homage to God without giving up the person's self-will. In other words, Man is still in charge without submitting to the authority of God.

Confusion: Satan's Smoke Screen

In case you have not noticed, the world is one confusing mess, and it is no wonder when man refuses to recognize God as the Creator of all that there is. Man will go to any length (no matter how illogical) to elevate himself to the position of being equal to or above God through his own self-effort. If you compare what the cults believe, you will soon see that in every description of God, it is a power or a force or a thing that Man is able to control and manipulate to his own liking. It all goes back to the Garden of Eden and believing the lie of Satan, "For God knows that in the day you eat thereof, you will be as gods." (Genesis 3:5)

All of these beliefs are a vain attempt to deny what Man already knows in his heart. He stubbornly refuses to bow before the Creator, whom he knows exists, and willingly chooses to remain ignorant. "But they *deliberately forget* that long ago by God's word the heavens existed and the earth was formed out of water and by water." (2 Peter 3:5, italics added)

No one is ignorant of God. We are clearly told in Romans 1:20 that we *all* have been given knowledge of our Creator. "For since the creation of the world God's invisible qualities—his eternal power and divine nature—have been clearly seen, being understood from what has been made, so that men are without excuse."

The struggle for godhood has been *the* battle all down through history, and the war is still raging in the hearts of Man. Man has set the stage for the battle by declaring his own godhood and that he has no need of a God to tell him what is good and evil. Mankind desires elevating himself to godhood in an attempt to encroach upon the Eternal Godhead and become one with God. In doing this, Man can choose by his own self-determination what it is that is right and wrong in obtaining his own happiness.

This is the rebellion towards God from which sin emanates. Rebellion is pride of self and is, in essence, self-love. Self-love has no room for the desires and needs of others and is self-seeking, self-centered and egotistical.

We all have heard the popular catch phrases of today, "love yourself," "be good to yourself," "look out for number one," "know yourself," "look within yourself," "pull yourself up with your own boot straps," and on and on it goes. Contrast this with what God says, "die to self," "serve one another," "love your neighbor as yourself," "look out for the needs of others," and "trust in God and not in self." The way of the world is self-focused; the way of God is other-focused.

Where does this self-focused attitude come from? The Bible says, "And even if our gospel is veiled, it is veiled to those who are perishing. The god of this age has blinded the minds of unbelievers, so that they cannot see the light of the gospel of the glory of Christ, who is the image of God." (2 Corinthians 4:3-4) Satan is the god of this world, and it is from him rebellion towards God first originated. This rebellious attitude had been passed from generation to generation beginning with Adam and up to the present day. Adam rebelled against God and by his life of rebellion, death was passed on to all Men. Christ (the second Adam) through His life of obedience even unto death, and through His death, life has been offered unto all Mankind. By Adam's rebellion, Paradise was lost but by the obedience of Christ, Paradise has been gained for whosoever will come to Him.

Chapter 15:

Paganism, the Fad Religion

◆◆◆

When dealing with Internet evangelism, the belief system we most often encounter falls under the large umbrella of the religion of Paganism. In fact, in the Yahoo! Groups we work in, under the subject area Religion and Beliefs, three years ago groups (then called "clubs") about Paganism composed almost 13% of them, second only to Christianity groups, which were approximately 59% of the whole in this subject category. At the time of this writing, the numbers have changed significantly. The Pagan groups have grown to 22% of all groups under Religion, and Christianity is now only 45%.

Paganism has become the fad religion of today's youth and is growing by leaps and bounds in a behind-the-scenes kind of way, out of sight of most mainstream Christians. The term "Paganism" brings to many people's minds days long past when scantily clad natives bowed down to trees, worshipped rivers, and feared the wrath of the earth gods if a crop did not produce an appropriate harvest. While those who practice Paganism today are more "civilized" than those of the past, the basic belief system has not really changed at all.

Trying to pinpoint a definition of Paganism can be difficult. If you are talking with a Pagan online, you will soon discover that the beliefs we give here as typical Paganistic beliefs might or might not describe what that particular individual believes. This is because it is a religion each individual formats himself into however he chooses it to be, choosing which gods and goddesses, if any, he will acknowledge and in what rituals he will choose to participate. All we can do in this book is provide the basic tenets that are true to many who consider themselves Pagans so you will have at least a starting place to begin the discussion with someone who considers himself a Pagan.

The word Pagan simply means a heathen, although the Pagans themselves prefer the definition *country dweller* or *one close to the earth*. A heathen would be one who does not believe in the God of the creation, but who worships the creation itself rather than the Creator of the creation. The only real difference between all of the various Pagan belief systems is the methodology of worship according to how *God, gods, goddesses, spirits, entities, forces, powers that be, energy* or any other description of the supernatural are perceived in their minds.

The origins of Paganism are nearly impossible to trace to any specific person or ancient writings. The roots are buried deep in the misty past of folklore and oral tradition. From a biblical perspective, Paganism is almost as old as the creation, originating from the time mankind first began not to acknowledge God as the Creator and instead desired to be their own gods in worship of the creation. The basic thought of Paganism is that God is in all and all is God (pantheism), so by becoming a part of the creation, this makes them gods themselves, which is essentially *self-worship*.

The Tower of Babel is a great example of the influence of Egyptian and Babylonian Paganism of the era. The purpose of the Tower of Babel was for mankind to ascend to the height of God in a desire to be gods themselves. The entire Bible addresses this conflict between man and God and has only two definitive groups of people: the Hebrew children being the children of God and the gentiles as the enemies of God. The Hebrew children worshipped the God of the creation whereas the gentiles worshipped the *creation* and introduced both the altering of God to fit their vain imaginations as well as the worship of many gods. Incidentally, to this day, there are still only these two definitive groups of people. The one is the group who recognizes God as the Creator and that there is no other God, and the other imagine themselves as becoming as God or are gods unto themselves.

In Paganism, the definition of God is confusing not only to themselves but is impossible for them to explain to others. A belief that "God is in all and all is God" requires an explanation of how it is that God created Himself when God *is* the creation. Most Pagans do not care to contemplate this vein of logic. When talking with individuals, regardless of their own peculiar mixture of beliefs, God is spoken of as a person in one moment, then in the next moment as an impersonal force, power, or energy. This confusion stems from the refusal to acknowledge a personal Creator, apart from His creation, and when it is thought through logically, it is the only explanation that is rational. Mankind is not ignorant of this; it is with willful intent they choose to ignore this fact. It is an attempt to replace a personal God, one to whom they would be held accountable, and to make a choice to reduce God to the level that is then either equal to or below Man himself. This futile thinking relinquishes any accountability they feel may be required of them.

Paganism is a broad set of beliefs, peculiar to each individual or group, that has one basic underlying belief that ties them all together: the worship of nature and/or the creation, sometimes referred to as "magickal" or "earth-based" religions. The two major groups under this heading are Neo-Paganism and Traditional (or Ancient) Paganism. The Pagans themselves may or may not actually use these terms to describe themselves. Those who are part of the Neo-Paganistic movement will be most reticent to call themselves Pagans, but fall into this category nonetheless. Proponents of the New Age philosophy and of Wicca (a form of witchcraft) fall under the classification of Neo-Paganism.

Ancient Paganism is not a religion you choose (according to the Pagans), but rather one you are born into or for which you are chosen. The beliefs are often quite varied from group to group and even from individual to individual. This is mostly true of the Paganistic beliefs of Nordic, Celtic, Germanic, Slavic, Finnish, Egyptian, Roman and Hellenic roots, based on the differing mythology from these basic cultures. Primitive religions would fall into this category as well, for example, being born into a certain primitive tribe and handing this belief down from generation to generation according to their own individual mythology.

There are some that do not belong to any group but who practice independent Paganism or Neo-Paganism and have altered or integrated their own beliefs into ancient Paganism or primitive religions. These beliefs sometimes include such as the American Indians' belief that the forefathers' spirits return back into the land or into animals tied to that land or a mixture of various primitive or ancient Paganistic beliefs and practices.

Most of what we encounter today from those who profess to be of a Paganistic belief is a hodgepodge mixture of Hinduism, Buddhism, primitive religions and an assortment of ancient and Neo-Paganism, which would best identify the New Age thought of today. Many times Christianity is perverted and twisted in an attempt to be forced into this mold as well under the label of "tolerance, unity and love." Paganism appeals to the "I did it my way" attitude that pervades much of modern society and offers a *customized religion* that "best fits me."

As one can readily see, this is the reason there are few apologetic books that are written on the subject of Paganism. It would be nearly impossible to have an exhaustive explanation of every belief, especially when new thoughts crop up on almost a daily basis. The varieties are as endless as the amount of individuals who profess to be Pagans in some form or another, and it would require an endless amount of writing to keep up. When trying to look at the big picture, it is a confusing mishmash of religious thought, but when the basics are focused upon, the confusion disappears.

Neo-Paganism

New Age integrates most of the Paganistic beliefs along with Jungian and/or Freudian psychology or often joins Paganism with a smattering of pseudo-Christianity. The identifying mark of New Age philosophy is an inherent belief that all religions and belief systems are equally valid and must be treated as such. Traditional Paganism, however, is rather exclusionary as far as being a member of their own particular belief system, whereas New Age thought attempts to embrace all beliefs. Pagans themselves will agree that it is a rather nebulous distinction, and there are no hard and fast rules concerning Paganistic beliefs.

While the Traditional Paganism[123] is more like the shamanistic beliefs of more primitive groups, it can often be mixed with Neo-Paganism in actual practice. To a degree, some forms of Wicca, such as Pow Wow Magick, may be more closely associated with primitive religion, while others would be closer associated with ancient Paganism. The same can be said of some of the ancient Paganistic beliefs, however. Some of these as well can be more closely associated with the practices and beliefs of primitive religions. At any rate, all of these descriptions of Paganism can be interchangeable at any given time according to the individual Pagan you may encounter.

Wicca

Some of the fastest growing sectors of Paganism are: Wiccans (with their own endless list of various beliefs and practices), New Age (also with many varying beliefs and practices), and an assortment of other magick- or earth-based belief systems that would best fit this category. It is impossible to generalize what Paganism is all about without having someone contradict you but, for the most part, we have compiled what you would most likely encounter as the heart of Paganism.

Wicca actually came on the scene rather recently, but as to the exact date, it is difficult to determine. We have seen dates of 1902, 1950, and 1970s. One of the best known Wiccans today, Silver Ravenwolf confirms its modern origins: "Wicca, as you practice the religion today, is a new religion, barely fifty years old."[124] However, if you talk to someone involved in Wicca, they are sure to make the same claim as the author of *The Teen Spell Book* when she said, "Earth-based religions, including Wicca, predate Christianity, Judaism, Buddhism, and Hinduism."[125]

As you can see, there are two faulty presuppositions inherent in this statement. First, it is presupposed that Christianity does not have its only ancient roots in Judaism. If Wicca can be considered much older than its true origin, whenever that may be, because of its roots, why are Christianity's roots not equally allowed as verification of its age? Be aware that the implication here is that since its roots are more ancient than those of Christianity, it surely must be more valid. Secondly, it is presupposed that the biblical account of creation is not true. If it is true, then there is only one God who created Adam and Eve, who were believers in Him. This would mean that any other religion, other than the one sanctioned by that God, would be a false, manmade religion and would obviously not pre-date the religion established by the one true God. Since Wiccans look to the Goddess as their main object of worship, they would like to believe that she existed before anything else, and because of this, they claim to pre-date Christianity.

The basic Wicca beliefs are rooted in Paganism because all Wiccans are Pagans (however, not all Pagans, as we have seen above, call themselves Wiccans). Wiccans deal more with the magical aspects of life, and many of them are quite proud to call themselves witches. It is difficult to have an exact count of the number of those who practice Wicca because they feel they would be persecuted if they reveal their spiritual beliefs. One website estimates 750,000 practitioners in the United States, which would make it the "5th largest organized religion in the United States, behind Christianity, Islam, Judaism and Hinduism."[126]

While not all Wiccans practice magic (a euphemism for witchcraft), most do in some form. Building on the beliefs we have already outlined for Pagans, the Wiccans add to this a more organized sense of ethics, looking to the Rede[127] for direction. The Wiccan Rede is: "If it harms none, do what you will."[128] This is coupled with another belief that some Wiccan sources call a Rede as well, that is often known as the "Threefold Law." This "Law" states that whatever one does, whether for good or for bad, will come back in kind three times as much. Because of this, you will find most Wiccans to be decent people, striving to do good to others. They tend to classify their use of magic as "good magick" and will tell you that Wicca is very similar to Christianity in that both use their religion to manipulate nature (and indeed, some who are of the Prosperity Theology[129] vein actually do sound more like

Wicca than biblical Christianity).

Wiccans will also claim that many Christians practice Wicca and do not have any problems integrating the two in their lives, which makes us wonder how they cannot see the obvious contradictions. Never before in the world's history has it been so accepted to admit to being a witch. The "new tolerance" boldly declares that Wiccan beliefs are equally as valid as Christian beliefs and by doing so it validates witchcraft as an acceptable religion in today's society.

Even in the U.S. Military, Wicca and Paganism are being more accepted as valid religions. Carl McColman, a Wiccan who has written a book to help those outside of it to understand his people better, talks about what he considers a positive step the Army has recently taken towards his religion. "In 1990, the U.S. Army published a guidebook for its chaplains in dealing with soldiers who practice a minority religion. This book includes a detailed, balanced, and fair description of Wicca and the unique spiritual needs of Wiccan and Pagan soldiers. The message is clear: in the army (as well as the other branches of the service), freedom of religion means that it's okay to be a Pagan."[130]

Cult Check

With Paganism, it is easy to see their denial of the Trinity, their repudiation of the Bible, and their trust in good deeds to make good karma for the after-life. Although the Pagan outlook on life might seem to give them the happiness they crave, we have worked with many Pagans who have found that worshipping whatever god you choose as you choose still leaves their heart empty and longing for more. Spending your life wondering if you are "good enough" to be joined as one with creation or to reincarnate to a better life form after you die weighs heavy on their hearts.

The same simple gospel that we have presented throughout this entire book is what the Pagans need to hear. Many of them have been disillusioned by what they thought was true Christianity, but that was, in reality, merely a works-based legalism under which only a perfect person could survive. Pagans are often surprised when they hear the true good news, the message of the grace of God.

Chapter 16:

How Paganism Has Infiltrated the Church

♦♦♦

Although the title of this chapter might be surprising for some, others will not be surprised at all. Because of the nature of BIBLE counseling, it is important to help people test what they truly believe against the unchangeable standard of the Bible. Even a pastor who counsels only the members of his church should not assume that their beliefs about God are correct just because they go to a Bible-teaching church. Some who come for BIBLE counseling, who even have their names on the church membership list, will be caught up in pagan and occult practices. In fact, there are some pastors who have incorporated pagan and occult teachings and techniques in their own preaching.

If there is any doubt that the Church has been infiltrated by Paganism, the occult and cultic teachings, let us look at a few statistics taken from a national opinion poll by the Chattanooga New Free Press, September 7, 1991.[131] These statistics will show how false teachings are stealing the heart out of Christianity.

Thirty-five percent of America's evangelical seminarians deny that faith in Christ is absolutely necessary for salvation. These are the ones in training to become the pastors of our churches.

However, in the Bible we read: *"Salvation is found in no one else, for there is no other name under heaven given to men by which we must be saved." (Acts 4:12)* and *"Jesus answered, "I am the way and the truth and the life. No one comes to the Father except through me." (John 14:6)*

Thirty to fifty-one percent of Protestant pastors and 30 percent of born-again Christians do not believe in the physical resurrection of Jesus Christ.

The Bible tells us, *"And if Christ has not been raised, your faith is futile; you are still in your sins." (1 Corinthians 15:17)* and also, *"They were startled and frightened, thinking they saw a ghost. He said to them, 'Why are you troubled, and why do doubts rise in your minds? Look at my hands and my feet. It is I myself! Touch me and see; a ghost does not have flesh and bones, as you see I have.'" (Luke 24:37-39)*

Fifty-three percent of those claiming to be Bible-believing conservative Christians say they do not believe in absolute truth.

Yet we see in the Bible: *"Then you will know the truth, and the truth will set you free." (John 8:32)*, *"Sanctify them by the truth; your word is truth." (John 17:17)*, *"Surely you heard of him and were taught in him in accordance with the truth that is in Jesus." (Ephesians 4:21)*, *"This is good, and pleases God our Savior, who wants all men to be saved and to come to a knowledge of the truth." (1Timothy 2:3-4)* and *"They will turn their ears away from the truth and turn aside to myths." (2Tim 4:4)*

Forty-three percent of born again Christians agree that it does not matter what religious faith you follow because all faiths teach similar lessons about life.

Once again, we can compare this to biblical truth. *"But he continued, "You are from below; I am from above. You are of this world; I am not of this world. I told you that you would die in your sins; if you do not believe that I am the one I claim to be, you will indeed die in your sins." (John 8:23-24)* *"Whoever believes in the Son has eternal life, but whoever rejects the Son will not see life, for God's wrath remains on him." (John 3:36)*

The Interfaith Alliance

If this survey is not frightening enough, let us introduce you to the "Interfaith Alliance" and the "Americans United for Separation of Church and State." Both of these political organizations consider fundamental Christianity as the single worst enemy standing in the way of the unifying of all world religions. Northminster Baptist Church pastor Rev. Dr. C. Welton Gaddy is the executive director of the Interfaith Alliance. The executive director of Americans United is Barry W. Lynn who is an ordained minister in the United Church of Christ.

Who these politically active groups consider "fundamental Christians" are those who believe the Bible is the infallible word of God that is sufficient for all matters of faith and doctrine and that Jesus is the only way to salvation. Both of these organizations are actively involved with the American Civil Liberties Union and are committed to destroying all vestiges of any public display and public confession of a belief in the God of the Bible.

Through their own words, they have denied the faith yet refuse to relinquish the title "Christian" in association with their names in an attempt to further muddy the waters and increase confusion in an already confused world. Here is an excerpt from a sermon presented to the congregation of Westminster church entitled, "How Does the Death of Jesus 'Save' Us?" by Dr. C. Welton Gaddy May 13, 2001.

> I want to be perfectly honest in this sermon. Your pastor is among those who feel that the sacrificial and substitutionary views of Jesus' death horrendously distort the nature of God and offer a false suggestion of the kind of life that Jesus inspires.
>
> What kind of God sends a holy child into the world to grow to adulthood for the singular purpose of dying an unjust death? Is this a sign of love? In such a mechanical, if not pagan, transaction, where do you find the presence of grace or love—God's grace and love for Jesus as well as for us? God is not a cruel overlord who must be appeased by the death of an innocent person before loving the highest order of creation. God is love.[132]

It is obvious that the Rev. Gaddy does not recognize Jesus as the "I AM," God manifested in the flesh.[133] He either fails or refuses to acknowledge that Jesus is God who paid the penalty for the sins that sinful man committed.[134] Rev. Gaddy does not understand that God, by the sacrifice of His own body[135] paid the penalty of the sin debt we owed in our place so we may have eternal life.[136] This selfless act of God is the demonstration of His love towards sinful man in that He offers forgiveness and the free gift of salvation[137] to those who acknowledge that they have sinned against a holy God.

Yes, God is love! "We know that we live in him and he in us, because he has given us of his Spirit. And we have seen and testify that the Father has sent his Son to be the Savior of the world. If anyone acknowledges that Jesus is the Son of God, God lives in him and he in God. And so we know and rely on the love God has for us." (1 John 4:13-16)

A visit to the web sites of both of these organizations shows that the clear target is what they call the "Religious Right." We would like to state that we are not defending the leadership of the Christian Coalition, and we are not in agreement with much of the doctrinal stance or the methodology of the political activism of the Christian Coalition. We do not consider this to be representative of *all* fundamental Christians. Nevertheless, we are concerned that the *real* target of the attacks from the Interfaith Alliance or the Americans United and the ACLU is not actually these individuals and this organization, but is in reality those who believe in the fundamental truths taught in the Bible.

Sadly, this attack is being perpetrated by those who call themselves Christians but yet deny that Jesus is the way, the truth and the life. This is indeed their choice to deny this, and it would be fine if that was where it stopped but such is not the case. The clear-cut agenda of these organizations is to silence Christians who *do* believe that Jesus is the only way, the only truth and the only life. Although they boast of their own tolerance, it is here that their own extreme intolerance is exposed for what it is because fundamental Christians are the only target of the hatred and intolerance of the unification of all religions. When they portray themselves as the epitome of love and tolerance, they hide their true feelings of hatred and intolerance towards the God of the Bible.

The Interfaith Alliance boasts of the diversity of their membership and lists representatives from nearly every Christian denomination plus representatives from the following beliefs: Animist, Baha'i, Buddhist (Theravada, Nichiren, Pure Land (Amitabha), Zen or Chan), The Church of Jesus Christ of Latter-Day Saints, Hindu (various schools), Humanist, Jain, Jewish (Conservative, Orthodox, Reconstructionist, Reform), Native American/Inuit (various), Shinto, Sikh Taoist, Theosophist, Unitarian Universalist Association, Wiccan, and Zoroastrian to name a few.[138]

The following is a quote from the web site of the Interfaith Alliance. In reading it, we have to be careful to see what the true meaning their words are saying. If we look closely, we can see what is actually being said by these nice sounding words.

> The Interfaith Alliance is a non-partisan clergy-led grass-roots organization dedicated to promoting the positive and healing role of religion in the life of the nation and challenging those who manipulate religion to promote intolerance. With more than 130,000 members drawn from over 50 faith traditions, local Alliances in 38 states, and a national network of religious leaders, The Interfaith Alliance promotes compassion, civility and mutual respect for human dignity in our increasingly diverse society. Our agenda aims to counter those, such as the Religious Right, who promote intolerance and degrade the value of a multi-faith nation. We affirm the duty of people of faith and good will to promote the healing and positive role of religion in public life, protecting religious integrity in America.[139]

We need to keep in mind that to counter fundamental Christianity, which they lump together under the title, "Religious Right," is their sole target. It then becomes obvious the comments they make are directed towards just this group. By stating they promote "compassion, civility and mutual respect for human dignity," they are implying that fundamental Christians are not compassionate, civil nor do they have respect for their fellow man. Fundamental Christians are labeled as those who "promote intolerance" and "degrade" others. By affirming that it is the "duty of people of faith and good will to promote healing," suggests there has been a negative group of people who are *not* people of "faith and good will" who have done damage that needs to be healed.

We must ask ourselves who, other than fundamental Christians, would the Interfaith Alliance be referring to when they say their purpose is to challenge "those who manipulate religion to promote intolerance?" This is a demonizing of fundamental Christians by trying to label them as an evil that is a threat to our society that must be eradicated.

> The Religious Right continues to storm the United States Capitol, state houses and school districts to advance a partisan political agenda that includes mandating sectarian prayer in schools; denying civil rights to all Americans; dismantling public education; revoking First Amendment guarantees, including the separation of church and state and freedom of speech; and fighting gun safety, campaign finance reform and efforts to protect the environment.[140]

This is totally a matter of perspective. What has always been considered a normal practice is what has just recently begun to be assaulted by such groups as the Interfaith Alliance and Americans United. For many years, prayer had always been an integral part in government institutes and public schools. Bibles in public buildings have always been the norm. In fact, reading from the Bible used to be an important part of the public school curriculum.

What we have here, however, is a group of people who dislike prayers devoted to the God of the Bible. Because of this, they have determined that the Bible is irrelevant and that they do not want themselves (or anyone else, for that matter) to be involved in this type of behavior, which would give the God of the Bible His due honor. They themselves have been the ones to storm the U.S. Capitol to try to undo the very principles of faith that were the foundation of this country. What is now considered to be unfair, intolerant, mean and hateful is fundamental Christians who refuse to deny

Jesus is the only way to God and that the Bible is indeed God's written word.

In a closer examination of the above statement on the Interfaith Alliance website, we can see that their use of terminology is merely hiding the truth of the matter. It is not the fundamental Christians who are demonizing others, but it is the Interfaith Alliance itself who uses euphemisms to cover their own, anti-Christian, political agenda.

Partisan political agenda: This means anybody who is not a part of their own political agenda. It also indicates how wide-spread this movement is, crossing over political lines and broadly encompassing anyone who holds to traditional moral values.

Mandating sectarian prayer in schools: This means that Christians who pray to the God of the Bible are offensive to others who are not Christians so this "evil" must be stopped.

Denying civil rights to all Americans: This means that we must not oppose homosexuality, abortion, pornography, drugs, alcohol abuse or any other things the God of the Bible calls sin. We must not only tolerate such people, but must hire them, even if it contradicts the moral code God has given us.

According to them, it is also un-Christian and narrow-minded to complain when someone dunks a crucifix in a bottle of urine with the inscription "Piss Christ" above it and calls it "art." When fundamentals are offended and speak against having their taxes used for such things, this is considered being insensitive to the feelings of others, and we are criticized for having no appreciation for the "Arts" and freedom of speech that is guaranteed under the first amendment. One can only imagine the world outcry if anything similar were done with any other symbol of a particular religious belief. Yet it seems that fundamental Christians are exempt from any respect for what they believe. No doubt there are other items the Interfaith Alliance and Americans United place under this label, but one would have to ask them as to what other civil rights they believe fundamental Christians are denying to all Americans.

Dismantling public education: This is a statement against those who desire to homeschool or wish to have vouchers to choose a school of their own choice for their children. This would include those parents who have decided sex education which promotes sexual promiscuity and teaches homosexuality as just another valid alternative life style is not what they believe is a necessary required study for their children. It also comprises those parents who believe the emphasis of the public education system should be on the fundamentals of education instead of on such things as environmentalism and multi-cultural studies and activities, which teach a flawed definition of tolerance to their children. While children are learning how to properly apply a condom, respect "mother nature" and learn the values of Yoga, self-realization and self-worth, they are failing miserably in the basics of reading, writing and arithmetic.

Of course, in the logical (or should we say illogical) reasoning in the minds of the proponents of the one world religion, it is the "evil" fundamentalists who refuse to pump more money into a failed public education system, and we then become the reason for the downward scholastic trend in the public schools. This is where they come up with the idea that fundamentals are homophobic bigots and racists, who desire to poison the waters, who have no respect for the values of others' religions and who desire to destroy the educational institutions of our children.

> Manipulating religion for partisan political gain is bad for both religion and government. It creates a civic culture in which adherence to a political agenda or ideology becomes a litmus test of faith. Any movement that seeks to establish "one true faith" as a national panacea to the complex problems facing our society undermines the integrity of our democracy and threatens principles inherent to the strength of our nation: religious liberty, equality, respect for diversity, and democratic participation.[141]

It would do the Interfaith Alliance and the Americans United both to heed this bit of their own advice. Their obvious partisan politics has been bad for government, public education and fundamental Christianity. The litmus test of these organizations has become acceptance of any and all faiths as long as the common denominator is denouncing fundamental Christianity.

If this is not so, we would like to ask both organizations to name groups other than fundamental Christians that are the object of their scorn. Who else would they be speaking of when they refer to "any movement that seeks to establish one true faith?"[142] Yet a good look at this accusation shows that they are attempting to establish what they believe is the "one true faith" that comes through the unification of all faiths with the exclusion of fundamental Christianity. Somehow, they have determined that fundamental Christianity "undermines the integrity of our democracy and threatens principles inherent to the strength of our nation: religious liberty, equality, respect for diversity, and democratic participation."

> While the leaders of the Religious Right whom we have quoted have made positive impacts in some areas, as public figures their inflammatory statements sometimes intolerantly deny basic liberties and potentially incite hate violence. Religious leaders that vilify Jews, gays, African-Americans, women, and our nations [sic] many minority religions are contributing to a culture that inadvertently comforts those who choose to express their hate with violence. Their words contribute to an environment that supports the demonization of certain people. When taken to its extreme by others, this leads to prejudice-based, hate-motivated acts of violence, including the highly publicized shooting sprees in Chicago and Los Angeles that were motivated by anti-Semitism and racism, as well as the tragedy of Matthew Shepard's slaying in Colorado driven by the anti-gay beliefs of his killers.[143]

This is the only platitude they offered towards the enemy. It makes one wonder what the positive impacts in some areas could be. Perhaps feeding the poor and giving aid and comfort to the sick? Perhaps speaking out and being actively involved against injustices perpetrated on the innocent and helpless? Could it be possibly the same things they value as well, but the real complaint is a confession of Jesus as Lord?

However, after the all-too-brief platitudes, the demonizing volume rises to a fevered pitch when they state, "their inflammatory statements sometimes intolerantly deny basic liberties and potentially incite hate violence." Again, let us look at exactly what they mean by the phrases they use.

"Religious leaders that vilify Jews": That means proclaiming Jesus as the promised Messiah, thereby indicating that Jews who do not believe in Him are not going to heaven.

"Vilify gays": This means calling homosexuality a sin, and considering it a lifestyle that is not natural and does not please God.

"Vilify African-Americans": This one is rather an obscure reference. There were no concrete examples to support why they would make a statement like this. We have no idea how they came to this conclusion unless the connection is made between school vouchers as being against the inner-city children who may be African-Americans and who they feel would be damaged by school vouchers. Another possible connection could be the attempt to label all white supremists as fundamental Christians. Once again, we would have to ask the Interfaith Alliance and the Americans United to explain this one.

"Vilify women": This means to believe abortion is a sin and that there is something honorable about being a mother who puts her family before her career.

"Vilify our nations [sic] many minority religions": Again, this means to proclaim Jesus as Lord and to present the gospel of Christ to the lost. Any time we stand firm on our belief that Jesus Christ is *the* only way to God we are "vilifying" any religion that does not believe this way.

According to the Interfaith Alliance, fundamental Christians "are contributing to a culture that inadvertently comforts those who choose to express their hate with violence. Their words contribute to an environment that supports the demonization of certain people." We have to wonder if the vilifying words the Interfaith Alliance uses to demonize fundamental Christians will contribute to an increase of hatred towards this minority group?

It is interesting, as this website continues, how they have drawn the conclusion that it is fundamental Christianity that was the catalyst that sparked the shooting sprees in Chicago and Los Angeles and caused two men to beat a homosexual man to death in Wyoming.[144] With this type of flawed logic, it would then be equally valid to place the blame of the shooting sprees that targeted Christians in Columbine and the shooting of church members in a Baptist church in Texas on the Interfaith Alliance and the Americans United because of their hate speech against fundamental Christians.

A link to the article, "Hate Speech Leaves Mark on Students" is strategically placed towards the end of the Interfaith Alliance's article, "When Religious Right Leaders' Speech Crosses Over to Hate Speech."[145] It is blatantly obvious that the intention is to make the association between these articles dealing with hate crimes and fundamental Christianity.

Americans United for Separation of Church and State (AUSCS)

The Americans United[146] is not quite as blatant, but the contents of their website makes it equally clear who the intended target is. Claiming to be champions of the protection of religious freedom, they target the same group as does the Interfaith Alliance, the fundamental Christians. The following quote from their web site shows this to be true.

> Americans United for Separation of Church and State makes every effort to challenge those who would take down the wall that separates church and state in this country. With that in mind, AU is proud of its role as the nation's leading opponent and watchdog of the Religious Right.[147]

If this statement is really true, then look at the issues that concern them, which they classify as supposedly taking away the freedom of religion.[148] Since the leaders of this group claim to be Christians, why should they feel their freedom to practice their beliefs are being threatened by the display of the 10 commandments in government institutions? Why should a Christian feel threatened by the appointment of government officials who hold the views of fundamental Christianity? Why should a Christian feel threatened by government funding of religious organizations for the purpose of alleviating suffering and pain? Why should a Christian feel threatened by prayer in school? Why should a Christian feel threatened by Bibles in public institutions? Why should a Christian feel threatened by Christian students evangelizing after school hours?

These are just a few of the issues being touted as a "threat" to religious liberty and which need to be championed by Americans United. None of these issues should strike fear into the hearts of true, fundamental Christians. The only real threat we should feel is the fear mongering of such organizations as these who seek to vilify and spread fear and ignorance of fundamental Christianity.

Why should any Christian feel threatened by these issues? The answer is really very simple. Only if one is not a Christian at all would these issues be a concern. What is at the heart of this issue is not the supposed injustice and intolerance by fundamental Christianity, but the real problem is with the God of the Bible. It is a systematic attempt to repudiate the God of the Bible and to replace Him with the one world religion where Man is his own god.

Ironically, though, not only is their hypocrisy exposed in promoting hatred and intolerance towards fundamental Christianity, it is further exposed with the accusation of fundamental Christians trying to use the political arena to further their agenda. The fact is that these websites are filled with pleas for money and articles that use guilt, fear and intimidation to strongly urge the use of politics to further their own agenda through world federations of governmental control over every issue of life. In other words, it is perfectly alright as long as it is *they* who control the masses through government agencies against fundamental Christianity, which is the threat to world peace. It is the one world religion that is the savior of the world and the protectors of the world against the "evils" of fundamental Christianity that stands in the way of Man realizing his own utopia.

Jesus said, "Enter through the narrow gate. For wide is the gate and broad is the road that leads to destruction, and many enter through it. But small is the gate and narrow the road that leads to life, and only a few find it." (Matthew 7:13-14) What the proponents of the unity of all religions have done to these words is to change it to, "straight and narrow is the way that leads to destruction and few will find it; broad and wide is the gate that leads to life and many will find it." Unfortunately, God is not persuaded by their new interpretation.

The words of Paul in Ephesians 4:13 that say, "until we all

reach unity in the faith and in the knowledge of the Son of God and become mature, attaining to the whole measure of the fullness of Christ," have been changed to mean "the unity of all faiths that deny the Son of God."

Love and tolerance have been redefined to mean love and tolerance of anything as long as it has nothing to do with the God of the Bible, love of anything as long as it is love of self and not of God; tolerance of anything as long as it is not anything the God of the Bible says is wrong. They have replaced universal salvation available to all with universal salvation of all except for fundamental Christians. The unconditional love of God has been redefined to mean even the rejection of His perfect sacrifice for the sins of the world. God's love is unconditional, but His salvation is conditional as far as confessing that Jesus is the way, the truth and the life and that no man can come unto the Father but by Him.[149]

Isaiah prophesied about how man would be in these last days in Isaiah 5:20, "Woe to those who call evil good and good evil, who put darkness for light and light for darkness, who put bitter for sweet and sweet for bitter." We live in a topsy-turvy world where good has now become evil and evil has become good. The goodness of God is being questioned as never before in the history of the world.

Paul also describes this present time in history in 2 Timothy 3:1-5, "But mark this: There will be terrible times in the last days. People will be lovers of themselves, lovers of money, boastful, proud, abusive, disobedient to their parents, ungrateful, unholy, without love, unforgiving, slanderous, without self-control, brutal, not lovers of the good, treacherous, rash, conceited, lovers of pleasure rather than lovers of God— having a form of godliness but denying its power. Have nothing to do with them." The prophetic accuracy of these verses is clear to anyone who reads them. Our society is perfectly profiled by this man who lived almost 2000 years ago.

False Teachers and False Prophets

False teachers and false prophets are nothing new coming against the church. It had already begun while the apostles were still walking upon this earth. We see several instances where it was confronted by various writers of the New Testament, as well as many of the early church fathers. Paul confronted the Pharisees who attempted to draw new converts back into legalism.[150] There were those who had already denied the bodily resurrection of Jesus and were confronted by Paul in 1 Corinthians 15:12-19. False teachers and false prophets were already in abundance as we see from the writings of Peter in 2 Peter 2:1-3. However, the Bible also says that in the last days, there will be an increase of deception through false teachers and false prophets, and this is what we see happening today.

Jesus said in Mark 13:20-22, "If the Lord had not cut short those days, no one would survive. But for the sake of the elect, whom he has chosen, he has shortened them. At that time if anyone says to you, `Look, here is the Christ!' or, `Look, there he is!' do not believe it. For false Christs and false prophets will appear and perform signs and miracles to deceive the elect—if that were possible." Here we can see the depth and intensity of the deception in the last days. Many who are not grounded in the truth of the Bible will be led astray by these false teachers.

Again, when Jesus was asked what would be the signs of the last days, He replied in Luke 21:8 "Watch out that you are not deceived. For many will come in my name, claiming, `I am he,' and, `The time is near.' Do not follow them." This is what we see in the world today, total confusion in what to believe and on almost a daily basis, some new idea, thought or religion is being proclaimed by some new false Christ (one claiming to be the "anointed one"), false teacher or false prophet that comes on the scene with new signs and wonders.

Much of this is what is behind the one world religion of unity at the expense of truth and the statistics we started with in this chapter are evidence of this very thing happening before our eyes. If there ever was a time in history that truth needs to be proclaimed, it is now. This is what is really at the heart of this book. There is a great need for solid, biblically-grounded counselors to be more than just counselors for those who are hurting but also to be evangelists, which we all have been called to be.

The time has passed to expect the pastors to carry this burden alone. We are all called to share and spread the good news of the gospel, and, in order to do that, we have to have a good understanding of just what that is. We need to heed the words of Paul in writing to Titus when he tells us to, "hold firmly to the trustworthy message as it has been taught, so that [we] can encourage others by sound doctrine and refute those who oppose it." (Titus 1:9) Again Paul impresses on Timothy the importance of this in 2 Timothy 4:2-3, "Preach the Word; be prepared in season and out of season; correct, rebuke and encourage—with great patience and careful instruction. For the time will come when men will not put up with sound doctrine. Instead, to suit their own desires, they will gather around them a great number of teachers to say what their itching ears want to hear."

The Marriage of Paganism and Christianity

In the false prophets of the Interfaith Alliance and the AUSCS, we see so-called Christians who are more willing to embrace the Pagan as their brother than fundamental Christians. Although this intermingling of Paganism and Christianity is not new, it has risen again in this era just as it did at the time of the tower of Babel. We see a strong rise in a coming together of those who stand in opposition against God, in their desire to set themselves up as their own gods.

These two organizations, and their goal of the one world religion, are prime examples of how the melding of Paganism and Christianity has been slowly growing, taking us almost unawares. We can see the leaven gradually infiltrating the Church in such a subtle way, and, just like leaven, a little bit will grow quickly until soon the entire loaf has been permeated.

The God of the Bible is being reduced to an impotent, jovial heavenly Father who winks at sin and who smiles on all religions equally, granting access to His presence through any type of worship we choose. We see churches abdicating their responsibility of evangelism en lieu of a "can't we all just get along" attitude that scorns the teaching of sound doctrine as being divisive.

We see Satan's masterful scheme weaving its way through our pews. His M.O. is still the same as it was in the garden centuries ago. First, he places a seed of doubt in the goodness and the motives of God. This appears in the form of a designer God, carefully crafted to our own specifications, who fits comfortably with the lifestyle we want to maintain.

Second, Satan convinces us that God doesn't really mean what He says. Surely He cannot mean that homosexuality is sin. Surely He cannot mean that we are to restrain our "natural" sexual desires. Surely He cannot mean that abortion is the same as murder. Surely the Bible really is not God's written word.

Then Satan comes through and encourages us to challenge what God has said. "Oh, come on," we hear him whisper in our ears, "you don't *really* believe all those stories in the Bible. They're really just nice little myths to entertain you." Did God *really* say...?

Lastly, Satan dresses up his own offers that appear to be better than what God can give us. He promises us the world but delivers us merely a load of manure. He promises us happiness but delivers an emptiness in our souls. His offers may look tempting, but they are as hollow as an old, dead tree. There is no substance to them. They are only wisps of dreams, always floating out of our reach, taunting us from afar.

The doors of the Church have been flung wide to Paganism because of our dissatisfaction with what we have and the refusal to acknowledge that it is Man's rebellion towards God that is the cause of the pain and misery on the earth. We find it much easier to blame God rather than ourselves.

The promise of paradise on this earth in the here and now is a very strong incentive to overcome, yet that promise is what the false teachers are promoting. False prophets and false teachers have always taught this: instant gratification and happiness by our own efforts because God is not doing anything to alleviate the pain and misery so we have to take control of our own future and trust in ourselves.

Of course, happiness is a very subjective thing. What makes one happy will generally be at the expense of somebody else's happiness. And after centuries of attempts, human effort has still not produced a resolution to this dilemma.

The biblical answer, however, is not the popular choice in our microwave world. God tells us that in this life there will be trials and tribulations, and we will never experience total happiness in this corrupt world. The promises of God, though, are that He will never leave us nor forsake us and will comfort us in times of trials and tribulations. Although the fulfillment of His promises will not be until His perfect time, we are assured that we will enjoy, not a temporary happiness, but joy with Him for eternity. We must make certain that we do not buy into the hedonistic philosophy that demands happiness now, even at the expense of the eternal fate of our souls.

Paganism's live-for-the-present, utopia-now ideology is destined to fail, along with Satan's master plan to steal glory from the God of the universe. The battle lines are being drawn and we need to be careful to choose God's side. Will we definitively stand on His side or will we try to straddle the line between Christianity and Paganism, hoping at the end that God will call us to be His own?

Let us not forget the sobering words Jesus gave us in Matthew 7:22-23, "Many will say to me on that day, `Lord, Lord, did we not prophesy in your name, and in your name drive out demons and perform many miracles?' Then I will tell them plainly, `I never knew you. Away from me, you evildoers!'" The choice is ours to make. We need to take it very seriously whether we will live only for the present or invest in the eternity of our future.

Chapter 17:

Pseudo-Christian Forms of Paganism

◆◆◆

In the next few chapters we will be exploring, in a more concrete way, how Paganism has infiltrated the Church of today. As we begin, we need to define our terms so we are certain that there will not be a misunderstanding in what we are saying. The first word we will define is *pseudo,* which means something that is a counterfeit or an imitation of the real thing.

Counterfeits are dangerous because they are so misleading. They *look* too much like the real thing that it can sometimes be almost impossible to tell the difference. Counterfeit bills appear on the surface to have great value, but when examined closely are exposed to be just worthless pieces of paper. Those who work in banks and where large sums of money are exchanged must be trained in how to spot a counterfeit bill from a genuine bill. To the untrained eye, one cannot see the difference between the two because on the surface, they look the same.

We all know that the goal in counterfeiting bills is to make it look as close to the genuine currency so as to deceive the unsuspecting person who may have received it as genuine currency having the value that it claims to have. The person who received the counterfeit bill may be totally convinced it is genuine and so happily takes it to the bank expecting it to have the claimed face value. It is not until the bill is presented to the one who knows the false from the real that it is revealed to be nothing more than a worthless piece of ink and paper, which has no redeeming value. In the same way, a counterfeit gospel has no redeeming value whatsoever and offers nothing but a false salvation.

A second word we must define is the word *Pagan*. The definition of what a Pagan is has changed somewhat over the years. The word Pagan is a Middle English word that originated from the Late Latin word "paganus" meaning civilian or a country dweller. *Paganus* came from the Latin word "pagus" meaning a village or a country.[151]

Originally, the Middle English word *Pagan* was used in reference to one who was not a Christian. A Pagan was defined as one who was not religious or who had no religion, or more aptly put, a heathen. A heathen is one who has no God, but his god is the worship of the creation rather than the worship of the Creator.[152] The choice for the word *Pagan* was intended to refer to one who was an "earth dweller," or in other words, who minded the things of this earth and whose eyes were not set on things above.[153] This is meant to contrast with those who would confess that they were only pilgrims or strangers on the earth awaiting a better country, a heavenly country.[154]

Simply put, there are only two groups of people on the earth: those who worship the Creator and those who worship the creation. The one group is earthly-minded and the other is heavenly-minded. The earthly-minded are called "earth dwellers" and the heavenly-minded are called "pilgrims" on this earth who are waiting for the new heaven and earth.[155]

Today, the word *Pagan* has been changed to mean one who is not of the Christian, Muslim or Jewish faith. Paganism has come to mean one who believes in many gods instead of the monolithic beliefs of Christianity, Islam and Judaism who profess only one God. Paganism has been redefined to be another religion that worships the same God as Christians, Muslims and Jews and is nothing more than a different path to the same God.

This redefining, however, is incorrect in two major areas. First, it is assumed that because Islam and Judaism believe in one God that it is the same God of the Bible and of Christianity. In our chapter, *The God of Abraham, Isaac and Jacob,* we will show how Judaism has forsaken the God of the Bible and how Islam may be based on the worship of only one God, but the concept of him has been derived from compiling many gods into one. The second wrong assumption is that Paganism is a religion that worships the same God as Christianity and is merely another path to the same God. It has been reasoned by the Pagans that to worship the creation is the same thing as the worship of the Creator and to honor the creation is to honor the Creator because the Creator and the creation are the same "one God."

However, Paganism is the belief in mythological gods and goddesses (origins unknown) and that Mankind can obtain the status of godhood or that we already *are* gods and goddesses who need to recognize our divinity. With this definition of Paganism, the original definition of *Pagan* in its broadest sense is the proper application of the word because it is the worship of self rather than God. It is in this sense that all religious thought is Man-centered and therefore is Pagan. Only Christianity is God-centered, centered on the one, true God.

The reason this chapter is entitled *Pseudo-Christian Forms of Paganism* is because of the mixture of two entities, Paganistic thought and Christianity, which produces a false, counterfeit form of religion that has a resemblance to Christianity, but is not worth the paper used to define it. This is why we call it *pseudo-Christianity*. When Christianity embraces the belief that Man can become gods, this is no more than another form of Paganism because Man is at the center instead of God.

The main focus on Paganism that we want to address is the belief in many gods (polytheism) when the Bible clearly proclaims there is only One God.[156] With that in mind, how can Christianity and polytheistic Paganism be joined together and yet still remain Christian?

Mormonism is the clearest example of the mixture of Paganism and Christianity, which we believe will become evident in the section of this book that deals with Mormonism. However, we hope to show how Paganism, in its broadest application, is at the root of all beliefs as we see Man displacing God and becoming his own god. By seeing Paganism for what it is, it becomes easy to unravel the confusion surrounding the various religions in the world by showing the common threads between them rather than give an exhaustive study of each one.

One more area needs to be addressed before the unraveling of the confusion grows clear. In modern Paganistic beliefs, the origins of the gods and goddesses are explained in one of two following ways: either the gods are a product of the cosmos or the cosmos and the gods and goddesses are one and the same.

If the gods are a product of the cosmos, then the cosmos birthed the gods and goddesses. This is the belief that matter is eternal, and life and intelligence emerged from the combination of matter and energy. With this belief, the cosmos *is* God, who is an unknown energy or power.

If the cosmos and the gods and goddesses are one and the same, the cosmos is God and the gods are the cosmos. In other words, there is no distinction between energy, matter, life and intelligence. All is God and God is all. All eastern religions, such as Hinduism and Buddhism, are based upon one of these two concepts of the origins of life and who or what God is or a mixture of the two.

Although most of the pseudo-Christian cults take the view of God who was the creator of the cosmos and is the source of life and intelligence, they have become Paganized by virtue of Man raising himself up as God and thereby displacing God. Man then becomes the center of worship rather than God. Not only does Mormonism take the view of Paganism of many gods and goddesses, it also takes the view of Paganism in the belief of the origins of life. In Mormonism, the gods and goddesses are a product of the cosmos. Another way of explaining this is that the cosmos birthed the gods and goddesses and the cosmos *are* God, the originator of life and intelligence.

One other form of a pseudo-Christian belief that is almost identical to Mormonism is the fairly new movement called the Word Faith Movement, that has permeated much of Christianity during the twentieth century. We will show this connection in the chapter about the Word Faith Movement.

In the furthest extreme application of the word Paganism, it is the desire for man to be their own gods and had its roots in the garden of Eden. From there, it had spread to all parts of the world and took on various forms in the folklore and practices of many cultures and was later on called a religion. All of these "religions" had abandoned the one true God, the Creator of all things, and had established the worship of a false god with man at the center of their worship. Thereby, when the word Pagan was originally introduced to describe these people, they were rightfully called a people who had no religion and were heathens because they no longer believed in God.

What we see today is the unifying of these false religions under the banner of love and tolerance. This is the vain attempt of Man believing that he can bring about world peace, unity and the brotherhood of man (utopia) upon this earth through his own works of righteousness apart from God. Although it may have the appearance of the worship of the God of the Bible, it is in fact the worship of a false god who has only a false future to offer.

What we see is a "unifying of faiths" and the "unity of the faith" coming to a climax. The true church of Christ will soon be raptured leaving the unified faiths to their own destruction before Christ comes back with His Church to set up a kingdom of true lasting world peace, unity and brotherhood built upon the righteousness of God.

Chapter 18:

Jehovah's Witnesses and the Impossible Dream

◆◆◆

In this chapter, the basics of the teachings of the Jehovah's Witnesses (JWs[157]) are to be used for an illustration of the importance of sound biblical doctrine when dealing with those who come for counsel. This study (as well as the rest of the chapters dealing with specific false teachings) is not intended as a thorough study of these particular false teachings. There are many excellent books that can give you detailed accounts of the origins and specific beliefs of each of these cults. Our purpose is to remain focused on the common threads that intertwine through all false teachings for the purpose of identifying them as contradictory to the written word of God.

As far as a thorough study of each of these, this is entirely left to the discretion of the individual to determine how much you may desire to study other beliefs. This may depend on your own personal counseling ministry. With Internet ministry such as we do, it is wise to be prepared to discuss any of the beliefs we have included in this text.

However, it is possible that you may not need to be as cognizant of these beliefs as one who deals more specifically with them. Knowing the basics, though, is important in order to perceive the roots of these in a person with whom you may be counseling. Even a pastor who counsels only his own people must be aware enough of these false beliefs as he delves into any particular person's basic beliefs about God to ferret them out if necessary. A pastor should never assume his preaching is the sole source of spiritual teaching members of his congregation are receiving.

Why are Some Drawn to Cults

As with all pseudo-Christian cults, JWs believe they are the only true church. To be a member of a church that God has chosen to be the exclusive recipients of special revelation knowledge gives the members a feeling of moral superiority over the rest of society. Many who are drawn into cults are concerned over what they perceive as a lack of morality and spiritual genuineness in the churches. Cults offer to fill this void.

Others who may be attracted to cults are those who have been convicted of a life of sin and desire to become better people. On the surface, this may appear to be a humbling experience, but it is actually the flip side of pride in self. This is still the attitude that we are basically good and can rid ourselves of the bad through strict regimental obedience to the laws. Although the motives may be good, it is still a refusal to acknowledge the depth of our sinfulness and to see our absolute need for the grace of God.

Another group of people who may be drawn to such cults are those who feel they have been shunned by or "victims" of society. Most cults with their strong emphases on separation from the "things of the world" appeal because they have a common hatred for those who are outside of their group. This kind of a "get even against society" thinking gives them a sense of belonging with those of like mind.

The strict codes of conduct required of legalistic churches appeal to the extremely prideful. Some appear to flourish and bask in the pride of their accomplishments towards obtaining their own salvation. For others, the extreme, strict codes give them a feeling of atoning for their own sins. They view salvation as the giving up of earthly pleasures (self-denial), which surely must be pleasing to God and in time will earn them God's approval. For others, it gives them a "God is on my side" feeling, and helps them to look forward to the day that God will take vengeance against those who treated them so badly.

It stands to reason that how one views God will be reflected in the type of religious beliefs one chooses. If God is viewed as one who demands absolute perfection when we know in our hearts it is impossible to obtain this perfection, how can we see God as other than a God without love, mercy and grace? If the God we serve is without love, mercy and grace, then we ourselves cannot give others love, mercy and grace because this reflects who our God is. When we study other beliefs, we begin to see what their view of God is and how this view is reflected in their literature.

This is very true of the Watchtower Society's writings, the foundation on which the Jehovah's Witnesses build their beliefs. In this statement from the Watchtower magazine, we can begin to see their concept of God from the words they choose to talk about "haters of God and His people," which would mean anyone who does not embrace the JW teachings and those who follow their beliefs. This would be especially fundamental Christians who consider them a cult.

> Haters of God and His people...are to be hated....We must hate in the truest sense, which is regard with extreme and active aversion, to consider as loathsome, odious, filthy, to detest. Surely any haters of God are not fit to live on his beautiful earth. The earth will be rid of the wicked and we shall not need to lift a finger to cause physical harm to come to them, for God will attend to that, but we must have a proper perspective of these enemies....We pray with intensity...and plead that his anger be made manifest....O Jehovah God of hosts...be not merciful to any wicked transgressors....Consume them in wrath, consume them so that they shall be no more.[158]

As you can see, the attitude expressed here reveals a God of anger and hatred, not a God of love and mercy. This type of God is one who requires a superhuman effort in order to be pleased, and anything less than perfection will fall short of His impossible standard. Many who are drawn into the Jehovah's Witnesses at first are lured by a promise of freedom, soon to find out it is in reality a nightmare of bondage. These are the ones who are smiling on the outside yet screaming on the inside to be set free from a life of fear, guilt and condemnation. They are the ones we can reach with the truly good news, the message of salvation by grace and not by works.

JW Beliefs

JWs teach a works-based salvation, which means they can never be assured of having obtained salvation. Faithfulness to the teachings of the church and perfect obedience to the commandments is required. For any JW to doubt or to leave the church is paramount to having left Jehovah and this results in a loss of salvation.

To begin with, the word "grace" to the JW means the chance to earn one's own redemption. It is viewed as an initial kick start. From there, you are on your own.

As with all pseudo-Christian cults, most or all of the fundamental beliefs of historical Christianity are either denied or altered in some way. Let us go back to our three basic fundamentals to see how the Jehovah's Witnesses match up.

The Trinity: JWs teach that Jesus is not God but was the archangel Michael who, when manifested in the flesh, became Jesus. After this, he took on a third manifestation, as the exalted angel Michael. They teach that the Holy Spirit is the invisible active force of God, but He is not God.

The authority of the Bible: JWs deny the authority of the Bible in all versions used by fundamental Christianity, and have devised their own translation of the Bible called the "New World Translation." This interpretation is according to the Watchtower publications, and it restates troublesome passages so the conflicts with JW doctrine are removed.

Salvation by grace: JWs deny salvation by grace and teach salvation by works. According to the teachings of the church, a JW can only begin his journey of gaining salvation through total obedience to the church, which begins with faithfully distributing literature and witnessing from door to door. Because of this, the witnessing is performed out of fear and obligation. Although sincere, it is not out of a genuine love for others but is part of the requirement towards salvation.

A JW is required to work towards obtaining total righteousness in this life just for the opportunity of getting to prove his worthiness during the millennium. Only faithful witnesses will survive Armageddon. If he has proven himself worthy to live into the millennium through his own sinless life, he earns the chance during the thousand years to work again towards perfection because he has still to face the final judgment. Even if the JW obtains perfection during the millennium, he still must face the final test of the final judgment when Satan and his hoards will be released to test their faithfulness to God. Most will not pass this final test.

What this means is that during his life now, he must work to be perfectly sinless so he will get the chance to spend a thousand years to possibly earn eternal life if he obtains perfection during the thousand years. But, if he should fail in one area, even at the last moment before the final judgment, he will have lost his salvation. What is expected of the JW is to obtain the status of godhood through works of his own righteousness and become as sinless as God yet still, in the end, he must prove his faithfulness.

The Rewards of Fear, Guilt and Intimidation

Is it any wonder that mental illnesses in JWs are 10 to 16 times greater than that of the general population?[159] The suicide rate is proportionately much higher in them than the general population.[160] Many JWs are suffering in silence, feeling trapped with no place to go and with alternatives that offer no hope. With no hope or assurance of ever being granted salvation, many JWs choose self annihilation. This is preferable to waiting for a merciless God to annihilate them after years of hard work to obtain sinless perfection in this life just to face another thousand years of the same torment. To be released from the present torment may appear to be the better choice of two evils, much like a choice of hanging to death by a nylon rope now or live in torment to be hung by a hemp rope later.

The next time you may encounter a JW in person or on the Internet, keep in mind that more than likely he or she is operating in shear fear of loss of his or her salvation on a continuous basis. The concept of being born again and having hope of entering into heaven is not even an option for the JW.

The only ones who have been "born again" are the 144,000 (the anointed) who have already been chosen (elected). This proclamation was made as a result of a failed prophecy, declaring Jesus was going to return in 1874. When it did not come true, the date was changed to 1914 and spiritualized. This sealed the end of the possibility of being chosen as one of the 144,000 and also of being one who lived under grace and mercy. These 144,000 are the ones who will be spirits ruling in heaven with God and Jesus. However, for the 99.9% of the rest of the JWs, the "other sheep," they must earn their salvation without the benefit of the election of God and being born again. If they become sinless and prove their faithfulness, they will then be granted eternal physical bodies to live on "Paradise Earth."

The sacrifice of Jesus for the sins of man applies only to the "chosen" who have already been selected. The JW has absolutely no plans or hopes of being of the 144,000. They are of the "other sheep" who must earn their way to enter into "Paradise Earth." Where the Bible speaks of grace, atonement, justification, and the free gift of salvation by faith, it does not apply to the "other sheep" but was only granted by God's grace to the "Elect."

As it is with all extreme legalistic religions, there are essentially two groups within the members. One group believes they have obtained sinlessness and sit in judgment of the less spiritual with an attitude of condemnation totally void of love and compassion. The other group knows within their heart they can never meet the requirements set forth, so they smile on the outside while they are dying on the inside, suffering in silence and isolation. A JW who dares question the authority of the church is subject to extreme threats of loss of salvation and faces being excommunicated and shunned by all members of the church. This includes his or her own spouse and children If they do not, they will also face the same punishment.

Although JWs appear to be sociable to the outside world because of their energetic door-to-door witnessing, in practice, they are required to associate only with other JWs. Because of this, many who have joined the JWs have already severed ties with non-Jehovah's Witness family and friends. This means that if they are shunned by the church body, they are left with absolutely nobody to turn to. This fear of being totally isolated coupled with being assured of having lost their salvation with no hope of ever being able to regain it (unless one fully repents and comes back to the church) is what leads many into extreme depression resulting in hospitalization and/or suicide.

Where Do I Go Now

Where does one go who has just been excommunicated out of or has left the "only true church" that God chose to divulge His truth through? What are a JW's options at this moment?

We have seen this pattern over and over and it has only four outcomes.

(1) The person can return to the JW church and live a lie of pretending to love a God who he hates and to serve a God who hates him, all the while pretending to be happy. In this case, he is clinging to a little flicker of hope that this God will somehow show a hint of mercy. However, the outcome generally degenerates into a life of extreme bitterness and hatred and contempt for God and for others.

(2) The person sinks into lower and lower bouts of depression that result in suicide or hospitalization. This is shutting down the total inability to reconcile the idea of a loving God with the reality of what he has experienced through who he thought was God. The teachings, attitudes and actions of those in the church were the reflection of the God they served. The idea of continuing to live under the hand of this type of God with no hope of change leads to an overwhelming despair.

(3) The person abandons any and all concepts of a God and decides to live for the moment and live a life in total opposition to what he has tried to live. More often than not, the attitude is, "If you want to annihilate me so bad, then I'll really give you something to annihilate me for."

(4) The person comes into contact with one who presents the true gospel of Jesus Christ, and with love and patience, leads him to the One who took the offense out of the way with His own blood and by grace offers the gift of eternal life to "whosoever will."

It can be difficult to witness to a JW because he or she is so certain the Watchtower Society is the only organization in the world that is teaching the truth. At first, you may need to begin by planting seeds of doubt in the reliability of their founders who have given them their foundational beliefs. During several periods of time in their church history, their leaders have made various prophecies, especially of Christ's return and the end times, which have not come true. By pointing out these false prophecies and showing them that even one false prophecy qualifies a person as a false prophet, you can often help them begin to question what they have been taught.[161] This is important to show there is no need to fear a false prophet. If this fear of the leaders can be removed, then they may be more receptive to listening to the truth.

Another item that can give a JW something to think about is to show the JW Genesis 3:8. Since the divinity of Christ is not believed, this is a good verse to show that it was the Lord (Jehovah) God who walked in the garden, not spiritually, but physically. Once they see that it requires a body to walk, it becomes easier for them to see that it was the Son of God who is the same Lord (Jehovah) God in the New Testament whose name is Jesus.

Realize ahead of time that the progress will be slow because the teachings have been so ingrained in them. Unfortunately, most cults take education in their doctrine much more seriously than most Christian churches, and the JWs you meet will be very well-versed in what they believe. If you are patient, you can slowly plant seeds of doubt that will eventually allow them to be willing to question what they have been taught as they see the inconsistencies.

While this type of scripture discussion can aid in bringing JWs to the truth, nothing is as effective as having a sincere love and concern for them. One of the best things to remember is to focus on verses that speak of salvation by grace and not of works and also that salvation is a free *gift* to *all* who call upon the name of the Lord. Show that God's grace has already been extended to all of mankind and not just the 144,000. Titus 2:11 tells us, "For the grace of God that bringeth salvation hath appeared to all men." Assure JWs that Christ died for the sins of the whole world and that salvation is made available for all who trust in the Lord Jesus for their salvation and not upon their own works.

You cannot imagine how many JWs long for this message, many who are trapped by fear, guilt and intimidation through the cultic teachings and tactics of the Watchtower Society. We recommend a thorough study of the teachings of the JW church in such books as *Cults and Religions* by Ankerberg and Weldon as well as *Kingdom of the Cults* by Walter Martin.

Satan's Tool of Legalism

Satan loves convincing man that there is some good thing in them that can be perfected through the works of the law. When man is convinced of that, then Satan is there (posing as God) to remind them of how much harder they must work. It is not long before it becomes apparent that this God is a sadist whose main goal is to toy with our minds by holding out a little glimmer of hope just to yank the rug out from under us. Salvation is always just a little tiny bit out of reach no matter how much effort is being expended. A God who we begin to serve as a God of love, soon turns out to be an evil sadist and before long, we are serving a God who we hate as much as it appears He hates us.

It is not only Jehovah's Witnesses who reverse the nature of God and Satan in their minds, but many others who confess to be Christians as well. The things that should be attributed to the nature of Satan are attributed to God, and the things that should be attributed to the nature of God are attributed to Satan. Where do they get these ideas? For the most part, they are a reflection of what is taught in their church and also through the attitudes and actions of those who represent the God they serve. It requires much patience and love to show them from the scriptures that what they have been taught is in fact a doctrine of demons. It is very difficult to lead them to Jesus because of the fear and hatred they already hold towards who they think is the God of the Bible.

In this, we can easily see the diabolical plan unfolding. Satan tries to turn the tables on God by painting Him to be an evil God and one who is devoid of mercy and grace. Satan appeals to the pride of man by presenting the Laws and saying, "You can do it.

This is what God expects of you to become just like Him." As soon as we are convinced in our minds that we can earn our own salvation through the works of the laws, and that this is what actually *pleases* God, the trap is set. This is the beginning of an endless rollercoaster of a ride of delusions, disappointments, frustrations, anguish and torment. It is not long until the picture of God is painted as a merciless God whose only desire is to bring harm and torment then, in the end, the person's eventual destruction.

It never occurs to the one who is caught in this trap that Satan is the one who "as a roaring lion, walketh about, seeking whom he may devour"[162] and who is the thief who comes "to steal, and to kill, and to destroy."[163] In the midst of the great confusion, it becomes too difficult to see that it is not God who is confusing, but it is Satan himself who is the author of confusion[164] and of the doctrine of devils.[165] This is the view Satan desires people to see of God while he desires to be thought of as the savior by having you question God's grace, goodness, mercy and love. The fact is that the picture Satan is trying to paint of God is actually a portrait of himself posing as God. If he can be successful in this, then it is not long before the Bible and the God of the Bible become nothing more than a cruel joke perpetrated on duped Mankind.

In dealing with JWs, you will see many similarities to those who are trapped in other types of legalism. It becomes an abusive cult that holds the person bound with chains of fear, guilt and intimidation. Patience and love are the most effective tools for working with anyone who is caught up in legalism. It is vital to keep pointing them to the God of the Bible, who is not only just and righteous, but also merciful, loving and gracious to those who seek Him with a humble heart. The true God gives salvation freely, through His own finished work on the cross and not through our own works.

Just as with legalism, the person often cannot see his own pride and air of superiority that has resulted from his own works of righteousness. These people need to have their own sinfulness exposed, compared to God's incredible holiness and seen as utterly inadequate. Until they can see the depth of their own sin, they will not really see a need for a Savior, other than themselves. When they can see the futility of trying to earn their own salvation through their own works, they will begin to catch a glimpse of the incredible wonder of grace, the grace that gives us our salvation through the mercy of a loving and gracious God.

Chapter 19:

Mormonism: On the Road to Godhood?

The old proverb, "All that glitters is not gold," is one with which most of us are familiar. During the gold rush of 1848, California was inundated by miners who were desperately seeking for a little glitter that would signal their inevitable wealth. Many, however, spent their lifesavings chasing this dream of prosperity, only to find their hopes dashed by those two little words, "fool's gold." It may have looked just like gold, but it was only a disappointingly shiny sham, driving some to end their lives in despair, cheated by the false glittering of a delusion.

We find this same type of delusion in the pseudo-Christian cults we are discussing in this book. At first glance, they appear to be a true, refreshing manifestation of the life-giving teachings of Christianity, but if we examine them closely, it does not take long to see the trap of despair they are setting for those they lure unsuspectingly into their clutches. It is with these cults that have the appearance of Christianity that we must be most on our guard. Whereas most Christians would never find themselves caught up in Islam or Buddhism, the cults that look Christian on the outside can be very deceptive. In fact, the large majority of those who convert to these pseudo-Christian cults come from mainstream Christian churches.

The Church of Jesus Christ of Latter-day Saints (LDS) is definitely one of these. Everyone has seen the shorthaired, clean-cut young men in white shirts and ties on their bicycles riding through the neighborhood. In the past ten to fifteen years, we have also been seeing an increase in public service messages put out by the LDS Church on both TV and in magazines. They present a picture of happy families, enjoying life together, centered around their faith in God. We have seen them place the Bible and the Book of Mormon together, side by side, declaring the Book of Mormon to be "another gospel of Jesus Christ." But is any of what we see in the media truly the reality of Mormonism?

Are Mormons Christians?

The first matter we must deal with is the validity of the claim Mormons make that they are Christians. Do they really believe in the same God mainstream Christians believe in? What do they really believe about God?

As we have stated before, in working with anyone, it is always important to define the terms we are using. This is especially important when talking to those involved in pseudo-Christian cults. They will use the same words as you, grace, salvation, Jesus Christ, God, but the meanings are usually quite different. It can often be quite effective to have them tell you what they mean when they use a commonly Christian term.

For example, when a Mormon talks of God the Father, the person about whom they are speaking is not at all the same God the Father as in the Christianity of the Bible. According to the LDS teachings, we meet Elohim, otherwise known as God the Father. There are many gods and Elohim was one who was commissioned to be in charge of the Earth. "The head God called together the Gods and sat in grand council to bring forth the world....In the beginning, the head of the Gods called a council of the gods; and they came together and concocted a plan to create the world and people it."[166]

The Christian concept of the Trinity is one God coexisting in three Persons. The Mormon understanding of God, however, is that there are many Gods, with Elohim being the one who was put in charge of Planet Earth. They consider themselves monotheistic because Elohim is the one they worship, yet as we continue to examine what exactly it is they believe, we will see that they are in reality polytheists, worshipping many gods.

Once Upon a Time

The story basically goes like this. Once upon a time, there were trillions of planets ruled by an unknown number of gods. One of these gods and one of his goddess wives conceived a spirit-child and named him Elohim. Through obedience to Mormon teachings, Elohim arrived at godhood, after going through the process of dying and being resurrected. Elohim and his goddess wives took up residence on a planet near the star Kolob, where they produced billions of spirit-children.[167]

Seeing a need to give his spirit-children physical bodies, Elohim called a meeting of the Council of Gods to see what could be done about this. The Council of Gods decided to create Planet Earth, where these spirit-children could take human form and learn what was good and what was evil. Because of the nature of this learning process, these spirit-children on Earth would need to have a savior to provide them with the way to attain their eventual godhood. The Council asked for volunteers to be the savior of this new world.

Two of Elohim's spirit-children vied for the position. Lucifer proposed that he would become the savior of the Earth by forcing all humans to become gods. His brother Jesus, however, gave his plan of becoming the savior by giving people a choice about whether they wanted to become gods or not. The Council decided Jesus had the better plan and appointed him to become the savior of the planet Earth.

Lucifer was not happy about the decision so he persuaded a third of all the spirit-children to join him in trying to take over the Earth. Those who followed Lucifer in this rebellion were all cursed with never being allowed to have physical bodies. They became the demons we know today. Those who followed and fought for Jesus were considered blessed and received their reward by being given the bodies that were born into Mormon families here on Earth. These were called "fair" and "delightsome" by the Book of Mormon.[168]

Throughout the writings held sacred by the LDS Church, we see a thread of racism that Mormons try, albeit unsuccessfully, to cover. Those who were descended from Cain were cursed with black skin. The Lamanites who fought against the Nephites and therefore against God were cursed with black skin. The spirit-children who chose neither Lucifer's side nor Jesus' side were cursed with black skin.

This is interesting to note because such a racist position does not appear at all in the Bible. In the Bible we see God saying that "all have sinned" and that Jesus gave His life for all[169]. There is no distinction between people in the Bible, neither by their nationality (Jew nor Greek), their status (slave nor free), or their sex (male nor female).[170] We are told in Revelation 5:9, "and with your blood you purchased men for God from every tribe and language and people and nation." *All* nations have been represented in this purchase, with no exceptions. It appears that the book of Mormon was under heavy influence by the issues at hand in the 1820s. In the United States, it was no secret that the personhood of slaves was in question and was one of the major topics of discussion of the day. In 1978, a "new revelation" was given to the Mormon Church that opened the all-white priesthood to blacks, but it did not change that the Mormon Church's doctrines still consider black skin to be a curse.

The story as you read it above is very evident if you read through the *Doctrine and Covenants*, and *The Pearl of Great Price (which includes The Book of Moses and The Book of Abraham)*. Something you will notice if you talk to most Mormons, however, is that they will deny these things when you inquire about them. And most likely they are speaking from what they know to be true.

Most people from Christian churches would not fall for the obvious fairytale-like quality of these beliefs of the Mormon Church, and it is not these beliefs that are presented to prospective converts. Instead, they are told that the LDS Church believes in God the Father, God the Son and God the Holy Spirit, the sinfulness of Man, salvation by grace, and the resurrection of Jesus, all seemingly "Christian" concepts.

We must note that in the LDS Church there are differing levels of understanding of these "basic" teachings. It could very well be that the Mormon you are speaking to may not be aware of these teachings of his church. This is how many of the pseudo-Christian cults work. They present themselves as Christian and, by the time the new convert begins subtly to be exposed to the (often extreme) differences, he is so caught up in the society of the church that he can easily be intimidated into going along with the crowd.

As with most of these pseudo-Christian cults, the worst thing is to be someone who has heard their "truth" and has turned their back on it. The eternal consequences are by far much worse for them than for someone who had no knowledge of the "truth" to begin with. These groups also foster a separation from family and friends who do not know this same "truth," and so isolate the person from the ones who love them the most. The church then becomes their new family and loved ones.

Once the convert has been so isolated and has become dependent on the church members for all social interactions, the idea of leaving involves more than merely giving up a set of religious beliefs. It involves cutting themselves off from all they have come to hold dear. This loss of their newly acquired society, coupled with the fear of losing their eternal rewards, is what keeps people trapped in these cults for years. Suspicions may arise in their minds, but are quickly squashed, often held silently inside of the new converts as they try to reconcile the inaccuracies they are seeing in what their church teaches.

Appearances become everything. Even if the teachings do not always make sense, one must keep up the appearance that all is well. We had a Mormon girl come to us and confess that she was considering having an abortion. The reason she was so distraught about being pregnant was because the LDS Church's teaching is that "unchastity is next to murder in seriousness."[171] In *Doctrine and Covenants* 42:22-26, 80-81, we see that the penalty for unchastity is for the person to be disfellowshipped or excommunicated. This girl was terrified that by carrying her child, conceived through an illicit, pre-marital relationship, she would lose all that she had ever known as she was growing up: her family, her friends and that she would be separated for eternity from those she loved.

She thought that as long as she had an abortion (which the LDS Church also speaks strongly against, but could be done without anyone knowing), she could hide it and still retain her position in the

LDS Church. Having an abortion seemed to be a better way of dealing with things than to have to openly admit her promiscuity, being excommunicated from her church and then cut off from her family.

Once again we can see the devastation caused by a legalistic doctrine. Mormonism may speak of salvation by grace, but their definition of grace is much like that of Roman Catholicism's. According to them, the amount of grace you receive is proportionate to the good works you do. You do good works and God gives you more grace. However, as we have stated many times before, grace that is earned cannot be grace.[172]

Instead of salvation by grace, Mormons work hard for their salvation. There are over 65,000 Mormon missionaries, pedaling their bicycles in countries all over the world, drawing over 750 new converts each day into the LDS Church. All of this work is towards their ultimate goal, which is godhood by the way of perfection in their life.

Although very few, only those classified as "sons of perdition," will not attain salvation of some sort, Mormons are still under the great stress of being perfect in this life so they will reach a stage of exaltation after death. "Exaltation," which is what they call the state of godhood, is only reached by the men who have perfectly followed the Mormon teachings throughout this life. Abraham, Isaac and Jacob did only what Elohim commanded them to do so they received their exaltation. David, on the other hand, did not attain this because of his sin with Bathsheba.[173]

A Mormon man's key to exaltation is to follow the Mormon teachings perfectly. A Mormon woman's key to salvation, however, lies not only in her following the Mormon teachings, but mostly in the obedience of her husband to those teachings. Her place in eternity depends on where her husband is. This is why you will never see Mormon women out evangelizing. Her role is to raise their many children in the teachings of Mormonism and to do all she can to make her husband worthy of exaltation.

How to Talk to a Mormon

The best thing you can do when talking to anyone who is caught up in a cult or false teachings is to have a genuine love for them.

True love for someone does not mean you let them continue in believing this false doctrine without saying anything. It means you do all you can to help them see the lies they are believing and, more importantly, the truth of the Scriptures.

The place to start with any pseudo-Christian cult is to have them define the terms they are using. Do not be afraid to ask them to explain what they mean when they use the word "God," or when they are referring to "salvation." Since the Mormons do ascribe a portion of authority to the Bible, you can often use it to help them understand what the Bible means by these various "Christian" sounding words.

As with any other false teaching, it is advisable to stick with the three major issues: the Trinity, the authority of the Bible and salvation by grace not by works. The Mormons have trouble understanding the concept of the Trinity because they believe you are referring to three separate Gods who rule over the Earth. This idea does not bother them because it is exactly what they believe. It is interesting to note that in Alma 11:22-31 it clearly states that there is only one God, and pointing this out to them can cause many Mormons to pause and avoid giving an answer.

We have included some excellent resources for helping to talk to a Mormon in Appendix G. The next time you see two clean-cut men with white shirts and ties at your door, take the challenge. The probability is that the reason they first got involved with Mormonism is because they were searching for something to fill that God-shaped hole in their lives. Unfortunately, they have gone to the wrong source for this. If we understand the serious plight of sinful man and the incredible wonder of God's grace, a strong compassion should overtake our hearts for those who are trapped in uselessly trying to find their own way to heaven. Under that smile lies a heart that needs Jesus. Let us never forget what the real stakes are the next time we hear our doorbell ring.

Chapter 20:

Penance, Purgatory and Paganism

❖❖❖

Many who pick up this book, might think it odd for us to include Roman Catholicism in our section on pseudo-Christian forms of paganism. Our purpose in this is not to insult anyone, but to point out the similarities in the beliefs and practices of Roman Catholicism and those of Paganism. We ask you to read through this material and judge it for yourself.

Let us remind ourselves of the basics of spotting a cult. First, all cults teach something different about the Trinity than what the Bible teaches. This appears in either adding to or taking away from the Godhead, and often shows itself as devaluing the role of Jesus as our sole redeemer.

Secondly, all cults diminish the authority of the Bible. Again, this is done by adding to what we have as our canon or taking away from it. If the authority of the Scriptures is in question, this shakes the foundation of Christianity because then there is no one standard by which we can compare what is sound doctrine and what is false.

Another way in which cultic thought undermines Christianity is by questioning the sufficiency of Christ's finished work on the cross. We can see this especially when salvation by grace is turned into a salvation by works.

As we examine the Roman Catholic beliefs and practices, we need to keep these three items at the forefront of our thinking. We urge you to compare the two. We think the contrast will be obvious.

Apostolic Succession

Roman Catholicism claims to trace its roots back to St. Peter and the quote in Matthew 16:18 where Jesus tells Peter, "And I tell you that you are Peter, and on this rock I will build my church, and the gates of Hades will not overcome it." In this verse, the Catholic Church says, Peter was given the authority to start the only true church. This is what is called the "Apostolic Succession."

In *Fast Facts on False Teachings*, Carlson and Decker tell us that Jesus was actually making a play on words when He used the word Peter and the Greek word for rock, which are very closely related. The masculine form, the name Peter (petros), is the form that refers to a small stone, merely a portion of a much larger rock. The form used by Jesus to tell what foundation His church would be built on, however, was the feminine form (petra), which means a large, foundational rock, such as the rock the wise man built his house upon. Peter could easily tell that Jesus was not conferring on him the entire weight of the future of the Gospel, but that the Gospel would be rooted in his confession that Jesus is the Christ, the Savior promised by God.[174]

This Apostolic Authority is the keystone, pardon the pun, of dealing with any Catholic person. Architecturally speaking, the keystone is the stone at the top of an arch by which all the other stones are held into place. Take out the keystone and the rest of the structure crumbles at your feet. In regards to witnessing to a Roman Catholic, all their other beliefs hinge on this one and, like removing the keystone, all their other beliefs will indeed crumble if they doubt the authority of the Roman Catholic Church in matters of faith.

The Roman Catholic Church claims to trace its authority in an unbroken line back to Peter, however, a study of history reveals that the first popes did not emerge until after the reign of Constantine (in the 300s AD). The Roman Catholic Church itself has difficulty documenting the lives of the earliest popes, and they rely heavily on tradition as their source.

Even establishing Peter as the authority in Rome to begin with causes a great deal of problems if not for Roman Catholic tradition. Paul's letter to the Romans is conspicuous in that it does not mention Peter in the long list of specific greetings he makes in Romans 16. It does not make sense that Paul would leave out such an important person as Peter in his greetings.

Another important passage in the Bible that pertains to this is found in 1 Peter 2:6 where Peter quotes from Isaiah 28:16, "See, I lay a stone in Zion, a chosen and precious cornerstone, and the one who trusts in him will never be put to shame." Here it is obvious that Peter himself is referring to Christ as the rock, and this rock is not laid in Rome, but in Zion. Peter would not have referred to Christ as the rock if he had really understood Jesus to be saying that he himself was the rock on which the Church would be built.

It is also significant to see that the location of the "rock" is in Zion, which indicates Israel, not Italy. Roman Catholic tradition puts Peter in Rome and by this establishes Rome as the governing seat of the Church. However, the Bible states that Jesus is the Cornerstone of the Church and that Cornerstone was located in Israel.

There are many other biblical arguments against the Apostolic Authority claimed by the Roman Catholic Church, such as the priesthood of *all* believers (1 Peter 2:5, 9; Revelation 1:6), the foundation of the Church being built on *all* the apostles (Ephesians 2:20), Paul being the author of the majority of the New Testament (12 epistles compared to Peter's two), Paul opposing Peter face to face for Peter's hypocrisy (Galatians 2:11-13), and the absence of Peter in the second half of the book of Acts. Each of these builds up a stronger case that the "rock" Jesus spoke of was the confession that Jesus is the Christ, not the rock of Peter the fisherman.

Why does the Roman Catholic Church cling so adamantly to this Apostolic Authority? If they were forced to accept that Christ, not Peter, is the foundation of our faith, then the power of the Vatican would be stripped and many of the Church traditions that are accepted as being part of the faith must also be repudiated. A typical response one receives when talking to a Catholic about the source of many doctrines is, "because the Church says so."

Marianism

It is apparent to even the most casual observer of the Catholic faith that Mary plays a dominant role in their beliefs. Her pictures and statues permeate every Catholic church, basilica and cathedral in the world. Apparitions of her appear to the faithful. Miracles are attributed to her power. Prayers are offered to her. Yet how does the Catholic view of Mary line up with what the Bible teaches of her?

To begin with, the Roman Catholic Church considers Mary as the "Mother of God." The logic they use is that since Jesus is God and Mary is His mother, she must be the mother of God. The flaw in this way of thinking, however, is that Mary was not the mother of Jesus' divinity, but only of His humanity. If Mary were the mother of His godhood as well, then Mary would have to be a goddess herself, and it would necessarily follow that Mary's godhood preexisted that of Jesus. This elevates Mary to a higher plane than Jesus and, by inference, makes her more powerful than the child she bore.

When confronted with this, Roman Catholics will deny that Mary is a goddess or that she has more power than her Son. Although the teaching of the Church in its catechism declares that God is the Father of Jesus' divinity and Mary is the mother of Jesus' humanity,[175] they still insist that she is indeed the "Mother of God."

Mary has been drawn into the redemptive process in a subtle yet obvious way by saying that through her consent to God's plan, her obedience, she was responsible for redemption being a possibility in our world. One must wonder what our fate would have been had Mary not given her "consent" to carrying the human body of Jesus. She is even contrasted with Eve, giving life to the world when Eve was responsible for death. In fact, it is said, "Death through Eve, life through Mary."[176]

Yet we see something different in the pages of the Bible. In Genesis 3:20, we see that Adam gave his wife a name: Eve, the mother of all the living. Since this name was given to her *after* the Fall, we can conclude that Eve's legacy was not to be the one through whom death entered, but the one who gave physical life to all. The emphasis on sin entering the world through Eve is not the same emphasis as what Paul has in Romans 5:12. "Therefore, just as sin entered the world through one man, and death through sin, and in this way death came to all men, because all sinned." Sin is inherited through the bloodline, which is passed on by the male, not the female. This is why we see in 1 Corinthians 15:21-22 that sin was passed on by the male: "For since death came through a man, the resurrection of the dead comes also through a man. For as in Adam all die, so in Christ all will be made alive." Jesus did not inherit the sin nature because He was not born of an earthly father.

All of this brings us to one of the central teachings of Marianism, Mary's sinlessness. Many Protestants, as well as many Catholics, do not understand what this teaching of the Roman Catholic Church is and how it contradicts one of the most foundational beliefs of Christianity: all have sinned (Romans 3:23). The Catholic teaching on this doctrine can be clearly seen in the catechism of the Roman Catholic Church, as stated by Pope Pius IX in 1854: "The most Blessed Virgin Mary was, from the first moment of her conception, by a singular grace and privilege of almighty God and by virtue of the merits of Jesus Christ, Savior of the human race, preserved immune from all stain of original sin."[177]

The Catholic logic is that obviously God could not be born of an unclean vessel, and so she must have been free from the stain of sin. Yet if God, in an act of grace, cleansed Mary from her sins in order to keep her as a sinless vessel, then the answer to sin is much different than the Bible tells us. If Mary was kept from sin by God's grace, then why did not God's grace reach to all and accomplish the same thing in the same way, and, by doing so, allow Jesus to avoid the horrible death He suffered?

When the Bible tells us that we are all sinners, the key word to note is *all*. There is no evidence from anywhere in Scripture that any human being was ever sinless, except for Jesus Christ. If they had been, their death for mankind would have sufficed as payment for all sin because they would have fulfilled the requirement for a sinless sacrifice. Mary could have died on the cross and Jesus would never have had to come down to earth. Yet Mary was not sinless because she had a human father by whom she, as all of us have throughout the centuries, inherited the nature of sin against which we are powerless to conquer.

Also, if Mary indeed were sinless by God's act of grace, then her consent to the redemption process was nothing more than a response over which she had no choice. She was unable to sin and therefore was also unable to make a choice whether or not to obey God in this. If one is pre-programmed to be sinless in life, then one has no choice but to be sinless. If Mary were indeed sinless, then she was merely a robot, doing what she had been programmed at the moment of her conception to do. She would have been incapable of doing anything other than obey.

Besides being sinless, Mary is called the "ever-virgin"[178] or *aeiparthenos*. You might notice in this word the same word that is used to describe the temple of Athena in Athens, the Parthenon, which comes from the Greek word for *virgin (parthenos)*. The concept of being the eternal virgin was not at all new to the time period when Christ was born. Athena, Artemis and Hera, goddesses who were being worshipped on a regular basis during that time, were all said to be eternal virgins, basking in the glow of the many cults of worship that sprung up around their virginal images.

In examining the Mary presented by the Roman Catholic Church, we see a stronger resemblance to the Greek and Roman goddesses of the time than to the Mary portrayed in Scripture. The typical pictures and statues of Mary are seen with a halo behind her head and the child Jesus in her arms. We need to note that similar statues have been unearthed from centuries before Christ, honoring the moon goddess and the sun god in her arms, looking almost identical to the statues of Mary and the baby Jesus we have now.

Mary is also called the "Queen of Heaven." In the Bible, we find references in Jeremiah 7 and 44 about the worship of the "Queen of Heaven" and God's anger at His people for perpetuating it. The title, "Queen of Heaven," has referred over the centuries to various pagan goddesses. It does not take much digging to find that one use of this term "Queen of Heaven," which the Catholic Church gives Mary, is the same title as held by Hera, the ever-virginal Greek goddess wife of Zeus. In studying Greek and Roman mythology of the time of the early church, it appears that instead of the image of Mary holding true to the Mary we see portrayed in the Bible, we see an eclectic Mary, pulling her characteristics from many other goddesses of the time in a strange mélange of pagan and Christian.

Very little is said in the Bible about Mary the mother of Jesus. In fact, after what we read in the Gospels, there is only one other mention of her throughout the entire rest of the New Testament (Acts 1:14). It seems odd that, besides Peter, another major player in the early church according to the Roman Catholic Church, Mary is conspicuously absent in the writings of Paul and the majority of the New Testament. Although we have no trouble with the idea that Mary was indeed a unique woman, who was blessed by the grace of God, the other claims that are made for her sinlessness and her eternal virginity have no basis in Scripture, only in the traditions of the Roman Catholic Church.

Traditions of Men
As with all teachings we hear, we must compare them to the unchangeable ruler of the Bible to see if they match up with that standard. The source of this teaching does not come from the Bible but from tradition. In talking with a Catholic, it does not take long to realize the authority that has been bestowed on tradition. Tradition encompasses the writings of the early church fathers, the writings of the popes, the apocrypha, pseudopigrapha and other documents of the Roman Catholic Church.

Even though the Bible is considered authoritative, it is put on the same level as these other sources and, at times, lowered to allow the authority of the extra-biblical source to rise above it. This has been sanctioned by the Roman Catholic Church and has become the foundation for many of the beliefs Catholics have.

The Catholic Church bases their belief in tradition on 2 Thessalonians 2:15, which says, "Therefore, brethren, stand fast, and hold the traditions which ye have been taught, whether by word, or our epistle." (KJV) Because Paul gives assent to traditions by word of mouth, it is assumed this includes the traditions recorded by the early church fathers. However, in focusing on this one verse, they ignore verses such as 1 Peter 1:18 and Colossians 2:8, as well as the confrontations Jesus had with the Pharisees in Matthew 15 and Mark 7. In these passages we see warnings against holding to the traditions to the extent of forsaking the Holy Scriptures. Clearly we see that God's laws should hold precedence over any man-made traditions there might be.

Jesus sums it up very well in Mark 7:13, "Thus you nullify the word of God by your tradition that you have handed down." Many of the traditions of the Catholic Church that have been handed down over the centuries do exactly that, "nullify the word of God." Whenever our traditions contradict the written word of God, we must be willing to give them up in order to stay true to the faith that has been handed down to us.

Mary's Role As Co-Redeemer

The subtlety of the twisting that false teachings do to the truth of the Gospel often amazes us. Make no mistake that these false teachings are very well thought out and formulated in order to assure the best possible chance to deceive those who hear it. The more one studies false teachings, the more apparent it is that the twisting is so intricate that it cannot have mere men at its root but without doubt is demonically inspired.

Because Mary has been credited with giving her consent to God's plan and through her obedience making a way for Jesus to come into the world to redeem us, the Roman Catholic Church has elevated her to the position of co-redeemer with Jesus. If it were not for her work, Jesus could not have redeemed us.

> This motherhood of Mary in the order of grace continues uninterruptedly from the consent which she loyally gave at the Annunciation and which she sustained without wavering beneath the cross, until the eternal fulfillment of all the elect. Taken up to heaven she did not lay aside this *saving office* but by her manifold intercession continues to *bring us the gifts of eternal salvation*...Therefore the Blessed Virgin is invoked in the Church under the titles of Advocate, Helper, Benefactress, and Mediatrix.[179] *(italics added)*

Yet in the very next paragraph of the catechism, they say that this does not in any way diminish the role of Jesus in our redemption. How can it be that adding Mary's work to what Jesus accomplished does not diminish His work? Basically the Roman Catholic

Church is saying that without Mary's cooperation, God could never have fulfilled His plan. Does this not reduce the efficacy of Christ's work on the cross? Does it not elevate mankind into a vital role for God's plan to be accomplished? Here again we see, as in other cults, the elevation of Man's works at the expense of God's grace. Mankind becomes the essential factor in our redemption, not God.

It does not occur to a Catholic that if Mary would have refused, God could easily have found a different woman to take her place. God's will will indeed be accomplished in this world, as it has been in the past, by whatever channel it takes for God to do so. God has even used dumb animals to make certain His will is achieved. However, God in His omniscience knew before Gabriel appeared to Mary that she would consent to His will. God knew she would say yes; otherwise He would have sent Gabriel to a different Hebrew woman. The vessel is not nearly as important to God as His will being done. God is more interested in finding willing hearts than perfect vessels.

The term "mediatrix" is the feminine form of the word "mediator." The Bible is very straightforward, though, on who the mediator is between God and men. Paul writes to Timothy about just this subject: "For there is one God and one mediator between God and men, the man Christ Jesus, who gave himself as a ransom for all men—the testimony given in its proper time." (1 Timothy 2:5; see also Hebrews 8:6, 9:15, 12:24) This verse does not leave any room whatsoever for more than one mediator, be it male or female. Jesus is the only one God acknowledges as a mediator between Himself and us. To add another rejects the sufficiency of Christ's work on the cross, denies the uniqueness of Jesus in all of humanity, and actually transforms the Trinity into a Holy Quartet.

"It Is *Almost* Finished?"

Questioning the sufficiency of what Jesus did on the cross is a common mark of false teachings. This is because Mankind finds it very difficult to believe that we could actually receive something from God without having to work on our own to earn it. Our pride motivates us to always want to put in our own effort and so add to the grace God has given us. Grace, however, by very definition, indicates that there can be absolutely *no merit* on our part. If there is even a modicum of our own merit on which our salvation is based, then it is no longer based on grace. (Romans 11:6)

When Jesus died on the cross, however, His words were, "It is finished." This statement did not give any contingencies whatsoever so there would be nothing else we could ever add to what our Savior has already done. Yet this is an area against which many Catholics and Christians struggle.

Catholicism itself is steeped in works-based salvation. A Catholic's life revolves around the works he must do in order to maintain his salvation and to pay penance for his own sins. As a matter of fact, penance is considered one of the seven sacraments (the sacraments "give birth and increase, healing and mission to the Christian's life of faith"[180]). But if we have to do penance in order to pay for our sins, then what was the purpose of Jesus dying on the cross? If His sacrifice did not pay for all our sins, then it was incomplete and imperfect and once again God must rely on Mankind to bail Him out of His imperfection.

In Hebrews 10:10-14 we read,

> And by that will, we have been made holy through the sacrifice of the body of Jesus Christ once for all. Day after day every priest stands and performs his religious duties; again and again he offers the same sacrifices, which can never take away sins. But when this priest had offered for all time one sacrifice for sins, he sat down at the right hand of God. Since that time he waits for his enemies to be made his footstool, because by one sacrifice he has made perfect forever those who are being made holy.

The sacrifice Jesus made on the cross paid for all sins, past, present, and future, and for us to try to add anything to that takes the effectiveness away from Christ and places it on our shoulders. The Catholic doctrine of purgatory is a perfect example of Man feeling the need to add something else to what Jesus has already done.

"All who die in God's grace and friendship, but *still imperfectly purified*, are indeed assured of their eternal salvation; but after death they undergo purification, so as to achieve the holiness necessary to enter the joy of heaven."[181] *(italics added)* Notice how Christ's sacrifice was not enough to purify us for heaven. The burden of purification is handed back into the "able" jurisdiction of the human because God cannot be trusted to provide what He demands of us.

Another factor of the Catholic teachings that unmistakably displays its works-based roots is their claim that outside of the Catholic Church, there is no salvation. Salvation comes through being a member of the Catholic Church, and not by any other means.[182] This is why a child is baptized into the Catholic Church as soon as the parents are able to, for fear their child might die before being baptized and be eternally lost. It is the baptism into the Church (a work we must do) that saves and not merely faith in what Christ has done for us.

Spells and Potions

In talking about the Roman Catholic's version of the Holy Eucharist, one who is unfamiliar with it needs to be aware of what exactly is happening during their mass. The priests speak certain words over the host (the bread), which is reminiscent of the spells said by Wiccans, and a magical transformation takes place. The common bread turns into the actual flesh of Jesus Christ. No, it does not look any different. It does not smell any different and it does not taste any different. But the Roman Catholic Church says that, whether we can perceive it or not, the transformation indeed does take place.

The wine, of course, transubstantiates into the actual blood of Jesus, according to the Roman Catholic Church. It is through ingesting this literal flesh and blood of Jesus that the Catholic maintains his salvation, as they partake anew of the re-sacrifice of Jesus. Does this sound confusing? When asked to explain it further, most Catholics cannot and will tell you, "This is why it is such a great mystery of God. We can't understand these things and merely need to take them on faith since the Church says it."

Because these two elements are in reality the presence of Jesus, you will notice the altars in Catholic Churches are roped off to the public. This would be because the altar actually contains God's presence in the host. Since the host is Jesus in reality, the wafers that are used today are precisely made so there will be no crumbs, lest one drop on the floor, thereby desecrating Christ. Drinking from the cup of wine is limited only to the priests in most Catholic congregations because of the fear of a drop being spilled.

Where does this tradition (called transubstantiation) come from? It is based on a passage in Matthew 26:26-28 where Jesus passes the bread and wine to His disciples and tells them it signifies His body and His blood. Ironically, on other matters that would require changing traditions of the church, the Catholic Church often chooses to take literal passages from the Bible in a figurative sense. In this particular passage, though, it is assumed that it must be literal.

If we look to the mythologies of the day, we can see how this idea of ingesting God for their salvation was also a well-known religious rite, practiced by the followers of Dionysus. Dionysus, also called "the dying and resurrecting god" was the Greek god of wine and revelry. In celebration of him, his followers would work themselves up into a frenzy, culminating in tearing a live goat to pieces with their bare hands and ingesting it. The live goat was thought to really *be* the god and by eating him, they were taking the god inside of them. This is how they became one with their god.

Catholicism has been known for assimilating aspects of indigenous religions in order to make its own beliefs more palatable for the population in general. For instance, the brand of Catholicism practiced in Latin America differs from what is practiced in Rome because of many local Indian traditions and rites that have been absorbed by those who now call themselves "Catholics."

A good example of this is the Day of the Dead in Mexico. It is a day where the local traditions say the spirits of the dead come back to walk the earth and visit their loved ones. Practicing Catholics see no difference between spending November 1 in church celebrating All Saints' Day, and then building altars in their homes to their dead loved ones, filled with all of their favorite things, to spend time with the dead on November 2.

While there are many other doctrinal falsehoods of the Catholic Church that we could deal with here, we would refer you to Appendix G for further reading on this subject.

As we look back to our list of three questions we use to test whether certain teachings are cultic or not, we can see that Roman Catholicism fits well into each of the categories. It adds to the Trinity by exalting Mary to her positions as "Queen of Heaven" and "Mother of God" and "Mediatrix;" it adds to the Bible by conferring the same authority to other writings and especially by replacing it with the authority given to the Roman Catholic Church; and it teaches a works-based salvation.

Chapter 21:

The Faith of our Fathers?

❖❖❖

As a BIBLE counselor practicing in a local church, it may be rare that a Jehovah's Witness or Mormon comes to us seeking help. Because of this, there is a tendency in our churches today to think that examining someone's doctrine when we counsel them is not necessary if they claim to be a Christian and especially not if they are a member of a solid, Bible-teaching congregation. While the authors believe this has never really been true, it is even more so a fallacy today.

It used to be that churches were rather insulated from the majority of the false teachings available. A study of cults and cultic thought was for intellectual seminarians and was considered more an academic "extra" than an essential. For most Christians, studying the various cults was a pursuit that was far distant from their daily lives, where they never encountered any such person who believed this way.

Unfortunately, this is no longer the case. Although it is still true that we may or may not associate with people who are Jehovah's Witnesses, Mormons, Pagans, Wiccans or the like, there is one cult group that is not only infiltrating our churches, but is being embraced by many, even mainstream congregations. It does not connect itself with specific denominations, and, where fifty years ago these teachings would have been denounced from most pulpits as obviously false, many Christian today praise the leaders of this movement and hold them in much higher esteem than those who teach sound doctrine.

We are referring, of course, to a movement that is often called the Word Faith movement, after the two distinctive factors that fuel these teachings. Other names that indicate the focus of this movement are: Name It, Claim It Theology; Health, Wealth and Power Theology; and Prosperity Theology. These names come from those outside of the movement, for those who are within the movement itself do not see it as anything other than a new moving of the Holy Spirit.

By far, we consider this one of the most destructive beliefs in the Christian Church today since it is everywhere we look. In fact, when non-Christians think of Christianity, the majority will mention the names of the leaders of this movement and point to them as what they assume all Christians are like. We must face the fact that, because of their high visibility through the media, these leaders are the only Christianity many people ever see. Our faith is under attack for its insincerity, its greed and its charlatanry because of these men yet when their doctrine is examined, it will not take long for a Christian who is truly grounded in the knowledge of the God of the Bible to see this as merely another doctrine of demons that Satan is using to make his last efforts during these end times.

Words, Words and More Words

Throughout this book, we have reminded the reader of the necessity to define terms when speaking to anyone about their beliefs. For instance, the Jesus referred to by the Mormons is the half-brother of Satan who is only one of many spirit-children of God; for the Jehovah's Witnesses, Jesus is the Archangel Michael in human form; and for Muslims, He is a prophet, inferior to Mohammed. The era we live in has put into question the very words with which we speak. The claim that there is no absolute truth is nowhere more evident than in the words we use.

In the Word Faith movement, we see confusion over two terms: "Word" and "Faith." At first glance, it might appear that these words are being used in their normal, biblical usage. However, when we take into consideration various writings and quotations from those who teach this theology, we soon see that there is more than meets the eye. As we show you quotations from these teachers, take careful note of what words they choose and how they use those words. You will soon see that one must be very careful to determine what is being said and to read between the lines.

Word Faith Theology at a Glance

All false teachings are subtle. After all, if they were glaring, they would be too easily recognizable as false. Yet this is precisely what makes them dangerous. When truth mixes with falsehood, it is like a little yeast that permeates the entire loaf. The entire message becomes tainted and cannot be trusted.

There are three major cornerstone verses this theology is based on: "For we walk by faith and not by sight." (2 Corinthians 5:7); "Now faith is the substance of things hoped for, the evidence of things not seen." (Hebrews 11:1); and "Through faith we understand that the worlds were framed by the word of God, so that things which were seen were not made of things which do appear." (Hebrews 11:3).

These scriptures are taken to mean that through faith and spoken words, what we cannot see ("not by sight," "evidence of things not seen," "were not made of things which do appear") can be materialized if "through faith we understand that the worlds were framed by the word of God." When we have this understanding (that the worlds were framed by the spoken Word of God), then if we need finances, for example, we do not *see* the needed money with our eyes, but through faith and spoken words (called faith-filled words) we can speak the needed finances into existence ("which do appear").

On the surface, this may appear to be a rather harmless teaching. Nevertheless, this is how doctrine built upon one error of faulty exegesis leads to other errors, which can soon snowball into a full-blown false teaching. In the following quotes, you must look carefully at the words themselves and not at who is saying them. Please do not let these false doctrines slide because you refuse to listen to anything negative about a particular teacher. Remember, in 2 Thessalonians 5:21 we are told to "test everything," and no human being should be above being tested. If the teaching of someone we esteem does not line up to what the Bible says, we should not excuse them for any reason. This is why we ask you to read these quotes for yourself before you read the names of those who have said them. If the teaching is false, it is false no matter who is behind it.

There are some serious implications behind this teaching if you follow through with what is being said. Essentially, they are saying that if we understand how God used His own Faith in His words to speak things into existence, all we need to do is use this same principle to do the very same thing. Let us think through the implications of this type of thought.

1. We can be like God and do the same things He can do.

2. We are then equal to God.

3. God did not have the power within Himself, but looked to outside forces and powers beyond Himself (called the force of faith and the power of words).

4. If God discovered these forces and learned how to apply them when He spoke things into existence, this would mean He is actually a lesser God than these forces are. If we are looking for the *real* God, we need to look farther back than God to these powers and forces that are the true gods.

5. If these powers and forces are personalities, then they are persons and would therefore be the *real* God we should be worshipping.

6. If these forces and powers are impersonal, then what is behind them and how did they originally come into being?

7. Either way, whether they are personal or impersonal gods, we cannot know who God is. He is reduced to merely another god among gods, and we find ourselves knee-deep in Hinduism, Mormonism, Occultism and Paganism.

8. With this being true, it should not surprise us when we catch glimpses of each of these belief systems within the word faith teachings.

I Do Not Believe This, Show Me

The following excerpts are from the leading Charismatic leaders and promoters of this theology. Some of the best materials to get in order to see what we are saying are small booklets that some of these teachers put out. One booklet in particular, *The Image of God in You*,[183] can be used to follow through on each of the points below.

"But first, you have to understand an important principle, a principle that's been in action since the beginning. It's the principle of the 'inner image.' God Himself gives us the first lesson about it in Genesis 1. There we can see Him using the principle of the inner image to create the Earth."[184] Notice that this clearly says that God was bound by a "principle," called an "inner image." We must also note that this mysterious "principle" had already been in action since the beginning, before creation, and that this principle is not the same as God. God had to acquire knowledge of this principle first in order to pass it on to us. It is obvious that God had to learn this principle before He could create the earth.

There is no biblical support for this "inner image" technique, however, imaging and calling upon mysterious powers to bring things to pass can be found in abundance in Hinduism, Mysticism, and various forms of Paganism. Before Wiccans cast a spell, they set up a "Cone of Power," using visualization techniques similar to what the above author has described. "Imagine the energy you have created encircling your group three times. Visualize in your mind's eye the energy spiraling up toward the moon....As your web of energy and light draws nearer the moon, visualize this cone of power protecting you from negative influences while helping to direct positive energy from the Goddess and God to you."[185] Many Wiccans we have spoken to say that spells are basically when they use inner imaging to visualize what they want to have happen.

"Now God didn't have any problems making the changes He wanted to make, did He? He took the principle of the inner image, added faith and the power of His words, and (pow!) darkness was changed to light."[186] God added faith? Does this mean God needed to acquire faith before He could create the Earth through the principle of the inner image with the power of His words? Where did this faith come from that He needed to add? Since faith must have an object, who or what was God's faith in? Was this faith in Himself or in some impersonal force, reminiscent of the Force in *Star Wars*? We can see how the false assumption of a principle of inner imaging has now turned into a redefinition of the creation story and a denigration of God's omnipotence.

"You have the same creative faith and ability on the inside of you that God used when He created the heavens and the earth."[187] This is a very bold statement that blatantly equates us with God. No longer is God omnipotent, but we are just as powerful as He is. We have the same ability to create our own earth if we apply this inner imaging principle so we can ourselves become the god of our own planet if we so choose. Here we see glimpses of Mormonism coming through their theology.

"God used words when He created the heaven and the earth....Each time God spoke, He released His faith – the creative power to bring His words to pass."[188] "What you need to use as the basis for your inner image and for the words you speak is the Word of God. The Word has supernatural power. And if you fill that Word with faith and speak it out, it will work for you to change your life and circumstances as surely as it did for God Himself."[189]

The capitalization of the term "Word" throughout the word faith writings is not by accident and indeed is quite significant. Although from time to time "Word of God" will mean the Bible, most of the time it does not have this connotation. And if we look closely at the statement above, we see that when the author speaks of the Word of God, he never makes reference to the "Word" as Jesus, as is obvious in John 1. Instead, he speaks of the "Word" as a supernatural power and a "that" in need of being filled with faith to work for you just as it did for God. If the Word of God is indeed Jesus as the Bible tells us, or even if it is in reference to the Bible itself, then why does he refer to the Word as an impersonal, supernatural power or as "that" instead of as the person of Jesus? Throughout the writings of the word faith teachers, we begin to see a redefinition of the Word of God into this creative force God used to form the world. If they would equate the Word of God with Jesus Christ, the foundation of all of their teachings would begin to crumble. This is no less than the denial of the divinity of Jesus, who is the second person of the Trinity, God, eternal in existence, by whom all things were created.[190]

"Faith is a spiritual force....It is substance. Faith has the ability to effect natural substance."[191] "God cannot do anything for you apart or separate from faith. Faith is God's source of power."[192] "God's blessings don't come because someone attended church twenty years. They come when you release something inside you that is a living, dynamic power and force and strength. That something is faith."[193] The authors' definition of faith is becoming clearer by the moment. Here we see that there is more to faith than merely believing or having trust in God. Faith is now a substance, a power, a living force, something tangible even, that is necessary before God can do anything at all. If this is so, then which is more powerful, God or this force called faith? If God cannot do anything without it, then obviously faith is more powerful than God, and therefore faith itself becomes the *true* God we should be worshipping.

As soon as we learn to properly apply this principle, it will change our lives. "What you are saying is exactly what you are getting now. If you are living in poverty and lack and want, change what you are saying....The powerful force of the spiritual world that creates the circumstances around us is controlled by the words of the mouth."[194] Here we begin to understand why BIBLE counselors might see many followers of this word faith doctrine come to their office. When they are lacking in finances or love or a good job or whatever they want in life, you can see where the blame is placed. It is because the person has said the wrong words or has not used this spiritual force of faith well enough. This causes a good deal of guilt and condemnation to be placed on the person who is evidently "weak" in faith because they are not getting what they are wanting in life. The spiritual leadership around them criticize them for their lack of faith and possibly even tell them that it is sin in their lives that are keeping this principle from working for them.

With this type of condemnation being placed on people, they buckle down and try even harder to have enough faith to make these principles work. Eventually, when they come up short time and time again, they usually become bitter towards God, angry because He is evidently asking them to do something they are incapable of doing. Many will turn their back on God at this point, hating Him for being so cruel and impossible to please. Others will turn into a pit of self-contempt, appearing to hate themselves for being unable to comply with God's way, yet in reality, loathing the God who abandoned them. The best way of helping them through this is to direct them towards the truth and expose these teachings for the lies they are.

Most people who are caught up in this movement know a good deal about what the Bible says, although the interpretations they use are merely parroting how the leaders have twisted them. It is important for them to see that the interpretations they have been exposed to are not consistent with other portions of the Bible.

Positive Confession

Let us continue on with the emergence of spoken words as a creative power and how it melds with the principle of the "inner imaging" we discussed earlier. "Jesus existed only as an image in the heart of God, until such time as the prophets of the Old Testament could positively confess Jesus into existence through their constant prophecies."[195] Here we see that even Jesus could not come into existence until someone (in this case the Old Testament prophets) positively confessed Him (that term means to speak aloud something that you want to happen).

This brings up some serious theological problems. First and foremost, the Son of God cannot be eternal if He spent the time from the creation of the world until the time Jesus was born as merely "an image in the heart of God." What does this say about His divinity? It is also interesting to note that it was not God Himself who positively confessed Jesus into existence, but the prophets of the Old Testament. Was God too impotent to bring Jesus into existence Himself? Does this make the prophets more powerful than God because they succeeded where God failed?

The word faith teaching is that God was completely *unable* to step in and confess Jesus into existence because of a "legal" reason. "Here's where we're gonna depart from ordinary church: Now, you see, God is injecting His Word into the earth to produce this Jesus – these faith-filled words that framed the image that's in Him....He can't just walk onto the earth and say, 'Let it be!' because he doesn't have the right. He had to sneak it in here around the god of this world that was blockin' every way that he possibly could."[196] "Depart from ordinary church?" This is quite the understatement! At the beginning of this statement, we see a direct contradiction to the previous quote from this author. Here he states that *God* was the one who produced the faith-filled words that brought Jesus into existence, whereas, in the last quote he said that the Old Testament prophets were the ones to do it. This, we assume, is what he refers to by saying that God "had to sneak" those faith-filled words in through the prophets.

In fact, throughout these teachings, God becomes an outsider to His creation, having given the dominion to the "gods" He created, Adam and Eve. "I want you to know something. Adam in the Garden of Eden was God manifested in the flesh....You see, Adam was walking as a God. Adam walked in God's class. Adam did things in the class of Gods, hallelujah."[197] Jesus "has got to be all man. He cannot be a God and come storming in here with attributes and dignities that are not common to man. He can't do that. It's not legal."[198] God could only come back into His creation through a "deal" He made with Abraham. If Abraham (or at least *some* man) would not have made this deal with God, then God would not have been allowed to send Jesus into the world to save us.

With all of this in mind, it becomes easy to see how the word faith teachings exalt Man to the level of God, and relegate God to a celestial "bellboy" who is at our command. As you get into these teachings, you find more twisting of the truth to the point where you eventually wonder where it will end.

These teachings assert that Jesus died spiritually, taking on the nature of Satan when He died on the cross, that He was the first born-again man, that all Christians are gods, and that if we have enough faith we can speak anything into being, just like God did. These are all tied together by the teaching that you must never "touch God's anointed."[199] This conveniently protects these self-proclaimed prophets from having their doctrine challenged by anyone. As with most cults, the follower who starts to see inconsistencies with their theology must either live in silent self-condemnation or leave the church, cutting off all connections with the people they have come to know and love.

Under these teachings, not only is Man elevated to godhood, but Jesus has been reduced to the level of a man who was born again. If Jesus is no more than a born-again man, that places born-again Christians on the same level as Him. Salvation is no longer found in the person of Jesus, but He becomes simply an example of how we can be our own saviors if we only learn what He has already learned and apply those same principles in our own lives. Salvation is gained through realizing the god within us and acting like the god we are.

Although there may be slight variations, it is these same foundational falsehoods that are at the root of the teachings of many well-known and well-respected TV evangelists and pastors, scattered across the United States and throughout the world. Because these people are so high profile via the media, their teachings are seen as biblical Christianity to the thousands who watch their broadcasts, and these teachings have spread like wildfire. Many are hailing it as a "great revival" and a new moving of the Holy Spirit. Those who follow these teachings label any who would dare to question the veracity of what they believe as resisting the moving of the Holy Spirit and threaten them by saying they may be in danger of blaspheming the Holy Spirit, thereby threatening their salvation. Fear and threats are commonplace among these teachers in order to keep their flock "faithful" to what they have been taught.

But will questioning these "anointed ones" be blaspheming the Holy Spirit? In 2 John 9-11 we read, "Anyone who runs ahead and does not continue in the teaching of Christ does not have God; whoever continues in the teaching has both the Father and the Son. If anyone comes to you and does not bring this teaching, do not take him into your house or welcome him. Anyone who welcomes him shares in his wicked work." Considering this passage, we cannot help but wonder about the hosts of popular TV and radio programs who embrace these teachers as dear brothers in the Lord. We must be cautious of the idea that everyone who calls himself a Christian is necessarily following the doctrines taught in the Bible.[200]

Helping Word Faith Adherents
Very few of those who are caught up in the word faith teachings are aware of the personal beliefs of those who are promoting this

false doctrine. Most are very sincere Christians who have been born again and who have a deep desire to know God on a very personal level and to please Him. These are the ones who have been exploited the most. Truth spoken in love, patience, understanding and compassion are essential in showing the errors in this false doctrine. The same rule applies as it would with helping those involved in all cults and false religions: gently show them a little at a time that what they have been taught is not the gospel given to the saints once and for all. Pushing too hard and fast will overwhelm the person being addressed and will just be met with more resistance.

One other thing that must be kept in mind is the tremendous peer pressure being exerted on those who may begin to have doubts. Fear, guilt and intimidation are all used by the leadership and fellow followers of the word faith movement to keep these people from "falling away." They are told they are being "blinded by agents of Satan," who are trying to remove the "Word" from them and that this will lead to their "eternal damnation," or even, that God will punish their children for their disobedience. Using Bible references can be helpful, but reason and logic need to be applied because, although the words in the scriptures may not have been altered, they have been altered in the mind through the redefining of words.

Seldom do those who are deeply involved in the word faith movement ask questions. Generally what they are led to believe is that they are "anointed" and have received special revelation knowledge that cannot be understood without this "anointing." It is this "anointing" that puts them above other Christians who cannot understand these principles, and so gives them an "inside track" to God's wisdom.

This leads them to view other Christians as not operating in the gifts, and therefore, these other Christians are in need of receiving the *Baptism of the Holy Spirit*, without which they are incapable of spiritual discernment. Almost without exception, what this means is that speaking in tongues becomes the evidence of having received the *Baptism of the Holy Spirit*, and without this evidence, it follows that none of the other gifts are present either.

When engaging in a conversation with one of the word faith followers, it is important to stay focused on the falsehood of the word faith teachings and not get off track by being drawn into a disagreement over the issue of the *Baptism of the Holy Spirit* and the evidence of tongues. More often than not, this is used as a diversion to avoid facing the real issues of the falsehood of what they believe to be true. The best approach is not to argue experiences and feelings, but to stay focused on what the Bible says.

Very few, if any, of the word faith teachings have biblical support and are based on supposed *new revelation knowledge* by "anointed" modern day apostles and prophets. Rather than argue this falsehood, questions need to be asked that will cause them to think and begin to question what they believe. We are dealing most generally with people who are imprisoned by the fear of losing their salvation if they dare question what they have been taught.

One other issue is pride. Not all, but many of the word faith followers are extremely full of pride because they perceive themselves as being special and above the general population of Christendom because they have been especially selected or chosen or anointed. We have essentially two different groups: those who believe they have arrived at godhood and those who are struggling to obtain that status. The latter are often ostracized for their lack of faith, the sin in their life that is causing God to withhold blessings of healing, finances and the power to bring these things to pass, and having their "true" commitment to God being questioned. Pride, and/or fear, guilt and intimidation is the glue that holds them to this false doctrine rather than humbleness, love, freedom and acceptance in the person of Jesus.

Questions to Ask

A good question to start with when talking with those who have been indoctrinated into the word faith teachings is: Be perfectly honest with yourself, how many "words of knowledge" or "prophecy" have you personally been given or have heard that came to pass 100%? When the answer is "not all" or "few" or "none," then ask, how can this be justified when the Bible says: "You may say to yourselves, 'How can we know when a message has not been spoken by the LORD?' If what a prophet proclaims in the name of the LORD does not take place or come true, that is a message the

LORD has not spoken. That prophet has spoken presumptuously. Do not be afraid of him." (Deuteronomy 18:22)

Emphasize that the mark of a true prophet of God is that the prophecy will come to pass 100% of the time, according to Deuteronomy 18:21-22. Stress that the Bible says this is an either/or situation. Either the prophecy comes to pass and the person is true, or it does not and the person is false. There is no in-between.

Often, when the person cannot answer this question, the response will be something along the line of: "We are human and prone to error from time to time." Do not accept this as a legitimate biblical response. Ask again how this excuse lines up with one who "Speaks in the name of the Lord" that if it is of the Lord, it will come to pass according to what the Bible says, as is stated in the above verse. Point out that there is a huge difference between human error and claiming to be speaking on the behalf of the Lord as a prophet. There is no such thing as a "prophet in training." In Ezekiel 13:8-9 we see God's opinion of those who put words in His mouth: "Therefore this is what the Sovereign LORD says: Because of your false words and lying visions, I am against you, declares the Sovereign LORD. My hand will be against the prophets who see false visions and utter lying divinations." How can we support people who claim that God says things that He obviously does not say (because it does not come true)?

Also, it is important to ask if these "prophesies" are *general* prophecies open to a wide range of interpretation, or if they are *specific* prophecies not open to various interpretations. Like horoscopes, the messages some "prophets" give out are so general that it would be unusual if they did *not* come true. The prophecies we see in the Bible are always specific, including many details so we can be certain they have been fulfilled. Speaking out general prophecies is a deceptive trick used by modern day psychics and fortunetellers, not the Holy Spirit of the Almighty God.

Another excellent question to bring up when in a discussion with a word faith adherent, is: If one claims to have heard directly from the Holy Spirit and yet what is spoken contradicts the Bible, and if you believe the Holy Spirit inspired the Bible, then how is it that the Holy Spirit would contradict Himself? Explaining this can only be accomplished and rationalized if the Holy Spirit is *not* God, the third Person of the Trinity. Instead, He would have to be understood as only a power to obtain and use that is subject to the prophets, and therefore *is* fallible. If the Holy Spirit is indeed God Himself, then for God to contradict Himself is an impossibility, indicating that one of the sources, either the so-called prophet or the Holy Spirit, must be false.

Two of the major focal points of the word faith theology are that all Christians were intended to be perfectly healthy and also very wealthy. These two things are obtained through speaking out our faith-filled words to make the inner image of these become a reality in our lives. However, if it is true that we can obtain health and wealth through faith in our words being spoken as the words of God, why did Jesus or the Apostles, or anyone else throughout 2000 years of Church history not explain this in such a way? Are we to believe this was a mystery hidden until revealed to us through modern apostles and prophets of God? This is what all pseudo-Christian churches teach; they dub themselves as the *true church* that has been restored through a special prophet of God who has revealed hidden mysteries and truth that had been previously lost, except to a select few.

Following through with that thought, if the Holy Spirit speaks through the prophets of today, and they are fallible, then this would mean the prophets of old were also fallible (because they both rely on the same Holy Spirit as their source of prophecy). If this were to be true, by what standard can we discern truth when one speaks as a prophet of God today? Most will respond that the Bible is what we must use to discern truth. However, it needs to be pointed out that it would be an unreliable source if the prophets of old were given the same latitude of error as are the so-called modern prophets of today.

Why would there be one standard for testing the authenticity of the prophets of old that would be different from testing the authenticity of a modern-day prophet? There is only one test (which we have already discussed from Deuteronomy 18:22), and if you believe the written word of God will never fail, then we have a major inconsistency. There is only one way to determine if someone is a false prophet, and that is if what he speaks does not come to pass. If the test is not passed, he is a false prophet. Period. Jesus warned that there would be an abundance of them especially in the last days. "For false Christs and false prophets will appear and perform great signs and miracles to deceive even the elect—if that were possible." (Matthew 24:24)

How many tests does one (who claims to be speaking for God as a prophet) need to fail before they are recognized as a false prophet? Would this not indicate that what they are hearing is not from the Holy Spirit, and if this is so, on behalf of what spirit are they speaking? This leaves only two options, the spirit of anti-christ, or speaking on behalf of themselves. Either way, it is not of God, and what they say must be dismissed as being not of God. And if they are speaking out of the spirit of anti-christ or their own spirits, then how can you trust in anything they say? How can you know when they are speaking godly things and when they are speaking on their own? In any case where even one prophecy has failed, you need not fear the threats, endure the condemnations, nor be intimidated or suffer with false guilt these types of leaders put on you.

When the leadership is exposed for who they are, then the rest of what is taught is soon to crumble. That is why the leaders of the word faith movement are quick to use their magical phrase, "Touch not my anointed." This is used to mean, "Do not question my authority because what I speak is direct from the Holy Spirit. If you question me, it is the same as rejecting God and is blasphemy of the Holy Spirit." Questioning doctrinal issues of any kind is conveniently condemned. "If you want to argue doctrine, if you want to straighten out somebody over here, if you want to criticize Ken Copeland for his preaching on faith, or Dad Hagin. Get out of my life! I don't even want to talk to you or hear you. I don't want to see your ugly face! Get out of my face in Jesus' name." [201]

As with all cultic teachings, fear, guilt and intimidation are used in manipulating the "flock" to keep them in line and to keep the cash flow coming into their pockets. Hinn is a good example of this when he verbally threatened the Christian Research Institute for exposing his false teachings.

"Now I'm pointing my finger with the mighty power of God on me....You hear this: There are men and women in Southern

California attacking me. *I will tell you under the anointing now*, you'll reap it in your children unless you stop....And *your children will suffer.* You're attacking me on the radio every night – you'll pay and *your children will*. Hear this from the lips of God's servant. *You are in danger.* Repent! Or God Almighty will move His hand. Touch not my Anointed...."[202] How would this type of threat make any of those listening feel about standing up against this type of false teaching?

Doug has personally witnessed many who were silently suffering and who have been immediately transformed when they realized that what they were being taught was a doctrine of demons (including Doug himself). The chains that held them captive were lifted from their shoulders, and they went on to become effective witnesses of the grace of God with joy in their heart. Jesus brings freedom. He is the way, the truth and the life,[203] and the truth will indeed set you free.[204] Truth is not a *thing*; truth is found in the person of Jesus.

Cult Check

Bringing us back to our three marks of a cult, we begin to see how the word faith teachings do indeed stack up. Since the heart of this movement is that we can be little gods, we can easily see how the word faith teachings elevate Man and denigrate God. Man becomes the one in charge and God becomes the biggest failure in the entire Bible: "I was shocked when I found out who the biggest failure in the Bible actually is....The biggest one in the whole Bible is God."[205] Jesus is relegated to an "emaciated, poured out, little, wormy spirit"[206] who was only released out of hell because of a technicality.[207]

Our true salvation comes when we learn the same principles as God has been using all along to create things, and we begin to use those principles for ourselves. This is how we regain our position of godhood that we lost in the Garden of Eden.

As for the mark of replacing the authority of the Bible with other extra-biblical writings, in the case of the word faith teachers, it is mostly extra-biblical sayings that qualify. Although a person who adamantly follows these teachers may know quite a bit about the Bible, you can be assured that their knowledge has been helped along by the words of their teachers. It is virtually impossible to find a word faith individual who has *never* read any books or listened to any of these teachers. Is this a doctrine people would come up with on their own through purely reading the Bible? No. It is a doctrine that has been built over several decades on false theology upon false theology to the point where it is now so far from the truth of biblical Christianity that it amazes us that those who are involved cannot see it.

But as with any other cultic teaching, those who get involved are usually not familiar enough with the Bible to tell truth from error, and, as we stated before with the fallacies of Neil Anderson's teachings, it is often difficult at the beginning to see the small portions of arsenic because they are so well hidden among the savory steak. Many of those involved in the word faith movement would not believe that their teachers believe such things as we have stated above, however, the quotations tell a different story. For this reason, one of the best resources we have found is the audiobook, *Christianity in Crisis*, by Hank Hanegraaff. There is also an accompanying book, but we have found the audio to be more impressive because it has the direct quotes from these men. There is no chance of someone saying, "He didn't really say that!" when they are listening to the actual person (many of whom have very distinctive voices).

We encourage you to look for these false teachings when you are dealing with people who come to you for counseling. This is the number one false teaching we face when we counsel with people online. We need to help our counselees, those around us, and even our churches to see the destructive errors in these faith teachings. Let us bring these people to an understanding of the truth through the person of Jesus Christ as He is revealed in the Bible, not as these men and women have made Him out to be.

Chapter 22:

The God of Abraham, Isaac and Jacob

◆◆◆

If your type of counseling is purely within a church context, the information in the next three chapters may not be as useful to you as the rest of this book. However, if you go into chat rooms online or go into any types of forums, you are certain to come across people who will be Jewish, Muslim or Atheists and knowing how to deal with them will be very helpful. We have added these three chapters because we believe they are important for Christians to understand and, in regards to BIBLE counselors, it is our opinion that studying the most popular false teachings will open your eyes to the root of problems people are bringing into counseling sessions. Our culture has definitely been influenced by all of the issues covered in these three chapters so a wise Christian will become familiar with them in order to protect himself and those he works with from these influences.

When it comes to the religions of the world, there is one teaching that sets Christianity, Judaism and Islam apart from the others, loosely joining them together under a type of umbrella of similarity. This is that they stand alone as monotheistic belief systems. Monotheism is the belief in only one God, and these three are unique in that they profess a belief in one God. For this reason, the question often arises: "Don't Muslims and Jews worship and believe in the same one God as Christianity?"

This might be true if Christianity believed that "one" God was a numerical "one" meaning one person who is God. While Christians do believe in one God, we also believe that the triune nature of God consists of three persons who collectively are the one true God. Because of this, the understanding of the God of the Bible would be both monotheistic and Trinitarian meaning one triune, personal God.

Yet the concept of the Trinity is difficult for our finite minds to understand. It appears to us to be a contradiction in terms to be one God who is three Persons. It is this supposed contradiction of terms as to why the Trinity is rejected that can sometimes lead to ridicule. The common misunderstanding is that Christians worship three gods, making it a pagan belief of many gods. Ironically, Islam and Judaism and all pseudo-Christian cults discount the Trinity on the grounds that it is a pagan belief, but we have already shown with the pseudo-Christian cults, that those who most often make the charge that Christianity worships a pagan god are paganistic in their own beliefs because they add to the godhead by becoming (or hoping to become) gods themselves.

Both Islam and Judaism reject the one triune God of Christianity and, therefore, both reject the possibility of God becoming flesh and dwelling among men. This would be understandable if one holds the belief of God as one person. From this view, it would be absurd for one to make the claim of being the Son of God when he was born of human flesh. However, it makes perfect sense when the triune nature of God is understood, and in fact, is the only view that ultimately makes sense of both the New and the Old Testament.

Most reject the Christian doctrine of the Trinity on the grounds that it is beyond comprehension and cannot be grasped, but this is not a valid argument for rejecting what the Bible teaches. If comprehension were the determining factor for rejection, then such things as eternity, how God created matter from nothing and even God himself would also have to be rejected. Besides, if we could comprehend everything about God, then *we* ourselves would be the gods.

Although Islam and Judaism are in agreement in the rejection of the Trinity and the denial of the divinity of Jesus, this does not make it two against one with Judaism and Islam standing together as serving the same one God and Christianity as the odd belief out. As we examine these two beliefs, it will become clear that their beliefs are not necessarily what most people believe they are. Through the doctrine of the Trinity alone, we have already separated the God of Christianity from both Judaism and Islam. But let us continue to examine what it is they believe.

Islam in a Nut Shell
As we give a brief explanation of the beliefs of Islam, keep in mind the common thread that ties all false religions and false teachings together: the denial of the Trinity, the challenge to the authority of the Bible and the denial of salvation by grace alone. Here is a short view of how Islam stands up to these three marks of a cult.

In regards to the denial of the Trinity or of God as He is revealed in the Bible, Islam teaches that Jesus was one of 28 prophets, but was not God, and was not even the most important of the prophets. The Holy Spirit is not God, but is a power or life source extending from God, a special aspect of God.

The Bible was translated incorrectly by Christians and is corrupted. The Koran is the uncorrupted word of God and is the main source of authority for all matters of faith and practice. Mohammad was the last and greatest prophet and was the agent to whom God revealed His words, and that revelation became the Koran.

Salvation may only be attained through maintaining a belief in the "Five Articles of Faith" and through strict adherence to the "Five Pillars of Faith" prescribed and set forth in the beliefs and practices of Islam. The notion of redemption (meaning what is done once for all) and forgiveness of sin is rejected. Salvation depends entirely on man's actions and attitudes. The Muslim can never be certain of his fate because he will never know if Allah will be merciful on the day of judgment or not.

A strong belief in the "Five Articles of Faith" is essential for the Muslim. These articles include a belief: (1) that there is one true God and His name is Allah, (2) in the existence of angels, (3) in the authority of the scriptures (This would be the Koran, Torah, Psalms and the Gospel of Jesus Christ, with the understanding that the last three have been corrupted by Christians and Jews, and that the Koran supercedes all other works.), (4) in the prophets with Muhammad as the last and greatest prophet, (5) in resurrection and judgment.

There are Five Pillars of Faith, on which the faithful base their worthiness to Allah, and they are: (1) the creed ("There is no God but Allah, and Muhammad is the Prophet of Allah," which must be repeated aloud and constantly.), (2) prayer (five times a day facing Mecca), (3) almsgiving (It is required to give one-fortieth to the destitute plus there are other rules and regulations for produce, cattle and so forth.), (4) fasting (each day during the month of Ramadan), (5) the pilgrimage (It is required of all Muslims to visit Mecca at least once in their life. This involves a set of ceremonies and rituals that centers around the Ka'abah shrine in Mecca.).

Is Allah another name for the God of Abraham, Isaac and Jacob?

Although the word "Allah" means "the God," when we examine who Muhammad's Allah was, we see it is a far cry from meaning the "One True God." It may seem like an insignificant observation, but this very definition of the word Allah already disqualifies it from both the God of Judaism and the God of Christianity.

"The God" was only meant to distinguish him from the other pagan gods that were worshipped by the pre-Islamic Arabs before and during the life of Muhammad.[208] Allah the moon god was married to the sun goddess and together, they had three goddess daughters named Al-Lat, Al-Uzza and Manat.[209] Once again we see how this ressembles the Mormon concept of gods and goddesses producing more gods or "spirit children" as the Mormons describe it to fit in with a perversion of Christianity. This is a very common root belief of Paganistic thought — gods and goddesses producing gods.

The Quarish tribe that Mohammad was born into had a central place of worship called the Ka'abah (formerly called Beit-Allah, or the house of Allah). The chief god of the Ka'abah was Hubal who shared the sanctuary with 360 other deities. This sanctuary was located halfway between Mecca and Medina in the town of

Qudayda. In the sanctuary was a square black stone and if you kissed the stone, it had the power to take away man's sins. The black stone represented Al-Lat (one of the three daughters of Allah) who was the goddess of "fate."[210]

The Koran tells of Mohammad returning to Mecca and driving all the other idols away, but it also confirmed that the black stone had the power to take away Man's sins so the central focus of worship has remained. (Sura 22:26-37)

Mohammad was influenced by the monotheistic beliefs of Judaism and Christianity through the reading of the scriptures. He created his own monotheistic religion by forbidding the worship of other gods and declared Allah as the "one God" to be worshipped. Allah replaced the chief god Hubal, who was being worshipped in that area, and the pagan practices of worship towards Hubal were then directed towards only Allah. One such practice was the kissing of the black stone (which all Muslims are still required to perform as part of the Pilgrimage to Mecca). The crescent moon was an ancient pagan fertility symbol of the moon god and can still be seen as the symbol of Islam today. This serves as a reminder of the pagan roots of Islam, from which it never fully broke away. In reality, it has merely been redirected and restructured.

It is very interesting how Islam and the more modern religion of Mormonism are identical in many ways. Mohammad and Joseph Smith both claimed that they had divine visitations from angels through whom God spoke in order to reveal the one true religion. Both were self-proclaimed prophets of God. Both were given divine messages that were recorded (the Koran and the Book of Mormon) and are the final authority on practices and beliefs for their religion. Both claimed that Christianity is pagan yet both Islam and Mormonism themselves are rooted in Paganism. Both Mohammed and Smith acknowledged being knowledgeable in the scriptures, and for this reason, it is highly likely that the Koran and the Book of Mormon are revisions of the scriptures because the similarities are too obvious. This makes it difficult to come to any other conclusion but that these newer "revelations" were based, at least in part, on the Bible. Both portrayed themselves as being on a higher moral and spiritual level than common man yet their lascivious life styles contradicted these claims.[211]

The fact that both Mohammad and Joseph Smith claimed to have received their knowledge from angels, it appears they both missed reading: "But even if we or *an angel from heaven* should preach a gospel other than the one we preached to you, let him be eternally condemned! As we have already said, so now I say again: If anybody is preaching to you a gospel other than what you accepted, let him be eternally condemned!" (Galatians 1:8-9, italics added)

Through the years, both Islam and Mormonism have undergone many changes and both try to downplay the failings of their founding prophets, their history and their roots. Their writings are still shrouded in a mystery that questions their authenticity, so that their origins can never be verified. When all is said and done, we have only the word of these two false prophets that what they received was from God. Millions have placed their eternal destiny on two men who basically said, "We alone heard, so you have to believe what we say is true. You must never question a prophet of God."[212]

Here we have two false prophets that are very much different in the divine revelations from the supposed same God. One has to wonder why God was confused in giving His only true message. The obvious commonality between Mohammad and Joseph Smith is that they both received another gospel from an angel, which makes them both false prophets.

Do Jews Worship the Same God as Christians?

By now it should be clear that the God of Islam bears little resemblance to the God of the Bible. "But surely," you are probably saying, "the Jews worship the same God as Christians. After all, they use the same books of the Old Testament[213] as we do." Let us begin with the basis of what the Jewish belief is.

All throughout the Old Testament up to the present day (for most), the hope of the Hebrew children has always been looking forward to the promised Messiah, the Savior, the One who would deliver the Hebrew children from their oppressors. When Jesus came to the earth, His ministry was to the Jews first, to show them the fulfillment of God's plan. The Jews who recognized Jesus as the Messiah and as their Lord and Savior are the ones who became the

New Testament Church, the body of Christ. It was through the believing Jews that God established the Church, and they, along with all others over the centuries who have believed in Christ, became the temple in which God would indwell, a temple that was not made with human hands. These Jews were not "converted" to Christianity, but were the very foundation of the Church. In fact, they were the first who were called Christians, meaning the followers of Christ, at Antioch.

The Gentiles, hearing the report of these believing Jews who proclaimed that Jesus was the promised Messiah, also became a part of the same body of Christ. These believing Gentiles then, in effect, became believers with the Jews who believed, and so became the same as the Jews: followers of Christ.[214]

The Church was established by Jesus, who was a Jew. The Apostles were all Jews that Jesus had called to follow Him. Paul, author of the greatest portion of the New Testament, was a Jewish Pharisee of the highest order. He had been an enemy of the Church and had persecuted it, but later he joined the ranks of the Christians. All of the first Christians were Jews, and all of the believers who gathered on the day of Pentecost were Jews. The visitation of the Holy Spirit on Pentecost was the fulfillment of the prophecy of Joel that God's spirit would be poured out on all flesh and that salvation had come to all who believe, Jew and Gentile alike.

The division between Jew and Gentile no longer existed according to human blood lines; it became a spiritual division, drawn by the blood of Jesus Christ. Today there still are only two groups of people on the face of the earth. A person is either a Jew by the circumcision of the heart or he is a Gentile of the heart. Those who are Jews by the heart are those who have received the Messiah into their hearts. Those who are Jews, although they may physically be of the Jewish people, are in spiritual reality uncircumcised, because their hearts have stopped following God's path. Everyone is either under the curse of the Law (Jew and Gentile alike), or they are free from the curse of the Law through Christ (Jew and Gentile alike). The non-believing Jews who rejected Jesus as their Messiah in effect joined with the non-believing Gentiles and became just as the Gentiles.

The Jews understood the scriptures and were fully aware of the prophesies, traditions and rituals that all pointed to the one who would be the fulfillment of these things. Those who accepted these as being fulfilled in Christ became followers of Christ, circumcised in the heart. Those who rejected them and who refused to see God's Messiah in Christ became as if they were uncircumcised. Their circumcision was merely in their flesh and had nothing to do with their spiritual position before God. They had become as Gentiles before God.

One prophecy the Jews were fully aware of was that the Messiah had to come and die before the destruction of the Jewish Temple as foretold by Daniel in Daniel 9:24-27. When the Jewish Temple was destroyed by the Romans in AD 70, the non-believing Jews knew they had missed the time of their visitation. With no temple left in which to perform their rituals, they lost their center of worship and their power and influence. They had nothing left but a religion of empty rituals and traditions that no longer had a purpose or meaning. No longer was there a need for the prophets; the prophets had already fulfilled their purpose and the scriptures had been fulfilled by Jesus. No longer was there a need for the lawyers because there was no longer the tribunal court of the Pharisees and Sadducees. Jesus had become the end of the Law, and He alone will judge the nations in righteousness.

The Jews were a people with no temple, no power, no influence, no purpose and no home. Even though they were scattered throughout the world, they did not lose their identity as Jews, but they did lose their identity of the twelve tribes of Israel. This identity was required in order for them to perform the temple rites, but when the temple was destroyed, their identity was also lost. Jesus became the High Priest and the priesthood was given to Him to distribute to the children of the Father.

However, God is faithful to keep his promise to Abraham, and in 1948 we saw the fulfillment of His promise when He gathered the Jews back into their homeland in present-day Israel. Although the majority of the Jews today do not recognize God's divine hand in the fulfillment of this prophecy, the Bible also says that, in the end times, there will be 12,000 of each of the 12 tribes of Israel who receive Jesus as their Messiah and will preach Jesus Christ crucified.

When we examine the Judaism of our time, we see it is nothing more than empty rituals and traditions. They are under the curse of the Law just as the rest of mankind. There was no other direction the non-believing Jews could go because all of what gave them meaning and purpose had been fulfilled in Christ. The believing Jews and the believing Gentiles, those circumcised in the heart, became the temple of God.

Today the inscription Ichabod, meaning "the glory has departed," is on the entrance of Jewish synagogues. Somehow, the Jews know in their heart that the God of Abraham, Isaac and Jacob dwelt with them at one time in their temple but has now left them — the glory has departed. It is only when they receive the Messiah in their hearts that they realize where God's glory now resides, in the temple of their hearts.

In answer to the question of, "Don't the Jews worship the same God as Christians?" the answer has to be no. The Jews do not worship the God of their Fathers, for if they did, they would have recognized the promise of God's Savior, who was Himself born of a woman, *Emmanuel*, God with us.

Do the Jews believe in the same God? No, they deny the Trinity by rejecting Jesus as God. Judaism denies the divinity of Jesus and rejects Him as the promised Messiah. To the Jewish mind, Jesus was a good man, but was not God. The Holy Spirit is not God but is a power extending from God. While the Jews use the same books in the Old Testament as we do, they view the New Testament as a Gentile fabrication and that through it the Christians perverted the meaning of the Old Testament. Salvation is obtained through obedience to the Law, not through faith in the One who made the Law. This is none other than a salvation-by-works doctrine.

In Zechariah 12:10 we read that a time is coming when the Jews and the whole world will see Jesus as He really is. "They will look on me, the one they have pierced, and they will mourn for him as one mourns for an only child, and grieve bitterly for him as one grieves for a firstborn son."[215] John tells us the same thing in Revelation 1:7, "Look, he is coming with the clouds, and every eye will see him, even those who pierced him; and all the peoples of the earth will mourn because of him. So shall it be! Amen." The mourning will be from those who refused to see Jesus for who He is, the Lamb of God who takes away the sin of the world, as they fully realize what that rejection means.

Let us do all we can to share this good news with the people of the world, whether they be Muslim, Mormon, Pagan, or Jew, so they will not have to mourn on that day, but can rejoice as they greet the One who died for them, the only One who alone is worthy of all honor and glory and praise.

Chapter 23:

The Unknown God

❖❖❖

On Mars Hill centuries ago, Paul was distressed when he saw the many altars to various gods the people of Athens worshipped. He even noticed that they had built an altar to "The Unknown God," in order to make certain they had not left out any deity. It was obvious to Paul that these people were desperately seeking something to fill that God-shaped hole in their hearts, and he felt compelled to introduce them to this "Unknown" God, the *true* God. In our society today, so many are like the Athenians, making altars in their lives to any thing or person who appears to be a god, but often they miss the only *real* God along the way.

Those who admit that they do not know whether God exists or not and who believe that even if He does, most likely He is unknowable, call themselves agnostics. In a broader sense, they are people who are not willing to commit themselves to believing in either the existence or nonexistence of God. Then there are others who have decided that there is no God: the atheists. Yet these two positions are not as far opposed as one might think. The two definitions become clouded and the line between them can become almost indistinguishable at times, depending on the one who claims to be one or the other and how they decide to use the definition that best suits themselves.

Atheism has come to mean a person who can state with absolute confidence that there is no God. But is this really possible? If a person can state with absolute confidence that there is no God, how can he make such a statement unless he possesses all the knowledge in the universe? Would it not be necessary to have indisputable facts and proof to back up such a confidence? And if he *does* possess all the knowledge in the universe, then would that not make him, by the very definition of the word, a god in his own rights? And if he is a god, how could he not believe in his own existence? It seems to us that those who call themselves agnostics are usually being more honest with themselves about the issue of the existence of God.

In actuality, the word "atheist" comes from the Greek word "atheos" meaning (a = *without* + theos = *god*) one who is without God. So the word "atheist" should not really mean that their belief is that there is no God; it should simply mean that they are without God. This then makes the definition of an atheist correct when it is defined as one who denies the existence of God. The denial of God does not make it a fact that there is no God, but because of their denial of God, they are without God.

One who claims to be an agnostic then is actually an atheist in accordance to the above definition of an atheist, and, on the other side of the coin, an atheist is actually an agnostic. Confusion often surrounds those who claim one or the other title. They try making distinctions between themselves and others who claim to be either agnostic or atheist. This is only another form of pride, the desire to think of themselves as "free thinkers," as people who are not influenced by the thoughts of others. They shun being "pigeon-holed." They want to pride themselves into thinking their own unique reasoning abilities have devised a way to justify the denial of God. They pat themselves on their backs, proudly feeling as if they have found something new under the sun.

Solomon already addressed this kind of thinking in Ecclesiastes 1:8-10, "All things are wearisome, more than one can say. The eye never has enough of seeing, nor the ear its fill of hearing. What has been will be again, what has been done will be done again; there is nothing new under the sun. Is there anything of which one can say, 'Look! This is something new'? It was here already, long ago; it was here before our time."

In considering the definition of an agnostic and an atheist, there are two words that seem to stand out: denial and commitment. At the heart of the issue, it is not really a matter of *if* there is a God. The real root of the matter is the denial of God and the refusal to make a commitment of any kind to Him. If truth be told, there is no such thing as someone who *knows* God does not exist. What the smoke and mirrors are all about is the attempt to justify why they should not trust in God.

Atheistic evolution, the "Big Bang," and other such philosophies are all about hoping to find the elusive "proof" that there is no God so as to find relief from the fear of what they *know* to be true in their hearts. We can say this with absolute confidence because the Bible says man is without excuse.

> The wrath of God is being revealed from heaven against all the godlessness and wickedness of men who suppress the truth by their wickedness, since what may be known about God is plain to them, because God has made it plain to them. For since the creation of the world God's invisible qualities—his eternal power and divine nature—have been clearly seen, being understood from what has been made, so that men are without excuse.
>
> For although they knew God, they neither glorified him as God nor gave thanks to him, but their thinking became futile and their foolish hearts were darkened. Although they claimed to be wise, they became fools and exchanged the glory of the immortal God for images made to look like mortal man and birds and animals and reptiles.
>
> Therefore God gave them over in the sinful desires of their hearts to sexual impurity for the degrading of their bodies with one another. They exchanged the truth of God for a lie, and worshipped and served created things rather than the Creator—who is forever praised. Amen. (Romans 1:18-25)

If mankind were truly a product of a chemical reaction that evolved from some mysterious primordial cosmic soup, the idea of a god or gods would have never entered into his mind. As an advanced chemical process, man would never be capable of even contemplating his own existence any more than a rock contemplates its existence. Who would argue that any other living creature, other than man, is aware of its ultimate death and ponders the reason and purpose for life? It is absurd to think a dolphin struggles with thoughts of an afterlife and the concept of a God. If man were but a mere advanced animal, then he would be ignorantly blissful, romping through the oceans of life awaiting the unknown next level of his evolutionary progress.

The argument that religion was a product of superstition and ignorance is illogical. If this were true, then how did the superstitions that lead to the belief in a god or gods enter the mind of the less intelligent? What is really being said is that as man evolved and gained more intelligence, then he became ignorant and became superstitious and thought up the idea of a god as a way to explain how he evolved to his present state.

If this were true, then as the chemical process of gaining intelligence continues to evolve, we should become *more* superstitious rather than less. This does not even make sense because, to use their logic, as one would become more and more intelligent, then man should become more and more conscious of God. But what we actually see is a reversal. As man increases in knowledge, he has become more and more arrogant and prideful in his own achievements and has entered into an era of trying to explain away God rather than acknowledging that there *is* a God. The fact is the reason man knows there is a God is because we are *not* a product of a chemical reaction. We are a product of His creation and were created in His image.

Nobody is Born an Atheist or an Agnostic

There is not a child born who questions the existence of God. Neither does anyone suddenly wake up one morning and say, "Hey, I don't think there is a God." While we have actually had atheists say that this was not true and that they could never think of a time they had a belief in God, we are not convinced this is true. They can proclaim this all they wish, but the fact is, God says there is not one person who can truthfully say they *never* believed there was a God. Romans 1:20 tells us, "For since the creation of the world God's invisible qualities—his eternal power and divine nature—have been clearly seen, being understood from what has been made, so that men are without excuse."

However, many have been turned from a belief in God through the things they experienced in childhood and on into adulthood. Our experiences are often what shape our view of God, and from there, we either move closer to God or further away from Him.

Usually, there are three basic reasons a person might turn away from God. One type of person who turns against God is one who was raised in an abusive home. They were abused sexually and/or physically, and they mentally struggle with wondering how a good God could allow such abuse to happen if He really does exist.

If the abuse came from the hands of the non-religious, then we need to point out that the abuse was a result of sinful man. The abuse did not come from the hands of God nor does He condone or approve of such things. This is why God hates sin because of the harm it brings on Mankind. This is also why God hates the sin but loves the sinner.[216] Because of God's love for all people, He withholds His judgment until the final judgment. If He did not, then none of us would be able to stand; we would all fall under His judgment, and no one would be saved.

Unfortunately, we are meeting more and more people who have been abused at the hands of someone who professed a belief in God. This is the most damaging kind of abuse because the one who has been abused sees God's character as the same as those who supposedly were representing God. In such cases, we need to show them that the God the abuser represented is not at all the God of the Bible. Often one of the best ways of reaching this type of agnostic/atheist is to expose them to the *true* God of the Bible and let them see how different He is from their perceptions of Him. These people will frequently throw up various questions about God, but many times these are a smoke-screen for the root question they have in their heart: How can a good, loving God have allowed me to be abused like I was? It is easy to understand how their hurts have clouded their reasoning. If God were indeed as sadistic as they have made Him out to be, then it is no wonder they would rather believe no God exists than to live in a world run by such a God.

If you can focus on the reason behind the words of people who claim to be atheists or agnostics, you can often help them to see the misconceptions they have about who the God of the Bible is. Sound doctrine, therefore, is the only thing to help them see the one, true God. We need to show them God's character, as revealed in the Bible, a balance of holiness, justice, love and mercy. God will indeed hold the perpetrators responsible for their actions and His justice will prevail.

Another reason people might question the existence of God is because they have seen more than their share of death, starvation, diseases, killing and other such things. This happens because of a similar view as those who have been abused. The question is essentially the same: How can a good, loving God allow such things to happen?

Once again we can explain that these things are the result of sinful man and rebellion towards God. These fail to realize that God never promised complete happiness in this life but that the promise of eternal bliss is reserved for those who trust in God. In this life we experience the pangs of sin as well as the good things in life so we can have a clear picture of good and evil in order to be able to choose who we will serve. We can choose to serve the God from whom all blessings flow or the god of this earth that has only death and destruction to offer.

A third type of person one might encounter as an agnostic or an atheist is one who may have been raised in a fairly good environment (religious or non-religious) who later in life makes a conscious decision to reject God. The reasons may appear to vary but they are simply because it interferes with their chosen lifestyle (generally sexual in nature) or may be a hindrance to gaining fame and fortune.

This is also a challenging group to reach because their life is centered completely on their own pleasures and self-gratification. More often than not, they are the ones who will argue the longest and loudest as to why there is no God. We have found that arguing evolution, the big bang and other supposed scientific evidences of "proof" that there is no God and disproving them scientifically is a complete waste of time. No matter how persuasive the evidence refuting these "proofs" may be, it will not change their heart because their rejection of God is purely for selfish motives. All one can do is to present the gospel message and leave the rest in the hands of God.

For one who may claim to be either atheist or agnostic, the first thing that needs to be done is to try and distinguish why they are what they now claim to be. Generally, if they are evasive to answer the "why," they more than likely are of the third group we have just mentioned. If their reason is because of their sexual preference, it soon becomes evident that this is why they reject the idea of God as the conversation will begin to focus on this aspect.

In regards to the first two groups mentioned above, the first group will express an extreme hatred for God. This is the tip-off that they are angry towards a God who they are trying so hard to convince themselves does not exist. If their anger is directed towards God alone, then chances are they were hurt by the hands of non-religious persons. These are the ones that may respond to the simple presentation of the gospel of salvation by grace and not of works.

If they express an extreme hatred towards Christianity, chances are they were hurt by the hands of a religious person. In this case, asking what church affiliation they grew up in can often open up the direction the conversation should take. If it turns out to be a pseudo-Christian church, then bring them into understanding that what they were subjected to was not representative of Christianity and of who God actually is. If it turns out to be a church that is generally one that teaches sound doctrine, then remind them that the abuser's concept of God is not to be taken as who God is. If they would have had a proper understanding of Him, they would not have abused them as they did.

Many Christians write off those who are agnostics or atheists because they feel they have nothing to offer them. However, we must always remember that behind all of these arguments and intellectual babble lies a soul for which Jesus died. If we can see them through His eyes, we will look for the roots, the foundational misconceptions they have about a God who loved them so much He came to earth to die for them. These ideas are merely guides to show some basic ideas for talking with agnostics and atheists. The more you work with them, the easier it will be to distinguish between what works and what does not. What works with one person might not work with another, but one thing is certain. They all need to hear the good news of the gospel of grace. Let us not back down from them, but let us prepare ourselves to talk to them intelligently and truthfully, as Peter admonishes us in 1 Peter 3:15, "Always be prepared to give an answer to everyone who asks you to give the reason for the hope that you have."

Chapter 24:

The Evolution Delusion

◆◆◆

This chapter is not intended to be an exhaustive study on either evolution or creationism, but it is only to touch on a few highlights of how irrational evolution is. As mentioned in the chapter on atheism and agnosticism, evolution is no more than a smoke-screen that is an attempt to try and provide proof that God does not exist. The atheist or agnostic will claim that evolution is not an attempt to disprove God. They will often insist that their belief is rooted in scientific fact and, in order to support their beliefs, they will point out that many Christians agree with the validity of evolution. But once again we must look past this smoke-screen technique to find what lies at the bottom of their desire to cling to this theory. It gives them an excuse and justification to continue on in their chosen lifestyle with the belief they can claim ignorance when they stand before the Lord. "Lord, if I just had known, I would have thought and lived differently."

Evolution was invented for no other purpose than to discredit the creation account and to undermine the authority of the Bible. If the first four chapters in Genesis can be discounted, then this casts doubt on the credibility of the rest of scripture, as well as the God revealed therein. If the creation account in Genesis is no more than an illustration to explain something that was too complicated for primitive man to comprehend, this suggests that man has evolved beyond the ignorance of primitive man and now realizes that the Bible was only a culmination of superstitions and myths. The real target is Jesus Christ, of course. If the creation account was a myth, then Jesus was a myth as well.

Personally, we do not know of anybody who has received Jesus as Lord and Savior as a result of refuting evolution. This is not to say that none have but this just has not been our experience. We have seen a discussion over this, though, erase any doubts in the minds of born again Christians who may have become confused as what to believe in regards to evolution.

Many Christians and several church bodies have embraced evolution mainly out of fear of being thought of as ignorant and anti-science by the intellectual elites of society. Some have embraced evolution with the false belief that it would make the church, and themselves, more socially acceptable so people would be more receptive to the gospel. The problem is that the gospel will never be socially acceptable unless the gospel itself is watered down to make it acceptable. If this is done in the name of being acceptable, then it becomes a false gospel with no eternal value. The shame of this is that most have not bothered to study the challenges against evolution and remain ignorant in believing evolution is a long-proven scientific fact.

Is Evolution a Fact?

The evolutionist will agree that evolution is a theory, but then they continue to say that evolution is a scientific fact based on a theory. This is where the word games of evolutionists come into play. First, evolution is still called "The Theory of Evolution" because it cannot be proven scientifically. In other words, it cannot be observed, duplicated or recreated in a scientific laboratory, so it is still a theory and cannot be a scientific fact. The argument a supporter of evolution will have is that it is not possible to prove scientifically because evolution occurs over such a long period of time that it cannot be observed, duplicated or recreated. This is a convenient way of making it impossible to contradict their theory. Since this is indeed true, how can they insist that it is a scientific fact?

For example, let us say we believe in leprechauns because we have read about leprechauns and believe the stories to be true. It becomes our theory that leprechauns are little green guys who turn objects into gold. We have also come to the conclusion that all gold was made by leprechauns. Now that we have our beliefs, we set out to prove our theory and begin a systematic compilation of our evidence, starting with gathering writings about them. We begin to gather little nuggets of gold in various places throughout the world where we have gathered the writings about leprechauns. Our proof that leprechauns make gold is because we have gold nuggets from the same vicinities we have writings about them. We systematically and scientifically recorded our evidence to prove our theory so therefore, based on our findings, we can say that all gold is made by leprechauns. Our evidence cannot be proved in a laboratory setting because it cannot be observed, duplicated or recreated, but for that very reason as well, it cannot be disproved. You cannot refute our findings through laboratory testing, thus it must be true.

Some might say this illustration is over simplified and silly to use in comparison with evolution. But is it really? It is not the storyline that is in error. The errors come when we begin with our own presupposition and then try to make our findings fit in with what we have already determined is the truth. When the gathering of data is done to prove whatever theory the person has already determined to be true, then no matter what data is found, the person will find a way of forcing the data to fit the theory instead of matching up the theory with the reality of the data. This is precisely what has happened with evolution.

The only thing that is "scientific" in the field of evolution is the scientific gathering of the information that presupposes that certain things are evidence of evolution. Most of this *supposed* evidence revolves around "this fossil looks kind of like that fossil," which is meant to prove evolution.[217] However, the scientific gathering and recording of this type of information is a far cry from the accumulation of what is in reality evidence for a scientific fact. We must remember that evolution began from a philosophy based on the presumption that there is no God and has worked backwards in trying to force-fit science into that presupposition. Instead of facts being found to support the theory, the theory has already been assumed to be the reality that the facts must be fit into, whether they actually do fit or not.

Another area of word games is for the evolutionist to say, "I suppose you don't believe in micro-evolution either." While what is termed "micro-evolution" can and has been observed, this process would be more accurately classified as adaptability, not evolution. Examples of "micro-evolution" would be such things as bears of the North Pole having a heavier coat of fur to withstand the cold climate of the North compared to a bear with less fur to adapt to the warmer climates of the South. This would also include such things as changes in gene expressions of breeding different breeds of dogs for example. In all incidences, the bear and the dog are still bears and dogs. Evolutionists contend that since micro-evolution is a fact, it stands to reason that macro-evolution can also occur. Macro-evolution is theorized as the same as micro-evolution but on a grander scale that we cannot see because the process is much slower in the change from species to species. Yet this is where evolution falls off the cliff of credibility. No scientific evidence has ever been produced to show that species can evolve from one species to become another species or that this has ever occurred down through the sacred mystical annals of the evolutionary gods. The latest scientific discovery of DNA placed the final nail in the coffin of the hoax of evolution. Only a vocal minority of evolutionist scientists are still trying to pull flesh over the skeletal remains of the dead and buried false prophet Darwin.

Atheistic Evolution

Most evolutionists with any capability to reason will acknowledge that evolution cannot prove the origins of life. Some will say evolution never made that claim, but this is where the dishonesty of that statement comes in. Even if not stated as such, the implication is very strongly suggested that if evolution can and did occur, then there is that remote possibility that a God was not required to be the spark that produced the first sign of life that began the rolling of the evolutionary ball. It is, in fact, the only true hope for those who want to believe in a God-less existence.

For the man who discounts the need for a God as the source of life, he is left with only one choice: spontaneous generation. Spontaneous generation means that life emerged on its own without any divine influence. There are two theories of spontaneous generation, which are: life emerged from dead organic matter (*heterogenesis*) or from inorganic matter (*abiogenesis*).

It was the belief of some people during the middle ages that such things as mice, worms, insects, etc. (subsequently all living creatures), were created by materials in their environment *(heterogenesis)*. Louis Pasteur proved that life could not spontaneously emerge from dead organic matter, and today heterogenesis is not even considered in the scientific arena as a viable explanation for the origins of life. However, Man was not daunted by this dastardly revelation by Pasteur; he simply jumped to the other theory. The theory of abiogenesis spontaneous generation became the promised messiah of the evolutionists that would finally explain away God. We will address the scientific "creators'" success rate of trying to produce life through lifeless chemicals further on in this chapter, but for now we want to address "Theist-Evolution."

Theist Evolution

The only difference between Atheist Evolution and Theist Evolution is that the theist believes God was the originator of life and that evolution was the channel He chose to use. At the root, this is saying that evolution is a scientific fact and that essentially the only disagreement between atheists and theists is on the origins of that initial spark of life. This may seem to be a harmless theory for the theist to embrace, but the problem is that it does not matter if it is called atheist or theist evolution. The fact remains that it did not happen. Although this may make one feel he or she is more accepted by the intellectual world, it does not change the fact that evolution bypasses the Genesis account of creation, replacing it with a manmade rewrite of God's version. As stated previously, this in turn causes confusion and doubts and challenges the veracity of the rest of the scriptures. Jesus, who is the Creator, referred to the scriptures and to the creation account itself.[218] If the account of creation were not accurate, then we could not believe Jesus and must assume He was fraudulent, and He therefore could not have been God.

When the creation account is bypassed, the original sin is taken out of the way and the sacrifice of Jesus for the sin of the whole world becomes nothing but a pointless act. It takes away the need for God's grace and declares that Man was not born with a corrupt nature but was born basically good, and Jesus came merely to set an example that Man is to follow.[219]

When the first four chapters of Genesis are explained away as nothing more than an allegory, this leads into all manner of heresies. Many heresies (although not all) have been addressed in this book and each one challenges the authority of the scriptures. Evolution is the chief proponent of escalating this challenge today, and it cannot be accepted by any Christian without having its effect upon the spiritual well-being of the individual.

Atheistic Evolution and the Spark of Life

Not only is the evolutionist fighting an uphill battle in the theory of evolution, for his theory to hold true he also has to explain how the cosmos came into being. For evolution to be plausible, the necessary ingredients had to have already been set in place for it to even occur. Of course, the popular explanation is the Big Bang Theory. The problem with both of these theories, Evolution Theory and the Big Bang Theory, is that they both go on the presumption that matter just somehow was and the origins of matter does not need to be explained in order to fit into the equation.

The Big Bang theorists explain that all the matter in the universe was compressed into an area the size of the head of a pin. Again we see the same problems: how do they know this and where did this matter come from? And what compressed it in the first place? For those who hold to this theory, no explanation is needed. This just has to be how it happened.

In time (always the vital ingredient in their formula), the force from the outside became so weak that the force from within this compressed matter became greater than the forces being exerted upon it from the outside, and it went, "BANG!!!!" Therefore, they theorize, all the matter in the vast universe that was compressed into the size of a pin head (an unsubstantiated theory in and of itself) went "boom" and it later produced order, life and intelligence. How did this mixture of cosmological energy (origins unknown) and matter (origins also unknown) produce the complexities of life and even DNA? The Big Bang theorists introduce the magic ingredient of time and chance to complete the theory, patting themselves on the back and tacking a bright, shiny label on it saying, "scientific fact."

We would like to inject our own theory that explains the Big Bang. No, on second thought, not a theory but a fact called, "The Fact of a Vain Imagination." "Because that, when they knew God, they glorified him not as God, neither were thankful; but became *vain in their imaginations*, and their foolish heart was darkened. Professing themselves to be wise, they became fools." (Romans 1:21-22 KJV, italics added)

The proponents of the Big Bang may feel like their intelligence has been insulted when their pet theory is bought down to this simple explanation, but the fact is when all the babble is cut away, this is exactly what is left of what they expect the general populace to believe. What is really sad is that a good portion of the population does accept it as a scientific fact, and, while they question creationism with overwhelming skepticism, they do not even question these theories as to whether they are true or not.

Conversing with an Atheistic Evolutionist

We have had discussions over these subject matters with many people and without fail, when we show them the absurdity of the Big Bang and Evolution Theories, it always winds up in an attack on the Bible itself and fundamental Christians. What makes this interesting is that we do not even need to mention the Bible during the discussions, nor to express our religious beliefs. If evolution was for any reason other than to discredit the creation account in Genesis, then why else is it that the Bible and fundamental Christianity is the first thing that comes to mind when the supporters of it feel backed into a corner?

Almost without fail, soon a long line of vulgarities begins to emerge and such things as, "I suppose you're one of those 'fundies' (*derogatory slang for fundamental Christians*) that believes in talking snakes and donkeys and in the God who killed children in the Old Testament?" We usually respond, "If you're asking if I am a Fundamental Christian who believes in the creation account in the Bible, yes I am. But what does that have to do with the discussion about evolution and the Big Bang Theory?"

If you are alert, you can see that what they are trying to do is to show the supposed "absurdity" of the belief in the creation account by making it sound ridiculous with the talking snake and donkey and the God killing children comments. Although difficult, we must resist the temptation at this point to let the subject become focused on these supposed absurdities and supposed contradictions in the Bible. We must keep it focused on creation vs. evolution. We can almost guarantee if we can keep focused on the main issue, the discussion will wind up as a stalemate, as we present the final statement that leaves them with having to make the choice between the two beliefs.

Neither of us is able to *prove* either evolution or creation because neither view can be tested in a scientific laboratory. This is our complaint with evolutionists claiming it is a proven scientific fact. We both agree that the existence of the universe is a fact because we are both living it and it is here to be observed. All that is left is the question of how did it all get here.

We must continually bring them back to the root issue. We believe evolution and the Big Bang are absurd to believe and they believe it is absurd to believe some "big white bearded guy" created all that we observe. We have to move away from opinions and look at what the evidence tells us is the most logical. We cannot base our belief on this matter on which we prefer to be true or which is easier to comprehend, but only which is more logical according to the evidence. Frankly, neither view can be comprehended and frankly, both views could be viewed as absurd, but which is the most logical of the two?

Let us examine the choices. Choice one says that life and intelligence emerged and evolved from lifeless chemicals created by the cosmos that were a result of a big bang, which occurred from matter and energy with unknown origins. Through time and chance, we exist and observe all that we see today.

Choice Two says that an eternal God, who is spirit outside of time and apart from matter, is the source of life and intelligence. He is the Creator of the cosmos, and the fact that we exist and all that we observe is the product of His creation.

There really are no other choices but these two, when it comes down to the heart of the subject. In comparing these two choices, it is not logical to persist in a belief that life came from non-life and intelligence from non-intelligence. It is a much more logical conclusion to believe an intelligent, living God gave life and intelligence to us. Indeed, it requires far less faith to believe in God than to believe in the magical force of sufficient time and chance.

As we work with those who adhere to the belief of evolution, let us remember to look past the outward expression and see their inward heart towards God. If we can do this, we will be able to cut through the thorny hedges of intellectualism to find the lost soul underneath.

Part 3

Introduction to Internet Ministry

Chapter 25:

The Cutting Edge of Mission Fields

◆◆◆

Imagine a city of over 70,000 people having not even one established church, only individual Christians who evangelize on a "hit and miss" technique. It would seem like the ideal place to plant a strong church in order to add stability to the evangelistic thrust, would it not?

In January 1998, that is basically what we did. We planted a stable place for the hurting and confused to come for help, and we planted it right in the heart of Yahoo! Chat on the Internet. On any given night in Yahoo! Chat, there are more than 70,000 people in chat rooms, wanting to connect with other people, many searching for balm to ease the wounds of daily living in this fast-paced world in which we live.

Two thousand years ago, Jesus sent His disciples out to preach the Good News to all corners of the world, commissioning them to, "make disciples of all nations, baptizing them in the name of the Father and of the Son and of the Holy Spirit." (Matthew 28:19) This great commission is still in effect today but has now taken on an entirely new dimension. Until now, few felt they were actually called to go to foreign countries to tell people there about the incredible news of God's grace to us through the sacrifice of Jesus on the cross. But all that has changed.

No longer do we have to think about uprooting our lives and getting typhoid shots and buying jungle gear to talk to those in other countries who have never heard of Jesus. All we have to do now is flip a small switch and we are instantly transported to virtually any country in the world. Our mission field is no longer a village of 100 people, but over 200 million users of the Internet.

It must have seemed an overwhelming task to the disciples when Jesus told them to preach to all nations when it took a week just to walk from one end of Israel to the other. The Internet, however, allows us to talk to someone from China and someone from Africa and someone from South America at the very same time! The disciples could never have envisioned being able to reach millions of people through a website or chat room, but it has become a reality in our time and culture. We are not suggesting that ministry on the Internet will take the place of actually going to real places and talking to people face to face, but it is indeed a cutting edge mission field of which we must take advantage.

Radio came first as the media by which preachers would be able to reach larger audiences than ever before. With the invention of television, Christians had yet another new venue to go to all nations to preach the Good News to them. However, when radio and television evangelists began, many people criticized them for using a media that was "of the devil" and said that God would never bless it. Many Christians are today viewing the Internet in a similar fashion.

While it is true that there is much on the Internet that is obviously "of the devil," the medium itself is not evil; it is what we choose to do with it. If Christians sit back and refuse to put a godly influence online, then Satan will be happy to take over the Internet and have it used solely for his purposes.

The Two-fold Purpose of an Online Ministry

The purpose of an online ministry is actually two-fold. Although the major emphasis is evangelistic, to be sure, there is also a very serious secondary emphasis: the protection of the elect. Recently, there has been a creeping of ecumenicalism into our mainstream churches and the very word "tolerance" has been redefined. No longer does tolerance mean that you can have your own beliefs yet still put up with those who think differently. It has now been redefined to mean that you must accept all beliefs as equally valid as yours.

As mainstream Christians, we cannot abide by this new definition. Jesus plainly says, "I am the way, the truth and the life. No one comes to the Father except through me." (John 14:6) Because of this statement by Jesus Himself, we are absolutely certain that there is no other way to God but through Him. Therefore, if this is true, then we must see that, although we can put up with those who disagree with our beliefs, we can in no way support any ideology that says that their belief in something other than God Almighty is equally as valid as our belief. How can this statement of Jesus' agree with Islam, for instance, that claims that there is one God, Allah, and Mohammed is his prophet, relegating Jesus to the position of merely another prophet and just a good man?

Yet this line of thinking has permeated our local churches, and in working with Christians online, you will soon see that many of them have no desire to question the accuracy of the beliefs of Jehovah's Witnesses, Mormons or even Pagans because they are buying into this false definition of tolerance. How dare we maintain a stand that our belief contradicts others because then we must say that someone is wrong?

Because of this, it is imperative that an online ministry overflow to our own brothers and sisters. We have witnessed many Christians, both young and old, who have begun to have a "crise de foi" *(crisis of faith)* because they have not only listened to the lies from these cultic beliefs, but also have erred in considering these beliefs as having a validity that they do not have. This is a technique by the enemy himself that paralyzes Christians, rendering them temporarily useless in the battle against him.

It does not take long for a mature Christian who is involved in chat room ministry to realize that the weaker brothers and sisters who witness these cultic claims need to hear the truth reaffirmed to them with a confident and Christ-assured attitude. When ministering to the unsaved, we must always take into consideration those who are saved as well. Sometimes, through comments and questions made by a believer, you can see that a confusion is beginning to form in his or her mind. When this occurs, the mature believer needs to determine if the present discussion will be edifying to our fellow believer or if perhaps a different time and place might not be better for continuing our talk with the non-believer. We need to be sensitive to the needs of others in the room.

Although this book can be used by anyone, we work from a perspective of Internet ministry. For this reason, we realize this work is geared towards those who have a heart for telling others about the wonderful grace of our loving Lord and who feel led to do so by way of the Internet. It is our hope that you will find help in these pages to establish a BIBLE counseling ministry of your own, and perhaps one that goes online in order to bring glory to the Almighty God. We are not intending this book to be a totally inclusive, in-depth dissertation on any of the included cultic beliefs or issues of comfort, but instead, the design is for reference that can be quickly accessed while you are chatting with someone online. Many of these issues may only be observed in those who are unbelievers online. We do not always use Scriptural arguments because many of the people you will be dealing with do not accept the Bible as an inerrant source of truth. If they do not believe in the Bible, you cannot build your arguments for validity on something in which they do not believe.

In this section, we would like to talk about the type of ministry we know best and to give some ideas for those who would like to start an online ministry for themselves.

Types of Internet Ministry Opportunities

The Internet is a series of computers that are linked together via phone lines or cables, which allow the computers to share information. This type of setup was originated by the government in 1969 and has blossomed into a networking that encompasses computers anywhere because of mobile links.

The original purpose of the Internet was to allow the government to share information between their computers across the nation and across the world. Universities soon joined in the task of making information available to the public through their computers. Soon the invention of electronic mail (e-mail) helped not only to connect people with information online, but it was the first step in connecting them with other people.

Human beings have been created as social creatures, with a built-in drive within us to interact with other people. As a result, e-mail was a stepping-stone that led to bulletin boards (also called forums), newsgroups, websites, instant messages, text chat and now voice chat in order to satisfy this desire for more personal contact.

An online ministry can focus on one or more of the methods above to share the Good News we have been entrusted with, but most ministries will use a combination of these methods. Let us take you through the various methods available so you can see the different ways that they can be used as both an evangelistic and discipleship tool.

Electronic mail is a very good method to use when you have already established a contact with someone. To witness under this medium, you will need to be patient and build up a relationship, earning the person's trust and friendship while sharing with them God's grace, rather like an electronic pen pal. An advantage of e-mail is that you can take time to carefully word and research your responses to your friend before your friend sees what you have to say. If you are a person who likes to choose their words carefully, this would be a good means of ministry for you. Another advantage is that you can focus your attention on one person instead of trying to deal with a multitude of different simultaneous conversations as in chat. This is probably one of the safest means of online evangelism and will protect the more tenderhearted from much of the harsh treatment other methods might lend themselves to.

A possible disadvantage of e-mail, however, is that it is a one-sided conversation and you have to wait to find out what kind of response you are getting. In other words, there is no immediate feedback to base your next statement on and sometimes you might not be clear about what the person is trying to share with you. Waiting for a response can often be tedious. Another disadvantage to e-mail evangelism is that you must first know a person to be able to e-mail them. While there do exist electronic pen pal services, the majority of the people you will e-mail will be people you have met through some other means such as chat rooms, forums, newsgroups or other acquaintances on the Internet.

Bulletin boards (or forums) and newsgroups have many of the same advantages and disadvantages as e-mail, but your comments are made public for many people to read and comment on and because of this, they take on a dimension of their own. Bulletin boards, or forums as they are sometimes called, are very much as their name implies: a place to post information, comments, or opinions where the public can see them and then respond to them. This has the same advantage as e-mail in that you can spend time researching your reply and then wording it carefully so it says exactly what you want, but in adding many viewers to the discussion, you will find that matters become more complicated.

If your ministry is to do evangelism through bulletin boards, be prepared for the following things. There will be some people who will be extremely picky about, well, pretty much everything. They will criticize you for everything from your doctrine to your spelling. They might call you "stupid" or "uneducated" if you do not have enough documented sources to back up your statements. Be assured that the Internet community is, for the most part, fairly educated or at least will do their best to make you think they are educated. You need to be well-versed enough to know whether the person who is looking down their nose at your ignorance has any validity to what he is saying or if he is merely putting on an intellectual mask that clouds the issues with unsupported statements. Many statements that are made about Christianity and are quoted as fact are in reality false and we must be ready to answer with the complete, unadulterated truth.

Newsgroups are basically a combination of e-mail and bulletin boards. The bulletin board format is followed, but it is sent to a specific e-mail list and since it is in the e-mail format, replies can usually be longer and more involved than forums or bulletin boards. In any of these formats, we strongly suggest that you read most of the recent posts before jumping in to make your comments. Many people who are anxious to jump on any anti-biblical sentiment blow their credibility with the others reading the board by blasting someone right off the bat. The members of bulletin boards, forums and newsgroups consider themselves as a type of community so it is wise to establish yourself in the community first before taking too adamant a stand or the other members will no longer bother to read your posts.

If you want to be effective, be aware of the thread of conversation you are jumping into. Get to know the personalities of the others in the community by reading their posts before you say too much. Think of it as walking into a room where five people are carrying on a conversation and you hear one person make a statement. On the basis of that statement, you begin a discourse on how the biblical account of creation is the correct view of the origin of the universe. Your statement might be 100% accurate, but it might not fit into the conversation flow and for certain the others in the group would probably feel a bit taken aback that you joined in so fast without really understanding what they had been talking about.

A Ministry Website

The "in" thing nowadays is to have your own website. Because of the very nature of the WWW, accurate statistics are difficult to determine, but we have seen some that say that there are more than three trillion websites on the Internet today, which averages out to be approximately 500 sites per person in the world. We think this estimate is rather high, but there is no doubt that websites are abounding. Families have websites; churches have websites; businesses have websites; colleges have websites; students have websites; just about anyone who wants to can make their own website over any subject they choose and say whatever they want. The availability of web space, however, shows us how necessary it is to take everything we read on the Internet with a grain of salt. It should also indicate to us the extreme competition our website in the sea of billions, if not trillions, of others.

There are two ways of having a website. One way is to secure a domain name and then find a server who will host your site. The cost of this type of setup will vary from server to server so if this is the route you choose to go, check around for prices and for technical assistance as well if you are not knowledgeable in designing your own site. Some charge a large one-time setup fee and minimal hosting fee, but others charge a smaller setup fee and also a larger monthly maintenance fee. One advantage is, however, that the URL address of your website will be much shorter than if you have a freebie site. Another would be a better e-mail management system if your ministry will be a group effort with several different people involved.

If you are on a budget, there are many things you can do online that cost absolutely nothing except your time and your original connection to the Internet. There are many servers who have made free website space available for merely the price of displaying one of the banners of their sponsors. Some of the major names are Angelfire, Geocities, Homestead, Tripod, and many more you can find by doing a search for free websites. Each of them has certain advantages and disadvantages to their setups, some are easier to use than others, so you will want to explore each of them for the aspects you find most beneficial according to your computer knowledge and your purpose. For instance, Geocities is very easy to set up even if you do not know much about computers, but the address can be rather lengthy and contains numbers that are easy for someone to mix up if you are trying to refer them to your site. Most people prefer words in a URL address as opposed to numbers because they are easier to remember. However, if you are a member of Yahoo, you can have a much shorter name that is connected to your chat name but is still part of the Geocities network. Unfortunately, as with all freebie sites you will have to deal with a fairly long name for your home page URL.

A website can be a good evangelistic tool if you want to write articles for people to read at their leisure. Websites allow the information to be available 24 hours a day whenever the person chooses to surf in. The challenge with websites is to make them as interesting as possible (both visually and textually) and to update often to keep people coming back. Also necessary is a good inclusion in as many search engines as possible. The most incredible site in the world is useless if nobody knows about it. This takes a good deal of time at first submitting your website and even when it is submitted there is no guarantee that you will have a lot of hits merely from being placed on a search engine.

Another way of advertising your website is through banners. There are many free banner exchange programs available, but be very cautious about this. Since it is a banner exchange, you will be required to put banners from the other members of the banner exchange on your site and you will most likely not have control over what banners are displayed. In exchange, your banner will be displayed on other people's sites and again, you will probably have no control over which sites these are. We suggest that you choose a Christian banner exchange that holds to certain doctrinal tenets so you will not pull up your homepage and see an ad for a porn site. Some banner exchange programs allow you to pay for more exposure for your banner. Again, this depends on the budget you have set out for this. If you have enough hits on your site, you will probably not need to pay for more exposure because the more hits you have on your site, the more credits you earn towards your banner being displayed on someone else's site.

Chat Ministry
The next area of ministry is in text chat, which encompasses Java, HTML and instant message chats. This is where Open Arms Internet Ministry began and so is the area with which we are most familiar and most comfortable. However, a word of warning: this is not an area for the faint of heart. It takes a special kind of person to deal with a chat ministry, just as it takes a special person to minister in any of the above ways. We have a friend who does not care at all for chat evangelism, but he has settled into a regular ministry on forum boards. On the other hand, we have tried forum evangelism but have found chat ministry much more to our liking. The message of Jesus is needed in all corners of the Internet and God will raise up people with just the right talents for each of these forms of ministry.

What we like best about chat is that it is in real time so when you pose a question to another person, he can answer you right then and the conversation continues almost as if you were sitting in a room talking to the person. We cannot even begin to guess how many chat rooms are on the Internet. Besides being available on most major sites, some people have chat rooms on their personal websites. The largest one is Yahoo! Chat (Yahoo has been the number one most hit on site several times) and is where we have planted ourselves and our ministry. In order to see just how many different chats there are, you can do a search for the word chat on any search engine online and you will come up with a huge list of entries (anywhere from three million or more websites!). It is best to find one chat that you like and stick with it. The key to having a successful chat ministry is dependability. The Internet is becoming known for being rather transitory so establishing yourself as a regular will be a major factor in your success.

There are some things to be prepared for with a chat ministry, however. Since chat is in real time, you must have your facts more readily at your fingertips because you will not be allowed the leisure of researching a topic and then coming back to respond. In fact, this is the very reason for this handbook. When you are engaged in a conversation with a Mormon and they ask you if you even know who Moroni is, you will not have time to read that book on Mormonism that you have sitting by your computer and then get back to them. Our purpose is to provide a resource for you that you can keep by your computer and will be able to see at a glance the major beliefs of many different cults that you will encounter in chat (usually more than one at a time). Then you will be able immediately to see answers to the most frequent questions they will ask you and the possible response you may give them. This handbook has been born out of over five years of being in the frontlines and dealing with these kinds of people on a daily basis.

Chat requires someone who can think quickly and who is prepared to field all those foul balls coming from every direction that are headed your way. Subjects can change quickly on the entrance of one or two new people. While typing skills are a must, the single most important characteristic in a chat evangelist is to have a sincere love and concern for those who are lost. If you have this, you will be able to look past the insults and vulgarities and will see into the heart of the person behind them, a person who desperately needs to become acquainted with the Author of life.

HTML chat was one of the first chats developed and is still used by some older browsers and those who are behind firewalls. It is a bit more cumbersome than Java because the screen must continually be refreshed for new text to come up. Because of this, if you are in a fast-scrolling room, you will find it difficult to really be a part of the conversation. If you have a choice and your browser supports it, you will find Java a much more satisfying way to chat. In Java you type in a line and as soon as you hit enter, it appears on the screen for all in the room to see.

Instant message programs such as ICQ, Yahoo! Messenger, AOL Instant Messenger and such are similar to a fast e-mail system that often allows you to see if the person you wish to contact is online so they can immediately respond to you. It can also give you the flexibility of sending files, URLs and voice messages. These programs also include a chat capability. In ICQ, you can have simultaneous transmission so you can actually see what the person is typing as they are actually typing it without having to hit enter. In counseling, this can give a lot of insight into the state of mind of the other person, whether they are seriously suicidal or are just saying it for attention's sake. ICQ also gives the added advantage of you being able to pick and choose who on your list you want to be able to see you as online. This is a great advantage if your ministry gets very busy because there will be times that you might need to be online to talk to one person and would not want everyone else knowing you are online.

Instant message programs can be used in a variety of ways to meet new people and tell others about Jesus. Also, they can be used for the edification of the Body. One lady passes around a verse of the day that is spread to all of the people on her contact list. Another we know is in charge of a prayer chain that passes along prayer requests to people all over the world.

The newest development in chat rooms and some of the instant message programs is voice chat. If you have a microphone, speakers and a sound card, you are now able to participate in verbal chats with the other people in the chat room. Although this area will see a profound growth in the near future, we do not believe it will replace text chat completely at the present because one of the main drawing factors of the Internet text chat is anonymity. It is very possible to text talk to the same person at different times with them using different names and pretending to be totally different people. This single factor is what makes Internet ministry so very unique. Because you cannot identify someone visually, as you normally would if they walked into your church, you have to pick up on very subtle clues as to the identity of the person (if they are trying to hide from you). In voice chat, it is much harder to hide from who you really are.

We need to take a moment and mention more about this factor of anonymity since this is *the* major ingredient in chat. The reason chats have become so popular is because people can be whoever they want to be online and nobody will know differently. Again, this is something that can be an advantage to ministering to them or a disadvantage. When people are free from others knowing exactly who they are, this will often cause them to go in one of two directions. Either they will be more open with you than they have ever been with anyone in their lives (which quickly opens the door to their heart and gives you the perfect opportunity to share the healing power of Jesus with them) or it will cause the evil intentions, which exist in all of us but are normally checked by the accountability with those around us, to gush out of them in a flood of hate, anger and vulgarities.

In the latter case, attempts to witness to that person will often be met with abusive comments and, depending on the thickness of your skin, can hurt you deeply. While we believe that everyone deserves to hear about Jesus, we also believe that some will harden their hearts to our message, and we need to be prepared for this. In Matthew 10:14, Jesus told His disciples that if anyone did not accept the message they brought, they were to "shake the dust off" their feet and leave. It could also be that you have planted the seed you were to plant and someone else will be brought along to nurture the seed you have planted.

In the next chapter, you will see close up how we have structured our Internet ministry and why we have chosen to handle things the way we have. While we understand that everyone's ministry will be unique, there is much we have learned over the years and we would like to pass this on to you as you take on this challenge of going out into the fields that are white with the harvest.

Chapter 26:

How Our Ministry Is Structured

◆◆◆

Open Arms Internet Ministry is an online BIBLE counseling ministry, which we started in January 1998. It began as a Bible study in Yahoo! Chat and soon progressed to biblical counseling as many would wander in and ask questions about how the Bible could give answers to their daily problems. We both had been doing this on an individual basis, but soon saw that the need was so great and that this mission field was wide open. We established a user room in the Society and Culture section of Yahoo Chat (which is where the Christian and Religion rooms were) on Monday and Friday nights and have continued them since that time. The rooms are open for two hours a night (because we found that the intensity of those two hours was very fatiguing for us) and as of this writing, we have had more than 28,000 come through our room and we and our counselors have personally counseled with over 5000 people.

In January 1999, we opened a Yahoo! Club (now they are called Groups) where those we establish counseling relationships with can join others for fellowship and have a safe environment to be involved with other Christians. We have been consistently listed in the top Christian groups since we opened, and are presently in the top five of advice groups.

Popularity, however, has never been God's method of measuring success. We have witnessed the meteoric rise of many clubs in Yahoo, zooming past us on the list of most members, only to fall stagnant or be torn apart by divisions (or worse yet, to be caught up in the false doctrine of tolerance, which we have discussed throughout the book). We believe that the reason our ministry has been growing steadily and producing life-changing results is because we are not in a race to gain the most members and instead desire a unity of beliefs, based solely on the Bible as the final authoritative source. As you have seen in the rest of this book, there are many false doctrines floating around on the Internet, and very few churches today are teaching their members how to distinguish fallacy from the truth.

One of the most destructive and anti-biblical lies being taught today is that doctrine is what pulls us apart and what causes disunity. We strongly disagree. In fact, it is just the opposite that is true. The better we know our doctrine, the closer we will become. If we all adhere strictly to what the Bible says, then we will be unified. The farther we stray from biblical teachings, the farther apart the Church will be torn. This is why we have tried never to compromise what we believe the Bible to be saying in order to keep disgruntled members as a part of our ministry. We believe that this is the single most important factor for a successful Internet ministry and is what has kept OAIM going longer than almost all other online chat ministries of which we are aware.

When we made the decision to start an organized ministry, we created a website as a base of operations, as it were, that we could refer people to for more information. On the website we included articles we wrote that pertained to the most frequent questions we received. It also gave us a more organized appearance to those who came into our room. As we said before, websites are easy to make and are a good way to start.

At the beginning, we had a small group of online friends (about five) who joined us in our room, some of whom helped us out. Our original intent was to have an online Bible study in order to teach others so they would have that solid doctrinal foundation, but we soon changed our plans. In Yahoo! Chat, we created a user room but in order for our friends to come in, we left it unsecured (open) to all who might want to join. However, because of the transitory nature of chat, with people surfing into a room for a few moments and then leaving sometimes, we decided that perhaps a Bible study was not what we wanted to do.

It was at this time that we created a user room and allowed it to be listed so people could see it and would come to investigate it. The first night we had 26 people come through our room, most of which stayed for a good portion of the two hours. If someone wanted to talk, we could take him or her to a private room and counsel them. This was fine as long as we had our friends to take care of the room while we were private with someone.

Unfortunately, this limited how many people we could help in a two-hour period. We knew that we needed helpers if we were going to continue this system so we found others in chat who were solid biblically and invited them to join us. We were staying rather steady in attendance (about 30-40) each night, but because we had more biblical counselors available, we were helping more people individually.

Then Yahoo restructured their chat and things started changing. Yahoo was forced to change its rules on restricting profanity and content of user rooms (until then Yahoo had mostly contained the sex rooms in one area and not just anywhere in chat). This brought with it a surge of unrestricted behavior and a major change in our operations. No longer could the person who created the user room secure the room at any time, which left us defenseless against people who came in spouting profanities merely for the reason that they could, hiding behind the First Amendment and declaring it freedom of speech.

We found the need for more organization in our room essentially so we could deal with those who came in simply to disrupt things. It was at this time that we instigated titles for those who were counselors with us. This was to allow those new to the room to distinguish whose counsel was from Open Arms and whose was not. We also included a staff page on our website so people would be able to go there and verify who the real OAIM staff members were. This gave us more control in the room because of the organization. If a counselor asked people in the room to put a disruptor on ignore, it was more likely to be done.

As our first year anniversary came around, we had about 2500 people through our Monday and Friday rooms, with at least 300 people receiving individual counseling. But we noticed there was a new feature that Yahoo was initiating: clubs. When we took advantage of this, it was definitely a direction from God. While the website was a good start as a home base, the club added a totally new and fresh dimension and gave our people a safe meeting place throughout the week plus a message board for posting prayer requests. Until this time, we really did not know just how many people our ministry had touched. Old friends, new friends, and people who stumbled upon us started to join our club.

We soon grew large enough to branch off into a teen club and a discipleship course club. Because of the expansion, we needed more counselors to handle all of the new members. It was at this point that we compiled an application to help us screen possible candidates. Since we do biblical counseling, our people are not required to have psychological degrees (which is in fact in opposition to actual biblical counseling), but we do require them to have a good working knowledge of the Bible and how to apply it to everyday problems. We composed a rather extensive application so we could be certain that our counselors' beliefs adhered strictly to the Bible. Through this means, we have been able to add more counselors to our ranks.

Again we wish to impress that unity in doctrine is very important in a ministry. If you are working closely with a group of others as you witness online, you need to be positive that you will not be contradicting each other when it comes to matters of doctrine. If you do so in a roomful of non-believers, you will soon find that your credibility is ruined and they will no longer listen to anything you have to say.

Once accepted by OAIM as a counselor in training (CIT), we provide a mentor (one of our counselors) to help the neophyte grow into his/her position as a full counselor. Some of our CITs have more life skill in biblical counseling than others, but all are required to go through a training course where they would receive real life scenarios, based on situations our counselors would actually face, and then they would respond as if they were counseling this person. The length of training depends on how much previous life skill the CIT has. At the beginning of their training period, we ask our CITs to counsel in the open room or with another counselor or CIT for two reasons. First, this would give our counselors and ourselves a chance to observe how the person did indeed counsel, and secondly, it would protect the CIT from possible situations that they were not quite ready for. Some of the stories we encounter online can be rather complicated and counseling in pairs is a very smart way of working.

Protecting yourself from false accusations is a real and apparent danger with this type of ministry, as it is becoming for almost any profession where someone is alone with another person. In order to counteract this, we try to have our counselors use either CheetaChat (which is a program that allows you access Yahoo! Chat, but gives you the advantage of being able to save the text of the chat) or ICQ (which is an instant message program that has a chat feature in which you can save the text). These texts are for reference only and if needed to settle a dispute. They are considered confidential by the counselors and are never used for any purpose other than helping the person involved. Yahoo! Messenger chat can now also save the chat text for future reference.

The Importance of Confidentiality

And this brings us to another very important factor of an Internet ministry. Confidentiality is an absolute must. If people know that you are going to hear their problems and then tell your friends online what they said, you will not have a ministry for long. People will start to avoid you and be very careful to choose their words so you will not spread their lives across the Net. You will need to build up a reputation that helps them to feel confident that they are safe in talking with you. An essential thing to remember is that trust is a very fragile thing that is destroyed so easily, but rebuilt only with painstaking slowness. It is much easier to maintain than to rebuild.

This is how the Lord has led us to structure our online ministry.

We offer this as a model that you may or may not choose to emulate. We are aware that there are many facets to the Internet and even more facets to the Holy Spirit, but if you allow Him to give you the vision for an online ministry, He will surely direct your path.

Appendices:

Practical Aids to Ministry

Appendix A:

A Word about Disrupters

♦♦♦

When we first began our ministry online, there were few disrupters in Yahoo! Chat. People could engage in a civil conversation with others in any chat room there was, whether a main room or a user room. Even if someone disagreed with you, they were, for the most part, polite and would merely agree to disagree. However, a couple of lawsuits against Yahoo have now changed that dramatically.

Some complained that enforcing rules about behavior and language in chat rooms was unconstitutional and violated the First Amendment right to freedom of speech. Unfortunately, this has lead to an unrestrained atmosphere in chat rooms online. In some ways, it has become a world where there are no police, no one to be accountable to, no responsibilities in regards to how one interacts with others. The evil in the hearts of man becomes blatantly obvious. I (Deb) personally had a student who told me how much "fun" he had going into Christian chat rooms and teasing and talking abusively with those in there. He is not alone in this new "sport." We believe that many people of all ages have started to view chat as just another video game and forget that the people on the other side of the screen are real people with real feelings.

The only option that is given to us by many chat rooms is to put people on ignore. This ignore issue has been a rather volatile one among Christians ministering in chat. In today's society, an online Hamlet might change his question to: "To ignore or not to ignore, that is the question." To answer this question, we went to the Bible to find any precedence for ignoring people through scriptural support. We found some interesting passages.

We recognize that many who are truly seeking God will come in with a mocking attitude, but a heart that is receptive to Christ. However, there are many who have indeed been given "over to a depraved mind to do what ought not to be done." (Romans 1:28) We have been the target of the evening's sport for many people while we have been trying to help people come closer to God. It becomes a game for some to see how many of their friends they can bring in and by doing so disrupt us from the ministry we are doing.

If you do a chat ministry, you will be faced with this question before long. Sometimes you might just have to experience these people before you realize that ignore is indeed a good thing. Be prepared for spammers (those who repeat a message on the screen so the screen scrolls and no one else can talk). You will also see those who are so angry with God that they will spend an entire evening (sometimes for many evenings in a row) going into Christian rooms to tell the Christians what mindless losers they are.

We soon realized that we were spending more time trying to talk with the few disrupters that we were not able to talk to those who were genuinely hurting. It was at this point that we had to determine our policy for dealing with disrupters.

Although we are a ministry and never profess to be a church, we wondered how churches would deal with the same situations we were dealing with. Let us give you an example of what it would be like. If someone walked into a church during the morning service, walked straight into the pulpit and began using foul language to declare that Christianity was a fraud and that everyone in there was a blind sheep just mindlessly following what they were being taught, how would the leaders of that church react? What would be the godliest way of handling just such a situation? Is it godly for a group of church leaders to sit by and make sure one person felt accepted and welcomed into their church at the expense of damaging the beliefs of many of their sheep? How many Sundays would the leadership of a church allow this to happen with the same person over and over again before they took strong action? How many times do we need to talk to the same people about spiritual issues when they have chosen over and over not to listen to a word we said?

The Bible gives us some concrete answers to these questions. Let us look at the life of Christ. What was Jesus' response to those who came to mock Him and His ministry? If you ask Christians around you, you will find that there is a prevailing image of Jesus as being meek and mild and never raising His voice to anyone. However, if you look in the Bible, you will see a different Jesus, one of authority and power who displayed a "tough love" to those who mocked His message. Observing the adjectives used to describe how Jesus talked can be very revealing. We see Him speaking *sternly* to the demons in Mark 1:25 and giving the man with leprosy a *strong warning* in Mark 1:43. Mark 3:5 tells us that Jesus looked at the Pharisees *in anger*. In Matthew 9:30 He *warned* two blind men *sternly* not to tell others about it. And we cannot forget Jesus' many statements to the Pharisees of His day, which were not at all gentle and according to our watered down idea of love. (Matthew 23 is a very good example of this.)

When we begin to look at Jesus' response to those He encountered, we note that Jesus did not go after those who rejected Him so He could continue to preach and tell them of God. We see this clearly in Matthew 19:16-26 where Jesus met the rich young man. There is no indication whatsoever that Jesus pursued this man to continue preaching the Gospel to him after he left. On the contrary, Jesus was still with His disciples and used this as an illustration of those who hear the truth but refuse to accept it. There is not one time that Jesus is shown either going after someone to continue talking with them or returning to the same person over and over to preach to him. That pattern we see in Jesus' life is that He preached and then moved on. When a farmer sows seed, he does not return to the same ground to sow more seed over and over.

Another example to see is the admonition Jesus gave His disciples when He sent out the twelve disciples. He told them, "If anyone will not welcome you or listen to your words, shake the dust off your feet when you leave that home or town." (Matthew 10:14, also Mark 6:11 and Luke 9:5) Since shaking the dust off of your feet was a great insult in that culture, this would indicate that staying there to continue talking to someone who was obviously opposed to God's message was not something Jesus expected them to do.

Although there are no examples of Jesus or His disciples continuing to preach to someone who was not at all receptive to the good news of the Gospel, there are, however, many warnings in the Bible about dealing with ungodly people. In Titus 3:10-11, we read, "Warn a divisive person once, and then warn him a second time. After that, have nothing to do with him. You may be sure that such a man is warped and sinful; he is self-condemned." "Have nothing to do with the fruitless deeds of darkness, but rather expose them." Ephesians 5:11 (See also 2 Timothy 3:1-5, 2 Timothy 2:16, 2 Timothy 2:23, Ephesians 5:7) In Romans 1, even God drew the line at ungodly behavior when He "gave them over" to their own sinful desires, to shameful lusts and to a depraved mind because of their continued rejection of Him (verses 24, 26 and 28). Because of this evidence, we believe that it is the more biblical action to put someone on ignore rather than let them distract from God's work that is going on in the room.

Our policy has been to talk to the person and determine whether they are seeking or merely in our room for sport. As you work with more and more people, this becomes very easy to determine in only a couple of exchanges with them in the room. If they are there for sport, we will ask all our counselors and other "regulars" to put that person on ignore. If one of our counselors feels particularly moved by the Holy Spirit to talk with the person more, we ask that they do so in a private message so the room does not see us divided in our response. This is a way of allowing for the Holy Spirit to work but yet maintaining peace in the room in order for the ministry to be able to function.

One of the complaints we get the most when we do this is that we are not doing what Jesus would do. However, as explained above, we believe we are doing exactly what Jesus would do if He had been doing online ministry. As we said before, this is a matter that needs to be settled early in your online ministry. If you are working with a group of people as you do your ministry, try to come to a consensus about how to handle disrupters before the situation arises.

There is one last thing for us to mention about disrupters. Sadly to say, some of the most hurtful disrupters are those who claim to be Christian and who come in and try to take over the room with all their "wisdom" from God. This is often an even more difficult thing to deal with than the non-Christians. As you can see from the other parts of this book, there are some cults that are masquerading as Christian but are teaching false doctrines. This will be more of an individual situation than the above mentioned and will require discernment as to whether it is more profitable to challenge their false doctrines or to allow them to continue to proclaim these things to the others in the room.

We advise you to be careful about judging the way a ministry is run before you have examined their reasons for what they do. If you disagree, ask them for biblical support for what they are teaching or doing. The only way an online ministry will survive the opposition out there is by grounding itself firmly in the infallible written word of God. If you hold fast to God's truths and "test everything" as it says in 1 Thessalonians 5:21, God will bless your ministry and use you in a mighty way. Keep a humble focus on God and your ministry will be effective.

Appendix B:

Most Frequently Asked Questions (FAQs)

◆◆◆

In responding to the following questions, depending on the direction of how the conversation was heading before these questions are asked, there will be several different responses. We often give you more than one so you can pick the one that fits best with what the person himself believes. There are no specific guides in determining which response would be the best; this knowledge comes only with experience in interacting with people of many varying belief systems.

If God is love, then why does He allow evil?
Response 1: In asking this question, you are assuming God is evil in allowing evil to continue. If this were the case, then why would God speak against evil and warn of impending judgment against those who do evil? An evil God would encourage evil, not speak against it.
Response 2: If it were not for the love and mercy of God towards Mankind, He would have destroyed Man long ago. It is Man that does evil things to Man, despite the fact that God has stated what is evil. It is much like the rebellious child of a family who is taught

better, but yet who continues to do as he wishes despite the instructions of the parents who know better. Is this then the fault of the parent, or of the child who chooses to do as he wishes?

Response 3: Is this question to imply that it is others who do evil and that our actions are excluded, or somehow are less evil than the other person's actions? The fact is, we all have done things to others that were hurtful, and the refusal to admit that perhaps our own "innocent" actions lead others to commit some action, that we may view as being of a greater evil than our own, is the result of pride. Pride is the inability to see ourselves as being just as evil as the other person. We should be thankful that God allows evil to continue because of His love and mercy, for if He did not, who of us would be left?

Response 4: What you are assuming is that God will not put an end to evil. We cannot forget that He will surely will put an end to evil one day. The question remains, when He does, will you be spared or will you feel His wrath against evil when the time comes to pass?

If God is all-powerful and can intervene, why doesn't He?
Response: For God not to allow even such horrible things to happen as murder and abuse, He would have to pronounce an end to all evil today, which would mean that many more would not be given the opportunity to receive Jesus as their Lord and Savior. It is still out of His love and mercy and long-suffering towards Mankind that He has not yet poured out His wrath upon an evil world. Still, we cannot lose focus on who it is that is evil. A lady came to us with this very question, devastated because a man she knew had killed his two-year-old daughter, leaving his wife a childless widow. If this husband had not chosen to do this evil thing, this little girl would not have been killed, and there would not be a childless widow suffering from this selfish act of evil. Once again, it is evil Man that does evil things to Man, despite the instructions God has given to Man not to do that which is evil. God's heart breaks, just like ours does, when such evil acts are committed, and we all have to suffer for the evils of Mankind. This is why God hates evil, because of the hurt it causes, and in His timing, evil will be destroyed because God is love.

If God is the creator of everything, then this would mean that God created evil, and does this not prove that God is both good and evil?

Response 1: God did not create evil; God created beings that were *capable* of evil. If created beings were not given free will to choose, this would not be an act of a loving God, but would be the act of an evil tyrant. Only a tyrant would desire his subjects to be under subjection to his will without a choice. Love does not enter into the picture of a person whose only desire is to control a person's thoughts and/or to remove the freedom to choose who he wants to be with or not to be with.

Response 2: Is this question to imply that since God is the creator of evil, He is in no position to judge what is and what is not evil, thus excusing your own sins and crying foul on the grounds that God is being unfair? This would only be true if God was both good and evil, a capricious god equaling those worshipped by the ancient Greeks. However, we must not dismiss that one can only be either completely evil or completely good. A mixture of either one discredits the other, therefore is impossible for a perfect God to be both. A coffee cup, for example, can only be a perfectly good coffee cup if it has no chinks or cracks. If it has one flaw, it no longer is a *perfectly* good coffee cup.

Response 3: This question only proves that you know what is good and what is evil. Where the problem lies is in what Man considers evil and what God considers evil. Here is the conflict. God also knows good and evil, but unlike Man, God hates evil and cannot be tempted by it because it is against His very nature. Man also knows what is good and evil, but unlike God, Man loves evil and is tempted by it because that is *his* very nature. We may know what is right and wrong, but we can never seem to *always* do what is right. It is this internal conflict of knowing what is good and what is evil and the inability to do anything about it is what makes Mankind compare himself to one another, tearing each other down in a futile attempt to make themselves appear to be less evil than others.

Response 4: This statement does not make any sense when examined closely. We see the conflict in everyday life between what we perceive as good and evil warring against one another. If God were both good and evil, He would be warring against Himself, and thus would be in the process of destroying Himself along with His creation.

What kind of free will is it when we only have two choices: we either love a God whom we hate or burn in hell? What kind of a loving God gives a choice like that?

Response 1: This very statement shows that you do have a free will, and that you are given the choice and that it appears your choice is eternal separation from a God whom you hate. An evil God would not allow a choice; He would force you to be with Him despite your protests. A loving God would not force you to spend eternity with Him since you hate Him.

Response 2: This question is to suggest God is an evil God, but on what basis? Would it not be because of what God considers evil is in conflict with what you considered evil, and this is why you hate God? For example, we can rail and protest against a society that says murder is wrong, and call the judicial system evil if we have to pay the penalty for murder which society has determined should be a just penalty. Would not this society be evil if it were to turn the other cheek and let a murderer continue to kill at will? It would be more accurate to say the murder is evil, not the judicial system. The murderer may think it unfair, but society would see it as perfectly fair.

Response 3: This is to question God's love and goodness, and is an attempt to shift blame from self to God. What is good and just is not relative. Something either is just and good or it is not. It cannot be a mixture of what one determines is just and good because everybody's concept would be different. There must be a standard by which to judge what is just and good to be compared against. If we are speaking of the Ten Commandments that we are protesting against, which one is not just or good? Since God is good and just, and He is love, why would one not love God? And if we truly did love as God loves, then we would admit that the commandments are good, because these are all things each of us wishes one would not do to us. However, this knowledge does not stop anybody from doing what is wrong in spite of what God says is right and just.

Appendix C:

Burnout and Internet Ministry

◆◆◆

As with any ministry, there is a very real possibility of burnout with an Internet ministry. It is easy to get caught up in the lives of the people online and spend more time there than is healthy. A new fad diagnosis in psychology is "Internet Addiction." We believe that, like all other things in the Christian life, there is a balance that must be found between being online and being involved in life away from the Internet.

Just as Jesus would go off to a solitary place to pray and be alone with God (Matthew 14:13, Mark 1:35, Luke 4:42) and He called His disciples to draw away from the crowds to rest (Mark 6:30-32), we believe that this is essential to the success of an Internet ministry. You will need to remember to give God the place He deserves and keep from using your talking *about* God as a replacement for your talking *to* God. Spend time with Him and in His written word. Study the word for guidance and so that you can "present yourself to God as one approved, a workman who does not need to be ashamed and who correctly handles the word of truth." (2 Timothy 2:15) This is the heart of any kind of Internet ministry, whether one to those caught up in false doctrines and cults or to those who have distorted beliefs about God and are struggling with life's problems because of it.

Here are some simple ideas to help you keep from burning out in an online ministry. We are sure that there are many more and several variations and adaptations that might work better for you as an individual. The most important thing, though, is to be aware of burnout and fortify yourself against it.

Since burnout comes from expending too much time and emotional energy in your ministry, one way to avoid it is to cultivate a life outside of your ministry. Be careful about letting your only friends be online ones. Have friends in the *real world* with whom you can go out and do activities. Do not cut everyone out of your life merely because your ministry is more of a solitary thing. This is an especially important thing to work on if you are single. Because you have more free time on your hands, you will need to keep this balance in perspective.

Another effective way of preventing burnout with an online ministry is to make sure you are solidly connected to a local church. God has given us the local church as a body of encouraging believers who will be there to spur us on to love and good deeds (Hebrews 10:24-25). It is necessary to be more than a *pew warmer* and get involved in activities so you can build strong relationships with others in the church. It is also good to have a steady source of solid biblical teaching coming in. Internet ministry is a rather draining type of ministry (well, most helping ministries really are), which makes it important to have godly input from outside sources to help nourish you (obviously the most important nourishment comes from God, but He can also fill us up through others). When you are involved in a church, you will also have a support group of believers who can keep your ministry in their prayers.

One of the things that has helped us the most in keeping from burnout is to designate at least one day as your "day off" from the ministry. At first it might seem odd to ask people to wait until the next day to talk to you, but we believe you will find this to be a useful day of relaxation that will refresh you to continue your ministry with renewed energy.

We are human beings and as such require adequate rest and food for our bodies to function correctly. If you find you are not being able to do these things because your Internet ministry is interfering, you should consider backing off for a bit and restructuring your ministry. Our bodies are the temple of God. When we care for them appropriately, we can better serve our Lord and thereby honor Him.

Appendix D:

Homefires

◆◆◆

Since the people we work with are in a needy emotional state, we felt a manual on doing Internet ministry or any type of BIBLE counseling would not be complete without a word about homefires. Anyone who is married and is working in a ministry of any kind knows that ministry can sometimes cause a strain between a husband and wife. This is especially true of an Internet ministry, which can encroach upon the household itself. If the spouse is a believer, much of this can be talked through by understanding the eternal perspective of the ministry. If the spouse is not a believer, however, the strain can become a true obstacle.

In either case, it is difficult for the spouse to sit back and watch and wait while the one he or she loves focuses on other people online. Unless there are two computers with Internet connections and the spouse is willing to be online and part of the ministry, there can be a sense of abandonment at times from a spouse who is relegated to merely sitting and watching things happen. Because of this, it is essential for the spouses to have an agreement about the limits of the ministry in their personal lives. There must be a compromise between the time spent in ministry and the time spent tending to the homefires.

For men who are doing online ministry, they need to be especially sensitive to their wives' intuition. Since the majority of the people they might talk to are women,[220] their wives might be the first to pick up on a growing improper relationship with another woman online. Good communication between husband and wife can be an excellent protection against an online affair. Wives are often much more aware of indications that another woman has feelings for her husband and will be happy to tell their husbands this if the husbands will let them. It is important, men, not to write this off as jealousy before discussing it. She might be seeing something you do not so consider her words carefully.

It is critical, though, to be aware of pure jealousy. This will most likely be prevalent in a non-Christian spouse who does not understand the eternal nature of the work you are doing, but Christian spouses are not exempt. If your husband or wife becomes jealous of the time you are spending online, you first need to evaluate whether you are being unreasonable about the amount of time you are online. Do you come home at night, gobble down supper, get online and stay there until too late to do anything but go to bed? Do you do your ministry every night or do you take nights off to be with your family? First look at this objectively for yourself, then talk to your spouse about his or her feelings. If you believe you are not spending an inordinate amount of time online, then you might want to ask your spouse if there is not something else behind the feelings he or she is having. Perhaps taking one night off and devoting it to your spouse by going out with him or her on a date might be a good thing to do.

It could be that your spouse is insecure in his or her place in your life. Check your own self first for any way you might be giving him or her this impression. If you are honest with yourself before God, He will reveal to you whether this is true or not. Insecurity in a spouse can be based on their own faulty beliefs about God and about what love is. It also might be rooted in a selfish desire to be more important in your life than what you are doing for God. Again, this is a faulty belief about God and marriage. In cases like this, remind your spouse that God's work is very important and that He must be given pre-eminence in our lives even over and above our spouses and families.

There is a balance that must be kept between families and God's work, however, that keeps in mind the responsibility God has given you in the marriage relationship. This is why some are mistaken in thinking Paul appears to be against marriage in verses such as 1 Corinthians 7:32-35. He understood that marriage gives us many blessings, but also adds to our responsibilities and therefore reduces the time we can be devoted to God's work. A wise minister for the Lord will work to keep this balance between his responsibility to the Lord's work and the responsibility to his family. And a wise spouse will see how the Lord is using their husband or wife and praise the Lord for allowing them to be able to support them in this kind of ministry.

Appendix E:

A Wife's Letter to Her Husband on Pornography

◆◆◆

This is a true story of the devastation pornography can have on a relationship. These events did actually happen, although the man this was addressed to denies it all. This letter was not written to hurt him or as a vendetta, but to show others that what society considers as "harmless," can in reality be dangerous in the end.

To My Dear Husband,

I'm sitting here watching you pack, too numb to cry, too sad to feel. How did we come to this? Why does it have to end this way?

I saw it coming, I guess, but thought if I pretended like it wasn't true, then it wouldn't really be. I don't even remember what was the first thing that began this rollercoaster of a marriage because I was trying so hard to play the ostrich, hoping the problem would go away.

I remember when I opened up our phone bill that once and saw $1000 staring at me, all made to 900 numbers. I confronted you with this and you repented, asking me to put a 900 block on the phone to help you with your self-control. I did, feeling as if I had locked away the alcohol from an alcoholic — until the next phone bill was $600, filled with calls to international numbers still for the purpose of phone sex, but that by-passed the 900 block. I felt like such a failure.

Obviously I was not enough of a woman to keep you from wanting these other women...or so I thought. I didn't know that this addiction had control of you, that it was the ruler of your behavior. All I could wonder was how far would your addiction drive you? And what would be left of us when it was through with you?

So, to counter the newest phone problem, I had the phone company do an international block on our phone. Finally, the problem seemed solved for a long time. I thought.

I was dusting the bookcases by the television one day and I found your stock of porn movies, all with obviously sexual titles. Again, when I confronted you with them, you told me you were merely intrigued and you were taking them back that day. I wanted to believe you, hoping that this was an isolated case. How gullible I was!

The next time I found them, I thought, maybe the reason he is so into these is because I'm not doing something right in bed. Maybe if I watch them, I could find out what I needed to change, how I needed to improve, how I could be so enticing to my husband that he had no need for outside stimulation. With a trembling hand, I put the first one in the VCR. I remember very clearly when you came home and found me trying to figure out what you saw in this poorly acted and loveless video. You scolded me profusely and told me that you were shocked that I would do something like that. I could never understand why it was okay for you to watch but not something you thought I should be watching.

Later that week, as we were making love, you put the video in the VCR in the bedroom and told me to watch it with you. That began the routine that would tear us apart. From then on, my body was never enough to excite you. You rarely touched me, caressed me, kissed me.

Sex became centered around you and your pleasure. I did all I could to make it enjoyable for you, but you still couldn't be aroused without first watching unrealistic bodies performing unrealistic acts, totally devoid of love and commitment.

Our lovemaking sessions became fewer and your time alone watching the movies became your obsession. Instead of enjoying my body anymore, you wanted to just watch me pleasure myself, or to just listen from another room instead of participate in loving your wife, playing the role of voyeur and reducing me to the same kind of whore you watched on your daily videos. Soon, even that wasn't enough so you added adult toys and then the fantasizing started.

I'm sure you had been fantasizing in your mind for a long time, but now it was becoming verbal and you concocted stories, fantasy stories, where you watched another man having sex with me. Now, in our marriage bed, there were three people, only in fantasy, yes, but as for me, it might as well have been as real. I felt as if you were wanting another man to come in and rape your wife in front of you in order to arouse you. I started getting scared that you would bring someone home to make that happen.

I remember the night that friend of yours came home with you and you let him stay upstairs in the spare bedroom. All night long I lay awake, afraid if I slept, I'd wake up to an unwanted threesome. You swore up and down that you would never ask me to do such a thing, but our lovemaking was increasingly bathed in fantasies of other men in bed with us, and I felt like you'd rather make love to anyone other than me.

You asked me what I fantasized about and seemed disappointed when I said that you were the only man I had ever been with and ever wanted to be with. I wanted you more than anything. Finally, in order to please you, my husband, I would lie about my fantasies, tell you that there were other men I had thought about, dreamed about. I hated every minute of it!

Your addiction was now beginning to effect our times outside of the bedroom. We would argue more and more and you would call me bitch and slut and call me ugly and fat. You even pushed me a few times. You threw things at me. I could never do anything right. And you didn't want to kiss me because I repulsed you. I just wanted to love you!

And then IT happened. You brought home an Internet account, under the guise of a present for me, and the end began. It wasn't long before I discovered your real purpose for getting the Internet in our home. I found seven responses to personal ads in our e-mail sent mail box. You told these women that you thought they were beautiful, sexy, luscious. All the words you used to use for me when we first married. You told them you were single. You even told them that you were bi-sexual. My heart shattered to pieces!

The websites you were visiting were becoming more and more degenerate until you confessed to me about finding a snuff site, where you could see pictures of someone killing someone while having sex with them. How utterly awful!!

I was terrified by this time! I was scared to sleep, this time not afraid of being raped, but afraid that I might never wake up again. I'd wait until you were asleep and then I'd sneak out to the couch and sleep a couple of hours before I had to get up and go to work.

Meanwhile, you were so engrossed in adult chat rooms and porn sites, that you wouldn't get a job and every day I saw us go further and further in debt. I would go to work in the morning, and you would sit at home amidst dirty dishes, messy rooms, dirty clothes and when I came home at night, you would greet me with, "What's for supper?" — still sitting in the middle of a dirty house, untouched in anyway. I quickly fixed the supper and then I left for my second job, always asking you if you would like to come and help me clean the offices. The response was always the same. No.

I would come home late and crawl into bed, so tired I could barely walk...and then early the next morning the same hell on earth would start again, over and over, until my body gave out on me and I had to quit my second job. You got mad at me, telling me that I was always sick.

Then one night I came home from work and found that our telephone had been cut off. I was livid. I had no idea how far behind we were in our payments because it dawned on me that I hadn't seen a bill for a couple of months. The day after work I stopped at the telephone office to find out how much we owed and how we could get it turned back on. Since we only have local service on our phone (you remember, I took all long distance off because you were calling your "family" and talking for hours and we couldn't afford the bills) so I didn't think it would be for more than $150.

Imagine my surprise when I found out we owed over $600!! When I asked for a printout of the bill, I hesitated to look at it. I knew what the calls were but I couldn't figure out how you had them charged to our phone! And then I saw it. Collect calls from all over the United States. It was easy to put together what had happened. You had talked to women in the adult chat rooms and you had them calling you collect!!

I asked you to leave. We said we needed to separate so you sold our tools, our couch and our tv set to get enough money for the train and an apartment. I loved you so much, but I knew we couldn't be together. We both cried on the way to the train station, but how could we continue the way they were? Two nights later, on our second anniversary, you called our neighbor collect and asked him to get me on the phone. You begged to come back, saying you had all your money stolen and you loved me so much that you couldn't stand to live without me. I let you come back.

That was seven months ago but things haven't changed at all...at least, not for the better. You came home, determined to beat your addiction, but it was not to be beaten down. You asked me to change the password to the Internet so you couldn't be online when I wasn't here and I agreed. It worked for a month or so, but then one morning at six you woke me up, ordering me to let you online. I refused since I didn't have to be up for another hour, and I knew what you would be doing while I lay there sleeping. You first began by threatening to erase the hard drive of the computer if I didn't let you on right then and then you turned to threatening me. You told me that if I didn't let you on, you could "take care" of me and no one would ever find me because you'd use boric acid to dissolve all the evidence away. Terrified, I typed in the password, twice, because the first time I typed it wrong, my fingers were so shaky.

I went to work that day, feeling so very hollow inside, wondering if I wouldn't be better off dead than to go home again. You pleaded and begged for me to come home and to forgive you. And again, I did. I loved you so!

Soon after, you went to visit your dad and came back telling me that you had a job offer there, far away from here. You then continued on to tell me that you couldn't live like I wanted you to live and how mismatched we were. I was stunned. When it sunk in what you were telling me, I became bitter and angry. I couldn't help but wonder if a woman from the Internet was tempting you away from me, although you always said no. I lashed back at you the only way I could, verbally. You came at me and hit me for the first — and last — time.

And here I sit, watching you pack, too numb to cry, too sad to feel. I have always loved you. I will always love you. You were my forever love. But your addiction is too much for me to live with. Good-bye, my husband, the man I vowed to keep myself for, to honor, to cherish and love forever. May God some day set you free.

Your Wife

An Update from the Wife

This letter was written over two and a half years ago and it still makes me cry when I read it. Many women who are presently being abused can relate to what I went through. My (now ex) husband was not normally a violent person, but when he spent time looking at pornographic images and chatting in adult chat rooms, his treatment of me was much more violent. There are so many other events that took place that were violent in nature, from his holding a meat fork to my throat to almost breaking my nose by pinning me down on the bed by pushing his angered face against mine.

I chose to be transparent by opening up this letter to others because I believe people needed to see the effects of pornography close up, but it has often had painful backlashes. I am amazed at how people seem to look for ways to hurt other people.

But I am still allowing this to be printed here for two reasons: to give hope to the hundreds of women who read it who are married to a man with such an addiction so they can see that they are not alone and to show men who read it that what they consider "harmless" viewing is the start of something very dangerous.

Women, if your husband is into porn, there are some truths you need to know. It has nothing to do with your body. If a husband truly loves his wife as the Bible says he should, then it is this love that will excite him when he sees her body. Many husbands are quick to quote verses where the wife is to be in submission to him, but they rarely quote verses that tell how the husband is to love the wife by giving himself up for her. Pornography is an unacceptable breaking of the marriage covenant. Jesus said that if a man looks on a woman with lust in his heart, he has committed adultery.

Please don't think the situation is hopeless, but take it seriously from the start. If there are signs of this type of behavior before you marry, reconsider. He is not going to change, no matter how much you love him. The *only* thing that can change him is a dynamic, living relationship with the God who created him. Don't settle for his promises of change on his own because it's not going to happen.

The best thing is one woman, one man, for life, nothing else added but a relationship with Jesus Christ.

Appendix F:

Helpful Links

◆◆◆

The following is a collection of links we have found helpful in building our online ministry. These range from the technical aspects of web building for the novice to opportunities for ministry. As of this writing all of these links are valid, however, the very nature of the Internet (which grows quickly) and books (which grow slowly) means that they may not be valid at the time you are reading this. It is almost certain that at least one or two of them may not work.

Also, this is not meant to be a definitive list. We are merely giving you a place to start if you are new to the online world. If you are comfortable with search engines, you will easily be able to find more, and probably even more helpful, sites on your own. When we started, we were both fairly new at the Internet (Doug had been online for six months and Deb had been on for only three months). We had to do some initial searching as to how to create a website, but there is much information on this if you are willing to look. Neither of us had any training in website creation. Now there are many freebie places to host your own website and they are quite helpful to novices. We have also listed resources for those who already know HTML and would like to have more control over how the content on your website is displayed.

Ministry tools and online resources are important as well. You will often come across those who have no immediate access to a Bible so having these URLs at your fingertips will be important to your ministry.

Webmaster Sites

http://www.thefreesite.com/   The Free Site

This is an excellent site for finding freebies in many different areas. The items we have connected to off of this site have been invaluable for both the basic building of our website and adding enhancements as we grew. They are adding to this collection all the time so it's good to check back often.

http://www.cbx2.net/index2.html   Christian Banner eXchange

A free way to advertise your site is to join a banner exchange program. You put other banners on your site in exchange for your banner being put on other people's sites. The only drawback with this is that you cannot control the content of the banners displayed on your site. This can be dangerous with a secular group because they sometimes do not have a conscience about whose advertisements they accept. We found this Christian banner exchange that requires those involved to agree to a specific statement of faith and code of conduct.

http://Free2Try.com/   Free2 Try

This site has many free things and trial offers. They cover a variety of subjects.

http://www.webreference.com/   Web Reference

This site has some very good free resources for webmasters to build your site, including links to JavaScript, Perl, and DHTML free scripts to cut and paste. They are even customized so you only have to put in the specific information you want to see and it will provide the custom script for you to cut and paste on your own website.

http://www.webposition.com/   Web Position

The key to a successful website is the traffic that sees it. This is a program that can help you increase your traffic by enhancing your META tags and other tips and resources that can boost your ratings on the main search engines. This site will give you a free trial version of it so you can see if it will be helpful to you.

http://www.thepromoter.com/   The Promoter

This service offers to promote your website by submitting it to several search engines. We've included this, but are not sure that the service is worth the results. The search engines are rather small and obscure and you will receive a *ton* of e-mail as a result of it. It also requires that you have their banner at the top of the page you submit.

http://www.gifwizard.com   GIF Wizard

If your page does not load in less than ten seconds, you will lose your viewer. Isn't that incredible? Our attention spans have certainly become short. Whether we like it or not, this is true. If there are too many graphics on the page, the viewer will lose interest and move on before the page is completely loaded. One way to prevent this is to use this GIF Wizard to help you reduce the size (and therefore downloading time) of the graphics on your page. This is a free online tool that examines the graphics on your page and gives you a summary of which ones need to be reduced. You decide if you want to have this program reduce them or not.

http://www.zdnet.com/downloads/   ZDNet Software Library

If you've been around the Internet very long, you will be familiar with the many downloads offered at ZDNet. Here you will find freeware, shareware and demos you can try out and use. There are many different types of programs including games and web building.

http://www.angelfire.com/   Angelfire Communications

This is where we started our website. The tools they have available have come a long way from when we first hosted ours there, and it has become much more user friendly. Unfortunately, a pornography site bought the URL http://www.anglefire.com (a transposition of the E and the L) and if someone mistypes your homepage address, they will be taken into a porn site. This was one of the motivating factors that resulted in us purchasing our own domain.

Ministry Helps and Opportunities

http://www.excite.com   Excite

This is a major site that has chat rooms, message boards, search engines and much more.

http://www.yahoo.com Yahoo

Here we have one of the largest sites online with groups, chat rooms, message boards and many other opportunities for ministry. It also has a good index that can help you find various sites and tools online.

http://www.crosswalk.com Crosswalk

This is a Christian site that has many of the same features of Excite and Yahoo, but from a Christian perspective. There are also devotionals you can sign up for and Bible study tools to use (the NIV is not included on this site).

http://Bible.gospelcom.net/ Bible Gateway

Here you can search the Bible (including the NIV version), read daily devotions and get a chuckle out of ReverendFun. You can also search for other Christian ministries.

Exposing False Teachings

http://www.letusreason.org Let Us Reason Ministries

This website will give you some of the best information out there for working with people caught up in false teachings. They have a large amount of articles on the word faith movement and other pseudo-Christian cultic teachings. This is our personal favorite.

http://www.equip.org Christian Research Institute

There are several articles and other aids to help you find pertinent information about various cults. You can also listen to audio of Hank Hanegraaff as the "Bible Answer Man."

http://www.watchman.org Watchman Fellowship

On this site you can find an extensive listing of cults, both common and obscure. (Their index lists over 1200 religious organizations and beliefs.) There are articles and other information as well.

Appendix G:

Recommended Reading List

◆◆◆

The following is a list of recommended reading. Although we might not agree in all points with all of these works, we believe that reading them can be beneficial to your study of the issues we have raised throughout this book.

Adams, Jay E., *Solving Marriage Problems: Biblical Solutions for Christian Counselors* (Grand Rapids: Zondervan Publishing House, 1983).

_____. *The Christian Counselor's Manual* (Grand Rapids: Zondervan Publishing House, 1973.

_____. *Competent to Counsel* (Grand Rapids: Zondervan Publishing House, 1970).

_____. *A Theology of Christian Counseling* (Grand Rapids: Zondervan Publishing House, 1979).

_____. *How to Help People Change* (Grand Rapids: Zondervan Publishing House, 1986).

Almy, Gary L., M.D., *How Christian Is Christian Counseling?* (Wheaton, Illinois: Crossway Books, 2000).

Almy, Gary and Carol Tharp Almy with Jerry Jenkins, *Addicted to Recovery* (Arlington Heights, Illinois: Christian Liberty Press, 1994).

Anderson, Barbara S., *The Counselor and the Law* (Alexandria, Virginia: American Counseling Association, 1996).

Ankerberg, John and John Weldon, *Encyclopedia of Cults and New Religions* (Eugene, Oregon: Harvest House Publishers, 1999).

_____. *Creation vs. Evolution: What You Need to Know* (Eugene, Oregon: Harvest House Publishers, 1998).

_____. *The Facts on Roman Catholicism* (Eugene, Oregon: Harvest House Publishers, 1993.

_____. *The Facts on the Faith Movement* (Eugene, Oregon: Harvest House Publishers, 1993).

Bobgan, Martin and Deidre, *James Dobson's Gospel of Self-Esteem and Psychology* (Santa Barbara, California: EastGate Publishers, 1998).

_____. *Competent to Minister* (Santa Barbara, California: EastGate Publishers, 1996).

_____. *PsychoHeresy: The Psychological Seduction of Christianity* (Santa Barbara, California: EastGate Publishers, 1987).

Bulkley, Ed, Ph.D., *Why Christians Can't Trust Psychology* (Eugene, Oregon: Harvest House Publishers, 1993).

Bullis, Ronald K. and Cynthia S. Mazur, *Legal Issues and*

Religious Counseling (Louisville: Westminster/John Knox Press, 1993).

Carlson, Ron and Ed Decker, *Fast Facts on False Teachings* (Eugene, Oregon: Harvest House Publishers, 1994).

Christianity, Cults and Religions (Torrance, California: Rose Publishing, 1996); pamphlet.

Copan, Paul, *True for You, But Not for Me* (Minneapolis: Bethany House Publishers, 1998).

Cory, Steven, comp., *The Spirit of Truth and the Spirit of Error*, vol. 1 and 2 (Chicago: Moody Press, 1986).

Decker, Ed, *Mormonism: What You Need to Know* (Eugene, Oregon: Harvest House Publishers, 1997).

Enns, Paul, *The Moody Handbook of Theology*, (Chicago: Moody Press 1989).

Ganz, Richard, *PsychoBabble: The Failure of Modern Psychology — and the Biblical Alternative* (Wheaton, Illinois: Crossway Books, 1993).

George, Bob, *Growing in Grace with Study Guide* (Eugene, Oregon: Harvest House Publishers, 1991).

_____. *How to Experience Victory over Depression: A Biblical Approach to Emotional Conflicts* (Dallas: People to People, 1982, rev. 1992).

Hanegraaff, Hank, *The Face That Demonstrates the Farce of Evolution* (Nashville: Word Publishing, 1998).

_____. *Christianity in Crisis with Study Guide* (Eugene, Oregon: Harvest House Publishers, 1997).

_____. *Christianity in Crisis* (Eugene, Oregon: Harvest House Publishers, 1993); audiobook.

Hines, William L., *Leaving Yesterday Behind: A Victim No More* (Geanies House, Fearn, Ross-shire, Great Britain: Christian Focus Publications, 1997).

Hunt, Dave, *Occult Invasion: The Subtle Seduction of the World and Church* (Eugene, Oregon: Harvest House Publishers, 1998).

_____. *A Woman Rides the Beast* (Eugene, Oregon: Harvest House Publishers, 1994).

Kruis, John G., *Quick Scripture Reference for Counseling* (Grand Rapids: Baker Books, 1994).

LaHaye, Tim, *Bible Prophecy: What You Need to Know* (Eugene, Oregon: Harvest House Publishers, 1997).

Mack, Wayne A., *Your Family God's Way* (Phillipsburg, New Jersey: Presbyterian and Reformed Publishing Company, 1991).

MacArthur, John F., Jr. and Wayne A. Mack with The Master's College Faculty, *Introduction to Biblical Counseling* (Dallas: Word Publishing, 1994).

Martin, Walter Ralston, Hank H. Hanegraaff, ed., *The Kingdom of the Cults* (Minneapolis: Bethany House, 1997).

Matzat, Don, *Christ-Esteem* (Eugene, Oregon: Harvest House Publishers, 1990).

McDowell, Josh, *The Best of Josh McDowell: A Ready Defense*, comp. Bill Wilson (Nashville: Thomas Nelson Publishers, 1993).

McDowell, Josh and Bob Hostetler, *The New Tolerance: How a Cultural Movement Threatens to Destroy You, Your Faith, and Your*

Children (Wheaton, Illinois: Tyndale House Publishers, 1998).

McDowell, Josh and Don Stewart, *Answers to Tough Questions Skeptics Ask About the Christian Faith* (San Bernadino, California: Here's Life Publishers, 1980).

_____. *Handbook of Today's Religions: Understanding the Occult* (San Bernadino, California: Here's Life Publishers, 1982).

Means, Pat, *The Mystical Maze* (n.p.: Campus Crusade for Life, Inc., 1976).

PsychoHeresy Awareness Ministries, comp., *Neil Anderson Warning Package* (Santa Barbara, California: PsychoHeresy Awareness Ministries, n.d.).

Rhodes, Ron, *The Complete Book of Bible Answers* (Eugene, Oregon: Harvest House Publishers, 1997).

Rhodes, Ron and Marian Bodine, *Reasoning from the Scriptures* (Eugene, Oregon: Harvest House Publishers, 1995).

Taylor, Paul S., *The Illustrated Origins Answer Book* (n.p.: Eden Communications, Films for Christ Assn., 1995)

Thurman, Dr. Chris, *Self-Help or Self-Destruction* (Nashville, Thomas Nelson Publishers: 1996).

Tripp, Paul David, *Age of Opportunity: A Biblical Guide to Parenting Teens* (Phillipsburg, New Jersey: Presbyterian and Reformed Publishing Company, 1997).

Walters, Wesley P., *New Light on Joseph Smith's First Vision* (Grand Rapids: Gospel Truths Ministries, 1996); pamphlet.

Appendix H:

Record Keeping

◆◆◆

Depending on how you utilize your BIBLE counseling skills, you will need to keep adequate records for what your ministry is. If you are doing a ministry that is structured like a regular counselor, you might want to have the person you are counseling fill out a form to give you a quick overview of their background, family structure, and their perception of the problem. If you desire to have a prototype like this to follow, you can find examples in Dr. Jay Adams' *The Christian Counselors Manuel* and in *Introduction to Biblical Counseling* by the Master's College Faculty, both of which we have included in our recommended reading list.

In the type of ministry we do, however, we do not have the ability to use a tool like this. Actually, we believe that, although the questions are valid to ask, they are again more behavior-oriented than they need to be. For us it is much more advantageous to actually ask the person the questions than to merely read something they have written down. This also gives us more of an opportunity to inquire about the person's understanding of who God is. The PDI (Personal Data Inventory), as it is called, is a carry-over from secular psychology. We believe it causes a distancing of the counselor from the "client" and enhances a sense of aloofness from the person to whom you are talking.

Items like this are considered by some to be integral and necessary parts of the counseling process, and if you feel more comfortable with using them, then it is your prerogative. It is our opinion, though, that it and the practice of charging for services appear to model the secular community more so than what the Bible gives us. Jesus did not require PDIs from the disciples before He would work with them. Whether you choose to use the PDI or not is up to you and how your ministry is structured, but we have chosen not to use these types of things in our ministry.

Because our ministry is online, we have slightly different record keeping needs than a ministry running out of a local church, staffed by laypersons. But no matter how your ministry is set up, you will still need to keep basic information about the people with whom you work. You need to keep information about what was discussed in your meetings with that person, at least to some degree. The notes do not have to chronicle every word spoken between you, but should give a good overview so the line of counseling can be seen. This is also to help aid you in remembering what you talked about with each person. At the beginning, it is easy to remember the problems of those you talk to, but as your ministry grows, you will need these notes to jog your memory and to remind you of homework assignments you might have given the person.

Also, if there is a situation where you are required to break confidentiality (see Appendix I for more on this subject), you will need to have documented why you chose to do this and what steps you took. This will be important for you to do so you can have proof of your responsible actions.

If your church is going to make the counseling ministry a sub-ministry of the church itself, the notes you will be required to keep will no doubt be much more extensive than if you are doing this independently on a friendship basis. The structure of such a ministry will be subject to the elders of your church and record keeping will be an essential detail you will want to discuss in depth. In setting up this type of ministry, you will most likely need to consult a lawyer for the particulars in your state. Your state may have specific guidelines that you will have to follow.

In an Internet ministry such as ours, the most important records we keep are how to contact the person via e-mail or their Yahoo! Chat ID. If you are doing Internet ministry, you will soon recognize how vital it is to write this information down meticulously. As the facts of their family and their lives unfold, you can write this information down with the other.

However you choose to keep records of what has been discussed and with whom, one thing is essential. You must make certain that the records are kept confidential. It would not do for your son to be playing around your computer and read through your notebook on the people you counsel. Notes should be securely locked away from others so you can assure those you are counseling that you respect their privacy. Again, we will deal more with this subject in Appendix I.

The main things to remember in regards to keeping records are that you need to have documentation of how you have helped any specific person in the past and what issues you have discussed.

Appendix I:

Confidentiality, 911 and Other Legalities

◆◆◆

These are important issues to make decisions on before you are forced to. Each of these matters requires careful, thoughtful contemplation and a written explanation of your view of them for those with whom you counsel if you are setting up a counseling ministry.

Confidentiality

Here is a copy of our confidentiality statement that we developed for OAIM. It is available on our website.

OAIM knows that when you come to us with your problems, you are trusting us with a very important part of your heart. We, as those who minister in this work of biblical counseling, want to be faithful to you in this respect. To this end, we have set down these guidelines within which we expect our counselors to work.

Because of the nature of the Internet and our counselors being on a volunteer basis, we cannot guarantee that the counselor you wish to talk to will be available at the time you need to talk. In order to serve you better, we do not wish to limit you to talking to only one specific counselor. However, please understand that if you are being counseled by more than one counselor, the counselors will be free to discuss between themselves the counsel they are giving you so they can work together for your best interests. This will ensure the highest quality of counseling for you. We do strongly suggest, though, that you try staying with one counselor as much as possible. We believe this helps to build a stronger counseling relationship between the two of you.

The counseling staff at OAIM works together as a team. In some instances, it may become necessary for a counselor to ask for guidance from another counselor in a situation where they feel as if they do not know how to proceed. But please understand that the information shared will remain only between the counselors and cits (counselors in training). The counselors will not go to other sources for help in working with someone.

At times it may appear to the counselors that there is a serious concern for either your own life or the life of others. If we believe there is a very real danger to human life, we are obligated, both by God above and by the state, to do our best to provide services that will protect human life. This may entail calling a nearby pastor, counselor, or law enforcement official. Rest assured that we do this out of our deep concern for you and will never do this for any other reason.

We ask you to understand the limitations of the Internet in regards to privacy. We do keep transcripts of the Monday and Friday chat rooms and often retain transcripts of counseling sessions (through chat, ICQ and Messenger, as well as e-mails), but again, these are archived for the counselor's use only (we counsel many people and it can often help to reread the last conversation before the next counseling session). However, we cannot guarantee that hackers do not hack in on conversations. As far as we are concerned, we protect the conversations with you as much as it is in our power. Please be careful about the archiving features of ICQ, Yahoo! Messenger and other such instant message programs. These often hold messages until they are manually deleted, and some even require them to be deleted from two separate locations.

In the case of a counselor being accused of improper behavior, correspondence and counseling transcripts may be subject to review by the other counselors and cits in order to determine the truth of the situation. Once again, please be assured that these materials will remain only among our counselors and cits unless legal situations or persistent false accusations require us to reveal them.

If you have any concerns regarding this policy, please let us know. Also, if you believe that there has been a breach of confidence by one of our counselors or cits, please inform us at oaim@oaim.org. Such matters are brought before the board of counselors and will be decided following biblical guidelines as stated here. We do not tolerate our counselors to be lax in this area and we see it as a grave offense.

Let us all work together to glorify the God who loves us so!

Confidentiality and 911

All counseling ministries have one common possibility for potential lawsuits: the confidentiality issue and a breach thereof. Having experienced a pastor's breach of confidence myself (Deb), I know the distress it can cause to a person who is already in an emotionally delicate state. For me it was a pastor who shared what I had said (in confidence) with his wife, who in turn decided to tell others in the church. The result was for my very close-knit family to be broken apart and scattered to various churches, and for me to be forced to find another church to attend.

Pastoral counseling, however, should not have results such as this. The trust a counselee has for a counselor can be quickly lost yet can take a very long time to be rebuilt. A counselor needs to keep this thought at the forefront of his mind. Most people who are being counseled have difficulty trusting others in the first place. Before speaking anything to another person, even a spouse, a counselor needs to consider this carefully. Some counselees will feel betrayed even knowing that the counselor has talked over these problems with a spouse or with another counselor.

A policy upfront, much as the one included above, that specifies who the counselor may confer with for help in working with someone can give both and assurance to the counselee and a standard policy of limitation for the counselor.

Making the Call

If one works with depressed or suicidal people, there will come a time when calling 911 will be deemed necessary. The majority of the women we work with online consider themselves depressed and often suicidal (the number one FAQ — frequently asked question — we get is, "If a Christian commits suicide, will they still go to heaven?"). It has been our experience, however, that most who come online talking about suicide are really merely hoping that someone will give them the answers that will stop the pain they are feeling. Someone who is truly suicidal does not usually sit at a computer typing out their feelings just in order to be with others.

Some suicidal threats are for attention and others are very real. It can be difficult for us as Internet counselors to determine which is which because we do not have as many clues as someone who is face to face with that person in a pastor's study or counseling office. There are ways, however, of seeing subtle changes in typing and wording that can tell how serious a person is.

When it comes down to someone we really believe is serious about killing themselves, we have made phone calls to 911 to ask for their help. Sometimes a welfare check (when the police stop in and see if things are okay) can be enough. At other times, there is a need to contact someone in the area (a local pastor or biblical counselor) to take over where we are limited. If you do Internet ministry, it would be good to make yourself familiar with how to find local police numbers and women's shelters if you need them.

In calling 911, we must be clear and precise about our situation, who we are and why we suspect someone is in danger, whether it be the person themselves or someone they intend to harm. Normally we try to contact the local police where the person lives, but if there is an extreme emergency, we have found most 911 services are willing to help out in long distance cases.

The saddest cases for us are those who come into our rooms once and we never see them again. We do not know if they actually went through with what they had planned or if what we said made a difference in their lives. In such circumstances, we can only trust in the loving hands of a good God. When we can, we try to make contact, but for some, we have no way of finding them. Some chat rooms are helpful to give out important information if there is a serious threat of suicide. The best you can do is be prepared and do all you can, and remember that God is in ultimate control.

Legalities

If you are going to take your counseling to a ministry level, you will need to investigate the legalities for it in your particular state. Each state has different regulations regarding religious counseling and it is important for you to know what rules govern your individual situation. Some states regulate what terms you can use and who can do religious counseling. It is better to be aware of where your state stands *before* any problems arise.

Appendix J:

How to Lead Someone to Christ

❖❖❖

The two extremes that must be avoided when leading one to Christ are an emphasis on sin that is void of grace or the emphasis on grace that avoids the consequences of sin. Both of these extremes will prevent people from seeing their total hopelessness of being lost in their sins and prevent them from obtaining the knowledge of the awesome grace of God.

If they do not see their total inability to purge themselves of their own sins, they will fall into a legalistic gospel. If they do not see their sins as serious, they will fall into a liberal gospel. Neither of these positions will lead to eternal life through Christ Jesus.

Strange as it may seem, the most legalistic churches (the ones that place the emphasis on purging themselves of their sins) have not seen the total ugliness of their sins or the grace of God. Their pride holds them back from seeing that the Bible says that all of our works of righteousness are as filthy rags (Isaiah 64:6), that all have sinned and that the wages of sin is death. (Romans 3:23 and 6:23) This is a finality: *all* have sinned and *nobody* will escape the penalty.

Another way of saying this is we are all walking dead men, dead in our trespasses. To have eternal death all one has to do is nothing because we are already dead in our sins. God already pronounced the death penalty on sin and nothing can be done about that. The only thing man can do is to be forgiven of sins and to be given eternal life as a free gift. This body is not eternal because in this body we have sinned, and it will die along with the corrupt nature. That is, the corrupt nature cannot be changed, altered or saved. It is already dead. All our own avenues must be put to a complete stop; there should not be even a hint of an escape from this truth.

The legalistic view points out the sins of Man and the consequences of sin but puts a stop to it here and places very little emphasis, if any, on the grace of God. As long as there is even a hint of a possibility that one can purge his own sins by works is to circumvent the purpose and the finality of the sacrifice of Jesus for the sins of Man, robbing the person of salvation.

The other extreme is to emphasize God's grace, believing it is extended to all without having to acknowledge their sinful condition. This leads people to believe that, because of God's grace, salvation is automatic. These are the ones who "turned the grace of our God into lasciviousness." (Jude 1:4, KJV) They are aware of the grace of God, but they never turn to the Lord Jesus for forgiveness of their sins. This would be the liberal gospel being taught in churches today.

The balance between these two extremes must be maintained. We need to show the finality of sin, even one sin, then the total hopelessness of their condition and the futility of trying to earn their own salvation by their own works. Only then will they see how wonderful and awesome God's grace is. When we serve God out of legalism, we serve out of fear of losing our salvation. When we serve from the standpoint of grace, we serve out of love and gratitude that produces good fruit.

Man's sinfulness

"As it is written, There is none righteous, no, not one: There is none that understandeth, there is none that seeketh after God. They are all gone out of the way, they are together become unprofitable; there is none that doeth good, no, not one." (Romans 3:10-12, KJV)

"But we are all as an unclean thing, and all our righteousnesses are as filthy rags; and we all do fade as a leaf; and our iniquities, like the wind, have taken us away." (Isaiah 64:6, KJV)

"For all have sinned, and come short of the glory of God." (Romans 3:23, KJV)

"Wherefore, as by one man sin entered into the world, and death by sin; and so death passed upon all men, for that all have sinned." (Romans 5:12, KJV)

"For the wages of sin is death." (Romans 6:23, KJV)

"And you, being dead in your sins." (Colossians 2:13, KJV)

"I said therefore unto you, that ye shall die in your sins." (John 8:24, KJV)

God's Solution

"But God commendeth his love toward us, in that, while we were yet sinners, Christ died for us." (Romans 5:8, KJV)

"For God so loved the world, that he gave his only begotten Son, that whosoever believeth in him should not perish, but have everlasting life. For God sent not his Son into the world to condemn the world; but that the world through him might be saved." (John 3:16-17, KJV)

"The gift of God is eternal life through Jesus Christ our Lord." (Romans 6:23, KJV)

"For by grace are ye saved through faith; and that not of yourselves: it is the gift of God: Not of works, lest any man should boast." (Ephesians 2:8-9)

We do not believe in having a formulated prayer for one to follow. After showing them from the scriptures of our lost condition and God's simple plan of salvation, this is the time to let the Holy Spirit convict them and simply ask if they understand it. If they say yes, then ask who Jesus is and have them answer.

Jesus simply asked Simon Peter, "Who do you say I am?" and Peter responded, "You are the Christ, the Son of the living God." (Matthew 16:16, NIV). It was this confession that the Father revealed to Peter and upon which the church was built.

We have to remember that all we do is present the gospel message and let the Holy Spirit do the rest. We cannot make someone accept Christ unless it has been revealed to them so this also needs to just be kept simple.

"How, then, can they call on the one they have not believed in? And how can they believe in the one of whom they have not heard? And how can they hear without someone preaching to them? And how can they preach unless they are sent? As it is written, 'How beautiful are the feet of those who bring good news!'" (Romans 10:14-15, NIV)

Other passages that show the simplicity are:

Acts 16:30-31. "He then brought them out and asked, 'Sirs, what must I do to be saved?' They replied, 'Believe in the Lord Jesus, and you will be saved—you and your household.'"

1 John 4:15. "If anyone acknowledges that Jesus is the Son of God, God lives in him and he in God."

Romans 10:9 "That if you confess with your mouth, "Jesus is Lord," and believe in your heart that God raised him from the dead, you will be saved."

Romans 10:13 "Everyone who calls on the name of the Lord will be saved."

Luke 12:8 "I tell you, whoever acknowledges me before men, the Son of Man will also acknowledge him before the angels of God."

When people see themselves as they truly are, sinners who are unable to change the sentence of death that our sin has caused, and they see Jesus Christ as He truly is, God Himself who came to earth in the flesh to pay the penalty for our sins, then they come to know Jesus in a real, life-changing way. Salvation is offered to all who are willing to give up reliance on their own works for salvation to throw themselves on the finished work of Christ on the cross.

Notes

◆◆◆

1 Many of the topics in this book are far too extensive to be included in one volume such as this and still maintain our purpose of helping people understand how to apply BIBLE counseling to help others. We strongly encourage you to research for yourself the reliability of the Scriptures, and, to that end, we have included a suggested list of reading in Appendix G for this reason.

2 The National Association for Consumer Protection in Mental Health Practices Press Release, Office of the President.

3 Aristides, "What Is Vulgar?" *The American Scholar*, Winter 1981-1982, p. 21.

4 Martin and Deidre Bobgan, *PsychoHeresy: The Psychological Seduction of Christianity*, (Santa Barbara, California: EastGate Publishers, 1987), p. 164.

5 Hans J. Eysenck, "The Effects of Psychotherapy: An Evaluation," Journal of Consulting Psychology, Vol. 16, 1952, p. 322.

6 Bobgan, *PsychoHeresy*, p. 180-181

7 Sigmund Freud, *The Future of an Illusion*, Translated and edited by James Strachey. (New York: W.W. Norton and Company, Inc., 1961), p. 43.

8 Thomas Szasz. *The Myth of Psychotherapy*. (Garden City: Doubleday/Anchor Press, 1978), p. 146.

9 Carl Jung. *Wholemind Newsletter: A User's Manual to the Brain, Mind and Spirit,* vol. 1, no. 1, p. 5.

10 1 Samuel 28

11 This is speaking in the sense of God's original design of a perfect world, without troubles or diseases.

12 *Psychology Today*, June 2000, "Voting for Mental Health," by Peter Carter, p. 10.

13 *Chicago Sun-Times*, December 14, 1999, "Mental Illness Ignored," by Maureen O'Donnell, p. 1.

14 J. Jacobi, *The Psychology of C. G. Jung*, 8th ed. (New Haven: Yale University Press, 1973), p. 60.

15 The United Pentecostal Church (UPC) is the largest branch of Oneness Pentecostalism, however, you may also find churches that use the word "holiness" and "apostolic" in their names. Although not all churches that use these titles will be Oneness Pentecostals (denying the Trinity), they usually will also be caught up in the legalistic trap.

16 The Jehovah's Witnesses will also challenge the Trinity in this manner.

17 We will be discussing the problems with Anderson's theology more in-depth in a later chapter.

18 The word "holy" means to be consecrated or set apart for a special purpose. We are called to be set apart from unbelievers and consecrate ourselves to the service of God.

19 Remember that while you can make observations of the possibilities of these physical things, it will require a medical doctor to actually make any diagnosis. Your role should be to merely suggest a physical exam to the person and not to diagnose what is wrong with them.

20 In reality, very few of those who are depressed will have a medical basis for their depression as is discussed in another section.

21 Eventually I was diagnosed as having Chronic Fatigue Syndrome.

22 Dr. Gary Almy, "Witnessing to the Mentally Ill," Defend the Faith 2001 Conference put on by Families Against Cults, P.O. Box 491, Carmel, IN 46082-0491.

23 Dr. Peter R. Breggin, M.D., *The Anti-Depressant Fact Book*, (Cambridge: Perseus Publishing, 2001), p. 18.

24 Breggin, p. 32.

25 Breggin, p. 21. "In reality, science does not have the ability to measure the levels of any biochemical in the tiny spaces between nerve cells (the synapses) in the brain of a human being. All the talk

about biochemical imbalances is sheer speculation aimed at promoting psychiatric drugs."

26 Breggin, p. 37.

27 "...two court cases raised the possibility that anti-depressants had caused violent and suicidal thoughts. One case involved an elderly man who fatally stabbed his wife and himself after being on Prozac for 11 days. The man's son and daughter are suing the drug maker. The second involved a 13-year-old boy who hanged himself after being on Zoloft (a chemical cousin of Prozac) for a week." Nancy Pearcey, "Drugs on the Brain," World Magazine, October 21, 2000, p. 23.

28 Gary Greenberg, "The Serotonin Surprise," Discover Magazine, July 2001, p. 67.

29 Ibid., p. 68.

30 Dr. Breggin, p. 26. "Impairing our emotional awareness and our intellectual acuity with psychoactive drugs such as SSRI antidepressants tends to impede the process of overcoming depression."

31 Dr. Bruce H. Wilkinson, *The Testing of Your Faith,* (Atlanta: Walk Thru the Bible Ministries, Inc., 1998.). 12 part audio cassette series. This can be ordered through Walk Thru the Bible Ministries at 4201 North Peachtree Road, Atlanta, GA 30341.

32 These questions are taken from sessions 1-2 of *The Testing of Your Faith* series. These are paraphrases of most of them, but the concepts are much more expanded in Dr. Wilkinson's teachings.

33 In Matthew 11:2-5 we see John the Baptist questioning if God really did know what he was going through. Jesus' response told him that He did indeed know what he was going through and God did care.

34 The beginning of the story of Job tells us that even Satan could not touch Job without God's permission. As the Creator of all there is, God is indeed in control of all that happens in His creation.

35 This is actually the true conclusion of existentialism, that the only real act I can control and which can give me meaning is to kill myself.

36 We are very strong believers in the eternal security of the salvation of the believer. For a more detailed explanation and biblical defense of this position, please see the chapter, *The Basics of*

Christianity.

37 Dan Allender, *The Wounded Heart*, (Colorado Springs: Navpress, 1990.) p. 179. Although Dr. Allender does sometimes rely more on psychology than on the Bible, we do respect his understanding of what true love is.

38 We will use the pronoun *she* here because in our work online, we have had only one suicidal man come online for counseling. It seems to us that men will usually take action instead of talking about it beforehand. This is not, however, to minimize the depression men feel. Women attempt suicide more often than men (an estimated three females for every male), but the statistics show that men will actually go through with it almost five times more often than women. Statistics for the U.S. can be found at http://www.suicidology.org/.

39 See our chapter, *The Basics of Christianity*, to learn more about the balance of these two concepts in the creation of man, dignity vs. depravity.

40 2 Corinthians 1:3-4 "Praise be to the God and Father of our Lord Jesus Christ, the Father of compassion and the God of all comfort, who comforts us in all our troubles, so that we can comfort those in any trouble with the comfort we ourselves have received from God."

41 See Appendix B for more of an answer to this FAQ.

42 See our chapter on "The Many Faces of Pharisaism" for more on this type of pride and self-righteousness.

43 Jeremiah 29:11 "For I know the plans I have for you," declares the LORD, "plans to prosper you and not to harm you, plans to give you hope and a future." Joel 2:25 "I will repay you for the years the locusts have eaten."

44 Romans 8:28 "And we know that in all things God works for the good of those who love him, who have been called according to his purpose."

45 Dave Hunt, *Occult Invasion: The Subtle Seduction of the World and Church*, (Eugene, Oregon: Harvest House Publishers, 1998), p. 439.

46 Ibid., p. 325.

47 Ibid., p. 326, from the original by Bruce Wiseman,

"*Psychiatry, The Ultimate Betrayal* (Freedom Publishing, 1995), pp. 357-358.

48 Philippians 4:6 "Do not be anxious about anything, but in everything, by prayer and petition, with thanksgiving, present your requests to God."

49 Flora R. Schreiber, *Sybil* (New York: Warner, 1973). Please note that this account of MPD is fictional.

50 Dr. Gary Almy, *How Christian Is Christian Counseling?* (Wheaton, Illinois: Crossway Books, 2000), p. 258.

51 Also see 2 Peter 1:5-7 "For this very reason, make every effort to add to your faith goodness; and to goodness, knowledge; and to knowledge, self-control; and to self-control, perseverance; and to perseverance, godliness; and to godliness, brotherly kindness; and to brotherly kindness, love."

52 See our chapter on *Roman Catholicism*.

53 Neil Anderson, *Victory Over Darkness* (Regal Books: 1990).

54 Steven J. Cole, Pastor, "Steak and Arsenic." This is from an article included in the *Neil Anderson Warning Packet* that is put out by PsychoHeresy Awareness Ministries, 4137 Primavera Road, Santa Barbara, CA 93110.

55 J.I. Packer, *Keep In Step With the Spirit* (Old Tappan, New Jersey: Fleming H. Revell Company, 1984), p. 159.

56 Neil T. Anderson, *The Bondage Breaker* (Eugene, Oregon: Harvest House Publishers, 1993), back cover.

57 These steps are taken from *The Bondage Breaker*, pp. 188-214.

58 This is very clearly seen in a counseling session Anderson has a transcript of on pages 48-52 where the man is never once told to confess his sin. Sin, however, is explained as some exterior thing that is really to blame for his problems. He is told not to feel guilty about things because in essence it is not his fault. Biblically, the man should have been told to confess his sins and turn from what he was doing to do what was right.

59 Ibid., p. 44.
60 Ibid., p. 190.
61 Ibid.
62 Ibid., p. 191.

63 Ephesians 1:9-10 "And he made known to us the mystery of his will according to his good pleasure, which he purposed in Christ, to be put into effect when the times will have reached their fulfillment—to bring all things in heaven and on earth together under one head, even Christ."

64 For more about setting ourselves up to be little gods in the Christian context, see our chapter, *The Faith of our Fathers?*

65 Anderson, *The Bondage Breaker*, p. 239.

66 This is reminiscent of the Roman Catholic tradition of praying the rosary. Most of the prayers are prayed to Mary, except for the "Our Father," yet its purpose is to help you focus more on Jesus.

67 Anderson, *The Bondage Breaker,* p. 244.

68 Ibid., p. 199.

69 Ibid., p. 201.

70 We will be dealing more with this in our chapter entitled, *The Great Addiction.*

71 For more on the word faith movement, see our chapter, *The Faith of Our Fathers?.*

72 Anderson, *The Bondage Breaker*, p. 64.

73 Steven Fernandez, "The Deliverance Model of Spiritual Warfare," *Reformation & Revival Journal*, p. 90, as seen in the *Neil Anderson Warning Packet* by PsychoHeresy Awareness Ministries.

74 Merrill F. Unger, *What Demons Can Do To Saints* (Chicago: Moody Press, 1991), p. 60.

75 1 Corinthians 6:19 "Do you not know that your body is a temple of the Holy Spirit, who is in you, whom you have received from God? You are not your own."

76 PsychoHeresy Awareness, "Memorandum: Reflections on the Freedom in Christ Seminar," June 24, 1992, *Neil Anderson Warning Package*, p. 12.

77 Ibid., p. 6.

78 Please note here that the evil spirit found the house "unoccupied." This indicates the person referred to never accepted Christ. Otherwise, the house would be occupied by the Holy Spirit.

79 Neil Anderson is one who made such statements in his earlier works. Since then he has taken a stance that people should not talk to demons to get information from them, but his ministry is

based on what he "learned" from the demons.

80 John 16:7-11 "But I tell you the truth: It is for your good that I am going away. Unless I go away, the Counselor will not come to you; but if I go, I will send him to you. When he comes, he will convict the world of guilt in regard to sin and righteousness and judgment: in regard to sin, because men do not believe in me; in regard to righteousness, because I am going to the Father, where you can see me no longer; and in regard to judgment, because the prince of this world now stands condemned."

81 To read a personal account of the effects of pornography on a marriage, see Appendix E, *A Wife's Letter to Her Husband on Pornography.*

82 Philippians 1:6 "...being confident of this, that he who began a good work in you will carry it on to completion until the day of Christ Jesus."

83 2 Samuel 11

84 1 Corinthians 6:18, 1 Corinthians 10:14, 1 Timothy 6:11, 2 Timothy 2:22

85 Jay E. Adams, *Solving Marriage Problems: Biblical Solutions for Christian Counselors* (Grand Rapids: Zondervan Publishing House, 1983), p. 20

86 Proverbs 27:17

87 Dan Allender, *The Wounded Heart*, p. 179.

88 For women, we see the training was to come from older, godly women in Titus 2:3-5. For men, we see the pattern in Titus 2:1-2, 6-8.

89 Ephesians 5:21-33; 1 Corinthians 7; Colossians 3:18-19; Titus 2:1-8; 1 Peter 3:1-7

90 Ephesians 5:33 "However, each one of you also must love his wife as he loves himself, and the wife must respect her husband."

91 Ephesians 1:13-14 "And you also were included in Christ when you heard the word of truth, the gospel of your salvation. Having believed, you were marked in him with a seal, the promised Holy Spirit, who is a deposit guaranteeing our inheritance until the redemption of those who are God's possession—to the praise of his

glory." And 2 Corinthians 1:21-22 "He anointed us, set his seal of ownership on us, and put his Spirit in our hearts as a deposit, guaranteeing what is to come."

92 Exodus 21:10-11 "If he marries another woman, he must not deprive the first one of her food, clothing and marital rights. If he does not provide her with these three things, she is to go free, without any payment of money."

93 Matthew 5:31-32 "It has been said, `Anyone who divorces his wife must give her a certificate of divorce.' But I tell you that anyone who divorces his wife, except for marital unfaithfulness, causes her to become an adulteress, and anyone who marries the divorced woman commits adultery."

94 For our purposes here, we will assume a relationship where the husband is the abuser. Although it might be much more rare, we do, however, acknowledge that sometimes it is the wife who does the abusing.

95 Romans 13:1 "Everyone must submit himself to the governing authorities, for there is no authority except that which God has established. The authorities that exist have been established by God."

96 We know that there are many Biblical counselors who say a husband can never "rape" his wife, but we strongly disagree. Any time sex is forced on another person, no matter what their relationship, it is rape and should be reported to the authorities by the victim.

97 Matthew 7:16 "By their fruit you will recognize them."

98 1 Corinthians 7:32-35

99 See also Romans 1:26-27 "Because of this, God gave them over to shameful lusts. Even their women exchanged natural relations for unnatural ones. In the same way the men also abandoned natural relations with women and were inflamed with lust for one another. Men committed indecent acts with other men, and received in themselves the due penalty for their perversion."

100 1 Corinthians 9:18; 2 Corinthians 11:7

101 The word religion comes from the Latin that means *to tie back*. We can see how religions are man's attempts to tie himself back to a relationship with God.

102 Hebrews 6:1 "Therefore let us leave the elementary teachings about Christ and go on to maturity, not laying again the foundation of repentance from acts that lead to death, and of faith in God."

103 This is a summary of these, written by Bill Bright, "The Four Spiritual Laws" (Campus Crusade for Christ, 1965, 1988).

104 Galatians 3:10-13, 19

105 Jay Adams, *Competent to Counsel* (Grand Rapids: Zondervan Publishing House, 1970).

106 In all fairness, Adams does have a book entitled *A Theology of Christian Counseling* (Grand Rapids: Zondervan Publishing House, 1979), but his other works speak little of applying actual doctrine to people's problems.

107 Romans 10:3 "Since they did not know the righteousness that comes from God and sought to establish their own, they did not submit to God's righteousness."

108 John 19:30 "When he had received the drink, Jesus said, "It is finished." With that, he bowed his head and gave up his spirit." And Hebrews 10:12 "But when this priest had offered for all time one sacrifice for sins, he sat down at the right hand of God."

109 Romans 4:22-24 "This is why "it was credited to him as righteousness." The words "it was credited to him" were written not for him alone, but also for us, to whom God will credit righteousness—for us who believe in him who raised Jesus our Lord from the dead."

110 Jude 3 "Dear friends, although I was very eager to write to you about the salvation we share, I felt I had to write and urge you to contend for the faith that was once for all entrusted to the saints."

111 Hebrews 9:12 "He did not enter by means of the blood of goats and calves; but he entered the Most Holy Place once for all by his own blood, having obtained eternal redemption."

112 John 3:14-17 "Just as Moses lifted up the snake in the desert, so the Son of Man must be lifted up, that everyone who believes in him may have eternal life. For God so loved the world that he gave his one and only Son, that whoever believes in him shall not perish but have eternal life. For God did not send his Son into the world to condemn the world, but to save the world through

him."

113 2 Timothy 1:7-10 "For God did not give us a spirit of timidity, but a spirit of power, of love and of self-discipline. So do not be ashamed to testify about our Lord, or ashamed of me his prisoner. But join with me in suffering for the gospel, by the power of God, who has saved us and called us to a holy life—not because of anything we have done but because of his own purpose and grace. This grace was given us in Christ Jesus before the beginning of time, but it has now been revealed through the appearing of our Savior, Christ Jesus, who has destroyed death and has brought life and immortality to light through the gospel."

114 Hebrews 2:14-15 "Since the children have flesh and blood, he too shared in their humanity so that by his death he might destroy him who holds the power of death—that is, the devil — and free those who all their lives were held in slavery by their fear of death."

115 A private message can be seen only by the one you are addressing and cannot be seen by others in the chat room.

116 For a better understanding, see our section on Oneness Pentecostalism in our chapter on *The Many Faces of Pharisaism.*

117 2 Corinthians 11:4 "For if someone comes to you and preaches a Jesus other than the Jesus we preached, or if you receive a different spirit from the one you received, or a different gospel from the one you accepted, you put up with it easily enough."

118 We will be discussing the effects of evolution in the chapter, *The Evolution Delusion.*

119 See our Appendix G for other recommended reading.

120 Galatians 5:1 "It is for freedom that Christ has set us free. Stand firm, then, and do not let yourselves be burdened again by a yoke of slavery."

121 Matthew 16:6, 12; Luke 12:1; 1 Corinthians 5:6-7

122 You can find these and many more cults compared in John Ankerberg and John Weldon's *Encyclopedia of Cults and New Religions,* (Eugene, Oregon: Harvest House Publishers, 1999).

123 Primitive religions would be closer associated with the shamanistic beliefs of witch doctors who invoke spirits to do their bidding through rituals and ceremonies, both for good and evil

purposes. These can include groups such as Native Americans, various African tribes, Central and South American beliefs of the indigenous Indian tribes, Eskimos of North America, etc. These Traditional or Ancient Pagans may be subdivided into Celtic, Germanic, Norse, Slavic, Finnish, Egyptian, Roman and Hellenic and many more less known or less popular ancient Paganistic beliefs and practices.

124 Silver Ravenwolf, *Llewellyn's 1999 Magickal Almanac* (St. Paul: Llewellyn Publications, 1998).

125 Jamie Wood, *The Teen Spell Book: Magick for Young Witches* (Berkeley: Celestial Arts, 2001), p. 5.

126 From the website, www.religioustolerance.org/wic_hist.htm; Internet; accessed 19 June 2003.

127 The word "rede" is an Old English word for "standard."

128 Carl McColman, *When Someone You Love is Wiccan* (Franklin Lakes, NJ: New Page Books, 2003) p. 100.

129 See our chapter *The Faith of Our Fathers?*

130 McColman, *When Someone You Love is Wiccan*, p. 175.

131 This survey is summarized from John Ankerberg and John Weldon, *Encyclopedia of Cults and New Religions,* p. xxx. The italicized entries that follow are the verses that show the Biblical truth.

132 Dr. C. Welton Gaddy, "How Does the Death of Jesus 'Save' Us?" given May 13, 2001 [online archive]; available from http://northmin.org/sermon.html; Internet; accessed July 25, 2001.

133 John 1:29 and John 8:58

134 Romans 5:8

135 Hebrews 10:5, Ephesians 1:23, Colossians 2:9

136 Romans 6:3

137 Ephesians 2:8

138 From the Interfaith Alliance Website. [website online]; available from http://www.interfaithalliance.org/Resources/resources.htm; Internet; accessed July 15, 2001.

139 Ibid., http://www.interfaithalliance.org/AboutUs/aboutus.htm.

140 Ibid, http://www.interfaithalliance.org/Rr/religious.htm.

141 Ibid.

142 It is ironic they would mention "one true faith." It almost

sounds like a confession that fundamental Christianity is the one true faith. After all, God *did* speak truth even through Balaam's donkey.

143   Ibid., http://www.interfaithalliance.org/Rr/context.html.

144   Although the Interfaith Allicance reported it happened in Colorado, Matthew Shepard was killed in Laramie, Wyoming.

145   Ibid.

146   The website for Americans United for Separation of Church and State is found at http://www.au.org/.

147   Americans United for Separation of Church and State website, [online]; http://www.au.org/relright.htm; Internet; accessed July 16, 2001.

148   http://www.au.org/press.htm

149   John 14:6

150   Galatians 3:1-14

151   William Morris, ed., *The American Heritage Dictionary of the English Language* (Boston: Houghton Mifflin Company, 1978).

152   Romans 1:25 "They exchanged the truth of God for a lie, and worshipped and served created things rather than the Creator—who is forever praised. Amen."

153   Colossians 3:1-2 "Since, then, you have been raised with Christ, set your hearts on things above, where Christ is seated at the right hand of God. Set your minds on things above, not on earthly things." Philippians 3:20 "But our citizenship is in heaven. And we eagerly await a Savior from there, the Lord Jesus Christ."

154   Hebrews 11:13-16 "All these people were still living by faith when they died. They did not receive the things promised; they only saw them and welcomed them from a distance. And they admitted that they were aliens and strangers on earth. People who say such things show that they are looking for a country of their own. If they had been thinking of the country they had left, they would have had opportunity to return. Instead, they were longing for a better country—a heavenly one. Therefore God is not ashamed to be called their God, for he has prepared a city for them."

155   2 Peter 3:13 "But in keeping with his promise we are looking forward to a new heaven and a new earth, the home of righteousness."

156   Isaiah 45:4-6, 22 "I am the LORD, and there is no other;

apart from me there is no God. I will strengthen you, though you have not acknowledged me, so that from the rising of the sun to the place of its setting men may know there is none besides me. I am the LORD, and there is no other... Turn to me and be saved, all you ends of the earth; for I am God, and there is no other."

157 Our abbreviation of Jehovah's Witnesses is in no way derogatory. We have often seen them refer to themselves in chat rooms in such a manner. It is merely a shortened form that is commonly used online.

158 *The Watchtower*, October 1, 1952, pp. 596-604.

159 Havor Montague. "The Pessimistic Sect's Influence on the Mental Health of Its Members: The Case of Jehovah's Witnesses," Social Compass, Vol. 24, 1977, pg.139.

160 Kjell Totland "The Mental Health of Jehovah's Witnesses." Journal of the Norwegian Psychological Association, In Press.

161 Deuteronomy 18:22 "When a prophet speaketh in the name of the LORD, if the thing follow not, nor come to pass, that is the thing which the LORD hath not spoken, but the prophet hath spoken it presumptuously: thou shalt not be afraid of him."

162 1Peter 5:8

163 John 10:10

164 1Corinthians 14:33

165 1Timothy 4:1

166 Joseph Smith, *Teachings of the Prophet Joseph Smith*, pp. 348-49.

167 Abraham chapter 3 (from the *Pearl of Great Price*).

168 2 Nephi 5:21 "And he had caused the cursing to come upon them, yea, even a sore cursing, because of their iniquity. For behold, they had hardened their hearts against him, that they had become like unto a flint; wherefore, as they were white, and exceedingly fair and delightsome, that they might not be enticing unto my people the Lord God did cause a skin of blackness to come upon them."

169 Romans 8:32 "He who did not spare his own Son, but gave him up for us all—how will he not also, along with him, graciously give us all things?"

170 Galatians 3:28 "There is neither Jew nor Greek, slave nor

free, male nor female, for you are all one in Christ Jesus."

171 From the official LDS website: http://www.lds.org/library/display/0,4945,11-1-13-49,00.html . Also see Alma 39:5.

172 Romans 11:6 "And if by grace, then it is no longer by works; if it were, grace would no longer be grace."

173 *Doctrine and Covenants* 132:37-39.

174 Ron Carlson and Ed Decker, *Fast Facts on False Teachings.* (Eugene, Oregon: Harvest House Publishers, 1994), p. 218.

175 The Holy See, *Catechism of the Catholic Church,* (New York: Bantam Doubleday Dell Publishing Group, Inc., 1994), paragraph 503, p. 141.

176 Ibid., paragraph 494, p. 139.

177 Pius IX, *Ineffabilis Deus,* 1854.

178 Although the Roman Catholic Church attributes continual virginity to Mary, there are many places in the Bible where brothers and sisters of Jesus are mentioned. We will bring up texts to refute this on our website online.

179 Ibid., paragraph 969, p. 274-275.

180 Ibid., paragraph 1210, p. 341.

181 Ibid., paragraph 1030, p. 291.

182 Ibid., paragraph 846, p. 244.

183 Kenneth Copeland, *The Image of God in You* (Tulsa: Harrison House, 1987).

184 Copeland, *The Image of God in You*, p. 4.

185 Jamie Wood, *The Teen Spell Book* (Berkeley: Celestial Arts, 2001), p. 69.

186 Copeland, *The Image of God in You*, p. 5.

187 Kenneth Copeland, "Inner Image of the Covenant," audiotape, side 2.

188 Kenneth Copeland, *The Power of the Tongue* (Fort Worth: KCM Publications, 1980), p. 4.

189 Copeland, *The Image of God in You*, p. 6.

190 Colossians 1:16; John 1:1-3; 1 John 5:7

191 Kenneth Copeland, "Forces of the Recreated Human Spirit," (Fort Worth: Kenneth Copeland Ministries, 1982), p. 8.

192 Kenneth Copeland, *Freedom from Fear* (Fort Worth:

Kenneth Copeland Ministries, 1980), p. 11-12.

193 Dr. Lester Sumrall, *Faith Can Change Your World*, (South Bend, Indiana: Sumrall Publishing, 1999), p. 4.

194 Kenneth Copeland, *The Laws of Prosperity* (Fort Worth: Kenneth Copeland Ministries, 1974).

195 Kenneth Copeland, *The Power of the Tongue* (Fort Worth: Kenneth Copeland Ministries), p. 8-10.

196 Kenneth Copeland, *The Image of God in You III* (Fort Worth: Kenneth Copeland Ministries, 1989), audiotape #01-1403, side 2.

197 Kenneth Copeland, *Following the Faith of Abraham*, (Fort Worth: Kenneth Copeland Ministries) audiotape #01-3001.

198 Kenneth Copeland, *The Incarnation*, (Fort Worth: Kenneth Copeland Ministries, 1985), audiotape #01-0402, side 1.

199 1 Chronicles 16:22 and Psalm 105:15 both say, "Do not touch my anointed ones; do my prophets no harm."

200 The major teachers of the word faith doctrines are Kenneth E. Hagin, Sr. (founder of Rhema Bible College and often called "Dad" Hagin, indicating his founding role in these teachings), Kenneth E. Hagin, Jr., Kenneth and Gloria Copeland, Charles Capps, Benny Hinn, Paul and Jan Crouch (founders of Trinity Broadcasting Network), Frederick K.C. Price, Jerry Savelle, Norvel Hayes, Earl Paulk, Paul Yonggi Cho, TD Jakes, Robert Tilton, Marilyn Hickey, Rodney Howard Browney, Lester Sumrall, Rod Parsley, and John Avanzini. It is difficult to have a complete listing since it grows daily. From this list it should be easy to see connections between these teachers and others you might know personally. If someone refers to any of these teachers in a supportive way, it should be a warning signal to their involvement in this movement.

201 Paul Crouch, "Praise-a-thon" program on TBN (2 April 1991).

202 Benny Hinn, presentation at World Charismatic Conference, Melodyland Christian Center, Anaheim, California (7 August 1992), CRI audiotape. Quoted in *Christianity in Crisis* by Hank Hanegraaff (Eugene Oregon: Harvest House Publishers, 1997), p. 344.

203 John 14:6

204 John 8:32

205 Kenneth Copeland, "Praise-a-Thon" program on TBN (April 1988).

206 Kenneth Copeland, "Believer's Voice of Victory" program (21 April 1991).

207 Kenneth Copeland, "What Happened from the Cross to the Throne" (Fort Worth: Kenneth Copeland Ministries, 1990), audio-tape #02-0017, side 2.

208 The Arabs, before the time of Mohammed accepted and worshipped, after a fashion, a supreme god called "Allah." (*Encyclopedia of Islam*, I.302) "Allah" was known to the pre-Islamic Arabs and it was one of the Meccan deities. (H. Gibb, *Encyclopedia of Islam*, I.46) According to Middle East scholar E.M. Wherry, in pre-Islamic times, Allah-worship, as well as the worship of Baal, were both astral religions in that they involved the worship of the stars, the sun and the moon. (*A Comprehensive Commentary on the Quran*, p. 36) In Arabia, the sun god was viewed as a female goddess and the moon as the male god. One of the moon god's name was called Allah. (Alfred Guilluame, *Islam*, p. 7.)

209 Allah, the moon god, was married to the sun goddess. Together they produced the three goddess (the daughters of Allah), Al-Lat, Al-Uzza and Manat. All of these "gods" were viewed as being the top of the pantheon of Arab deities. (*Encyclopedia of World Mythology and Legend*, I.61)

210 George W. Braswell, Jr., *What You Need to Know About Islam & Muslims*.

211 This is not limited to Mohammed and Smith. Most cult leaders follow exactly this same pattern, holding their followers accountable to a higher moral code than they themselves want to follow.

212 This is the same idea we hear from today's self-proclaimed prophets. They expect people to believe them because they say it is from God, and the catch is that one must never question what a prophet of God says.

213 Please remember that Jews do not call those books the Old Testament. The term, "Old Testament," implies that there is now a New Testament that has superceded it. Since the Jews do not believe the Messiah has come yet, the Bible they have contains the

same scriptures, but is usually referred to as the Torah (which would be the first five books) or the Tanakh or the Law, the Prophets and the Writings. Some feel comfortable with the term Bible as well. When speaking to a Jewish person, your views will be much better respected if you do not call it the Old Testament.

214 Galatians 3:28

215 This can be a quite effective verse to use when speaking with those who are Jewish. If their concept of God is purely spirit, then how could Man pierce Him? And when was it that Man pierced God? It becomes easy to show them how this was a prophecy about the Messiah, Jesus.

216 John 3:16-17 and Romans 5:8

217 This can especially be seen in the truth behind the "Nebraska Man." A fossil tooth was discovered in Snake Creek, Nebraska and was presumed to be that of a primitive ape-like man. Within five years, the tooth was revealed to be that of a type of wild pig. While the original discovery received mountains of publicity, the final conclusion was kept quiet and almost swept completely under the rug.

218 Mark 10:6-9 and 13:19

219 This is in reality the precise teaching of the New Age Movement. The "Christ-consciousness" is within us all, and we can access it by following the same path Jesus took.

220 The majority of those we have worked with over the years have been women. We believe this is because when women have a problem, they find their solutions by talking about those problems. Men, on the other hand, do much of their thinking internally and then speak only once they have drawn their conclusions. We have worked with men, but the sessions are much shorter and they usually want us to get to the bottom line quickly so they can go and think about it and process it inside before they come to a conclusion. Sessions with women can be longer and more in number because of this.

Index

❖❖❖

abuse, ...29, 32, 56, 76, 78, 79, 80, 82, 83, 84, 85, 86, 100, 145, 147, 148, 151, 157, 207, 291, 292, 293, 334, 352, 386
Adams, Dr. Jay, ...ix, 138, 167, 359, 365, 385, 387,
addiction, ...113, 114, 116, 117, 119, 121, 123, 127, 132,135, 339, 348, 349, 351, 352, 384
adultery, ...145, 352, 386
agnostic, ...287, 288, 289, 290, 292, 293, 294, 295
alcohol(ism), ...113, 114, 135, 207, 347
Allah, ...279, 280, 281, 309, 394
Allender, Dr. Dan, ...76, 382, 385
Almy, Dr. Gary, ...63, 64, 90, 360, 380, 383
American Civil Liberties Union, ..203
Americans United. *See* Americans United for Separation of Church and State
Americans United for Separation of Church and State, ...203, 204, 207, 208, 210, 211, 390
Anderson, Neil, ...50, 95, 96, 97, 98, 99, 100, 101, 104, 107, 275, 363, 380, 383, 384
anointed, ...214, 230, 267, 268, 269, 270, 273, 274, 386, 393
anorexia, ...78, 114
anti-depressant, ...61, 62, 64, 65, 66, 67, 380
anxiety, ...x, 89, 109, 110, 169, 170
AOG. *See* Assembly of God
apologetics, ...177

Apostolic Succession, ...246
armor of God, ...110,
Assembly of God, ...171
atheist, ...177, 277, 287, 288, 289, 290, 291, 292, 293, 294, 295, 298, 299, 300, 301

Barden, R. Christopher, ...20
BIBLE Counseling, ... ix, 13, 14, 15, 17, 18, 21, 25, 28, 35, 69, 115, 142, 146, 150, 155, 156, 158, 166, 172, 200, 310, 319, 343, 365, 379
biblical counseling, ...ix, x, 18, 27, 30, 33, 35, 51, 61, 66, 68, 69, 115, 116, 157, 158, 167, 169, 171, 322, 362, 365, 369
Big Bang Theory, ...289, 293, 300, 301, 302
binding demons, ...100
bipolar, ...91
blank slate. *See* tabula rasa
Bobgan, Martin and Deidre, ...20, 21, 360, 379
bondage, ...40, 41, 42, 96, 101, 104, 123, 127, 182, 228, 383, 384
Book of Mormon, ...15, 238, 240, 281
Breggin, Dr. Peter R., ...64, 381
Buddhism, ...24, 187, 196, 197, 222, 237
bulimia, ...78, 114

channeling, ...189
chemical imbalance, ...64, 65, 381
Christian Coalition, ...204

Christianized Pharisaism, ...38
Chronic Fatigue Syndrome, ...380
Church of Jesus Christ of Latter-Day Saints, ...205, 237, 238, 239, 240, 241, 242, 247, 392
church, role of the local, ...86, 147, 150, 151, 155, 157, 158, 259, 309, 340
Cole, Pastor Steven J., ...95, 383
communication, ...16, 138, 344, 357
companionship, ...138, 139, 143, 150
Copeland, Kenneth, ...273, 392, 393, 394
Creationism, ...294, 301
credentials, ...18, 19, 20, 96, 104

Darwin, Charles, ...16, 298
deliverance ministries, ...50, 91, 93, 94, 95, 102, 103, 104, 107, 108, 109, 110, 111
demonic possession, ...30, 31, 106
depression, ...32, 40, 41, 59, 60, 61, 62, 63, 64, 65, 66, 67, 68, 69, 75, 76, 79, 83, 91, 117, 168, 170, 171, 231, 361, 380, 381, 382
Descartes, René, ...22
Diagnostic and Statistical Manual, ...88
diet, ...116, 122, 123, 126
disorders, ...87, 88, 89
divorce, ...123, 145, 146, 150, 151, 386
DSM. *See* Diagnostic and Statistical Manual
Durlak, Dr. Joseph, ...21

Effexor, ...65, 66
emotional problems, ...14, 17, 27, 49
empiricism, ...24
eternal security, ...168, 169, 182, 381
evolution, ...177, 289, 290, 293, 295, 296, 297, 298, 299, 300, 301, 302, 303, 360, 361, 388
Eysenck, Hans J., ...20, 379

faith-filled words, ...266, 267, 272
fatigue, ...62, 63, 122, 131
Fibromyalgia, ...62

finished work of Christ, ...16, 33, 143, 378
forgive(ness), ...50, 78, 82, 83, 99, 100, 122, 125, 186, 204, 279, 351, 376
free will, ...23, 81, 335, 336
Freud, Sigmund, ...16, 25, 26, 27, 87, 196, 379
fundamentalists, ...21, 208

Gaddy, Rev. Dr. C. Welton, ...203, 204, 389
gay, ...151, 209, 210
generational curse, ...102, 103, 107
genes, ...152
gluttony, ...124
grace, ...ix, 15, 16, 32, 35, 38, 39, 40, 41, 43, 44, 45, 49, 50, 52, 69, 78, 84, 87, 94, 100, 104, 119, 122, 124, 125, 130, 135, 136, 143, 162, 163, 165, 166, 168, 169, 170, 172, 179, 180, 182, 183, 184, 185, 186, 190, 203, 226, 227, 228, 230, 231, 232, 233, 234, 235, 238, 240, 242, 243, 245, 249, 251, 252, 253, 254, 274, 279, 293, 294, 300, 308, 310, 311, 361, 375, 376, 377, 388, 392
Greenburg, Gary, ...66
grief, ...68, 76

Hagin, Kenneth, ...273, 393
Hanegraaff, Hank, ...275, 358, 361, 362, 393
happiness, ...53, 54, 55, 56, 57, 124, 138, 190, 199, 216, 217, 292
hedonism, ...53, 88, 217
Hinduism, ...189, 196, 197, 198, 205, 222, 262, 263
holiness, ...18, 37, 54, 55, 57, 152, 163, 165, 169, 183, 234, 255, 292, 380
homosexuality, ...88, 114, 137, 151, 152, 153, 154, 207, 208, 210, 216
hormones, ...60, 61, 65
Hunt, Dave, ...88, 161, 362, 382

image of God, ...24, 190, 263,

392, 393
incest, ...79
inner image, ...263, 264, 272, 392
Interfaith Alliance, ...203, 204, 205, 206, 207, 208, 210, 211, 215, 389
Internet, ...x, 13, 14, 59, 93, 109, 115, 193, 225, 229, 307, 308, 310, 312, 313, 314, 315, 316, 317, 318, 319, 320, 323, 324, 339, 340, 341, 343, 349, 351, 355, 357, 366, 367, 369, 370, 372, 389, 390
Islam, ...198, 220, 221, 237, 277, 278, 279, 280, 281, 282, 309, 394

Jehovah's Witnesses, ...15, 155, 181, 225, 226, 227, 228, 229, 230, 231, 232, 233, 234, 259, 260, 309, 380, 391
Judaism, ...197, 198, 220, 221, 277, 278, 279, 280, 281, 285
judging, ...23, 29, 37, 40, 43, 44, 49, 82, 104, 167, 229, 230, 245, 279, 280, 284, 291, 331, 332, 335, 336, 385
Jung, Carl, ...16, 26, 33, 34, 87, 196, 308, 379, 380
JW. *See* Jehovah's Witnesses

Koran, ...279, 280, 281

legalism, ...35, 36, 38, 39, 41, 43, 44, 45, 143, 172, 182, 184, 199, 214, 233, 234, 376
lesbianism, ...149, 153
Lewis, C.S., ...127
liberalism, ...182, 184
local church, ...14, 86, 95, 147, 150, 151, 155, 157, 158, 259, 309, 340, 366
Locke, John, ...23, 24
logos, ...22
loneliness, ...138
loss of salvation, ...42, 45, 169, 228
Lynn, Barry W., ... 203

magickal, ...195, 197, 198, 389
manic-depressive disorder.
See bipolar
Marianism, ...248, 249
marital problems, ...32, 138, 139, 145
marriage, ...56, 137, 138, 139, 140, 141, 142, 143, 144, 145, 146, 147, 148, 149, 150, 151, 215, 344, 345, 347, 349, 352, 359, 385
McDowell, Josh, ...177, 362, 363
mental illness, ...x, 30, 31, 63, 64, 66, 90, 229, 380
mental problems. *See* mental illness
micro-evolution, ...298
Mohammad, ...260, 281, 309, 394
Monotheism, ...238, 277, 278, 281,
Mormon, *See also* Church of Jesus Christ of Latter-Day Saints,
MPD. *See* Multiple Personality Disorder
Multiple Personality
Disorder, ...90, 383

nativist view, ...23
Neo-Paganism, ...195, 196, 197
New Age, ...187, 195, 196, 197, 395
New World Translation, ...15, 228
Nirvana, ...187
nouthetic, ...18, 167

OAIM. *See* Open Arms Internet Ministry
occult, ...26, 88, 188, 201, 262, 362, 363, 382
Oneness Pentecostalism, ...42, 43, 171, 380, 388
Open Arms Internet Ministry, ...125, 315, 320, 321, 322, 369, 370, 371
overeating, ...78, 114, 116, 117

Packer, J.I., ...95, 383
Paganism, ...ix, 14, 23, 43, 193, 194, 195, 196, 197, 198, 199, 200, 215, 216, 217, 219, 220, 221, 222, 245, 262, 281
panic disorder, ...89
paraprofessionals, ...21
Paxil, ...65, 66
Pentecostal, ...42, 43, 171, 380, 388
personality disorder, ...89

Pharisaism, ...35, 36, 38, 43, 44, 167, 382, 388
Phen-fen, ...65
physical illness, ...30, 31, 169
pleasure, ...53, 100, 101, 113, 124, 127, 128, 133, 134, 146, 151, 152, 226, 292, 348, 384
PMS. *See* Premenstrual Syndrome
pornography, ...113, 124, 129, 135, 153, 207, 347, 352, 357, 385
Positive Confession, ...266
Post-Partum Depression, ...61
Premenstrual Syndrome, ...60
pride, ...14, 36, 39, 40, 44, 48, 49, 55, 78, 83, 100, 101, 119, 121, 127, 130, 132, 161, 162, 167, 166, 169, 170, 184, 185, 190, 226, 233, 234, 253, 270, 288, 290, 334, 375, 382
prophecy, ...230, 232, 270, 271, 272, 273, 283, 284, 362, 395
Prozac, ...65, 66, 381
psuche, ...22
psychiatry, ...26, 63, 64, 65, 88, 89, 90, 381, 384
psychoanalysis, ...27
psychology, ...ix, 20, 21, 22, 25, 26, 27, 28, 29, 30, 33, 34, 47, 48, 49, 62, 63, 87, 88, 89, 91, 93, 96, 98, 99, 156, 196, 322, 339, 360, 361, 365, 379, 380, 382, 391
purgatory, ...94, 245, 254
purging, ...114, 375

qualifications, ...18, 22, 62

rape, ...65, 68, 79, 147, 349, 350, 386
rebuking the devil, ...101, 106
recovery groups, ...33, 150, 360
Religious Right, ...204, 205, 206, 209, 211
responsibility, ...22, 28, 43, 89, 90, 110, 115, 122, 133, 135, 146, 147, 156, 215, 345
Roman Catholicism, ...242, 245, 246, 247, 248, 249, 250, 251, 252, 255, 257, 360, 383, 384, 392

Sabbath, ...44, 124
salvation by grace, ...15, 39, 41, 43, 162, 182, 183, 184, 185, 228, 232, 240, 242, 245, 279, 293
sanctification, ...95, 134, 164, 165
Satan, ...x, 14, 15, 40, 48, 79, 80, 93, 94, 96, 101, 106, 107, 161, 179, 182, 188, 189, 190, 215, 216, 217, 229, 233, 234, 260, 267, 269, 308, 381
secular counseling, ...30
self-centeredness, ...48, 68, 98, 138, 139, 153, 190
self-contempt, ...77, 78, 122, 125, 136, 266
self-esteem, ...47, 48, 49, 50, 52, 53, 55, 99, 360
selfishness, ...48, 51, 117, 121, 138, 139, 141, 153, 161, 293, 334, 344
self-righteousness, ...36, 83, 84, 167, 170, 382
serotonin, ...64, 65, 381
Seven Steps to Freedom, ...94, 96
Seventh-Day Adventism, ...39, 41
sexual abuse, ...79, 80, 82, 83, 84, 85, 86, 157
shame, ...78, 115, 124, 125, 156, 172, 247, 296, 330, 339, 386, 388, 390
singles, ...137, 148, 149, 150, 151, 152, 340, 349
Smith, Joseph, ...281, 282, 363, 391, 394
sound doctrine, ...32, 168, 170, 171, 172, 173, 176, 181, 182, 215, 245, 260, 293
spiritual problems, ...15, 28
strongholds, ...108
submission, ...352
suicidal thoughts, ...59, 75, 76, 77, 79, 170, 171, 381
suicide, ...26, 48, 75, 76, 77, 78, 168, 229, 231, 372, 373, 382
Swindoll, Chuck, ...96
Szasz, Dr. Thomas, ...26, 379

tabula rasa, ...24
temptation, ...101, 110, 111,

118, 129, 133, 134, 135, 302
Theosophist, ...205
three marks of a cult, ...14, 33, 43, 87, 274, 279
three questions, ...69, 79, 90, 106, 257
thyroid, ...60, 63, 65, 66
tolerance, ...199, 204, 205, 206, 208, 212, 213, 223, 309, 320, 362, 389
transubstantiation, ...256
Trinity, ...15, 42, 43, 172, 180, 184, 188, 199, 228, 238, 243, 245, 253, 257, 264, 272, 278, 279, 285, 380, 393

Unger, Merrill, ...105, 384
Unification Church, ...181, 187
unity in the faith, ...172, 213
UPC. *See* Oneness Pentecostalism

victim mentality, ...79
Voodoo, ...189

Wicca, ...170, 195, 197, 198, 199, 206, 255, 259, 263, 389
Wiccan Rede, ...198
Wilkinson, Bruce, ...69, 381
witchcraft, ...x, 195, 198, 199
word faith movement, ...32, 222, 260, 269, 273, 275, 358, 384
works-based, ...168, 169, 170, 199, 228, 254, 255, 257
wrath of God, ...24, 289

Yahoo, ...193, 307, 315, 317, 319, 320, 321, 322, 323, 327, 358, 367, 370
Yates, Andrea, ...41

Zoloft, ...65, 66, 381

Printed in the United States
86663LV00003B/43-63/A